Fine Lines of Faith

Toni K. B. Popé

FINE LINES OF FAITH

A STUDY OF THE TORAH'S OUTLOOK ON HUMAN SUFFERING

Based on Malbim's commentary to Iyov

Rabbi Eliezer Parkoff

FELDHEIM PUBLISHERS *Jerusalem / New York*

Library of Congress Catalogue in Publication Data
Parkoff, Eliezer.
Fine lines of faith / by Eliezer Parkoff.
p. cm.
Includes bibliographical references.
ISBN 0-87306-669-3
1. Suffering—Biblical teaching. 2. Malbim, Meir Loeb ben Jehiel Michael, 1809-1879. 3. Bible. O.T. Job—Commentaries. 4. Suffering—Religious aspects—Judaism. I. Title.
BS1199.S8P37 1994
296.3'11—dc20 93-48518
CIP

First published 1994

FELDHEIM PUBLISHERS
POB 35002 / Jerusalem, Israel

200 Airport Executive Park
Spring Valley, NY 10977

Printed in Israel

10 9 8 7 6 5 4 3 2 1

Dedication

This book is dedicated to my parents,
Mr. and Mrs. Meyer Parkoff,
for their constant encouragement and support in my development towards *Rabbanus* and Torah education. It was their dream that I follow in the footsteps of my respected grandfather, Reb Yitzchok Dov Parkoff, ז״ל, one of the founders of Yeshiva Torah Vodaath. In the merit of this book, may they be blessed with health and happiness for many years to come, and may my father be granted a רפואה שלמה בתוך שאר חולי ישראל.

Acknowledgments

I wish to express my thanks to Hashem *Yisborach* for granting me the ability to complete such an undertaking as this book has been. May it enlighten many eyes and be a source of inspiration to all who read it.

In every *ben Torah*'s development there are certain individuals whose indelible imprint upon him is clearly evident. There are three very special people about whom I feel a deep obligation to make special mention of my sincere appreciation for all they have done.

I have had the unique opportunity to study in Yeshiva Torah Ore, Jerusalem, under the great Torah personalities, one of the *Gedolei Hador, Moreinu V'Rabbeinu Maran Rosh HaYeshiva Hagaon HaAdir HaRav* Chaim Pinchas Scheinberg, שליט״א. Under his tutelage and guidance I have grown in learning and have developed a deep appreciation of true Torah values. His *shiurim* are comprehensive studies of all aspects of Torah (Gemorah, Halacha, and Mussar) and he has taught us to try to emulate him and delve into all aspects of Torah knowledge in the deepest fashion possible. In my mind I have fond memories of his warm and heartfelt *mussar shmuezim* which kindled the flame within me to devote myself to the cause of *harbotzas haTorah* and inspiring the youth of our generation to Torah-true *Yiddishkeit*. May God grant him and the Rebbetzin health and happiness and the ability to continue serving the *Ribbono shel Olam* and *Klal Yisrael* for many years to come. Amen.

I also feel very humble for the great honor to have been able to study under and be in the presence of one of the greatest *Baale Mussar* of our generation, *Rabbeinu Maran HaMashgiach HaGaon HaTzaddik HaRav* Avrohom Yaakov (Zeidel) Epstein, שליט״א, *Mashgiach Ruchani* of Yeshiva Torah Ore. His advice and comments were indispensable in the writing of this work.

I also express my deep gratitude to the son-in-law of the *Rosh Yeshiva*, my revered *Rebbe HaGaon HaRav* Chaim Dov Altusky, שליט״א, Associate *Rosh Yeshiva* of Torah Ore, Jerusalem. I have had the opportunity of listening to his *shiurim* in Gemorah and Mussar for many years. His suggestions and elucidations on various aspects of the manuscript have been invaluable.

I am especially indebted to the esteemed Rabbi and educator HaRav Avrohom Pincus, שליט״א. Originally a *talmid* of the famous world-renown *Mashgiach* of Yeshivas Mir in prewar Europe, *Maran HaGaon HaTzaddik* Rav Yerucham Levovitz, זצ״ל, he served in the prestigious positions of Rav of the South 5th St. Shul, as *Menahel* of Yeshivas Kaminetz Yerushalayim. He graciously gave much of his valuable time and bestowed a tireless effort to check over the manuscript to ensure a final work of high Torah quality.

To the *Rosh Yeshiva*'s son, my dear friend, the *Menahel* of Yeshiva Torah Ore, Rav Simcha Scheinberg, שליט״א, for his advice and assistance which further augmented the quality of the book.

To my dear devoted colleagues, Rav Moshe Finkelstein, Rav Dovid Krohn, and Rav Moshe Lewis, Rashei Yeshivas Shaare Chaim, Jerusalem, as well as the entire staff of Yeshiva Shaare Chaim, Jerusalem. Their selfless dedication to *limud* and *harbotzas haTorah,* together with their efforts to become the very embodiment of Torah ideals, have been a constant source of inspiration. To my good friends and *chavrusos* Rav Moshe Lewis and Rav Hershel Pincus, I owe a special debt of gratitude for reviewing the manuscript and offering invaluable comments and insights. I wish also to thank my good friend Rav Zvi Zobin and my dear *talmid* Yitzchok Mickler, for looking over the manuscript in its early stages.

To my dear friend Yaakov Feldheim and his capable staff for offering me professional and courteous service during all the stages of publication.

And especially to my brothers Yitzchok Dov (Steve) and Gershon Yoseph (Jerry). Our lengthy conversations and correspondence were the seeds that eventually developed into this work. This book was written with them in mind. May Steve and his wife Barbara (Basya) and their children Seth, Susan, and Heather, and Jerry, and his wife Shulamis Leah and their daughter Bayla Bracha, be blessed with finding spiritual fulfillment and much *nachas* throughout their entire lives.

Finally, but most importantly, to my dear wife, Bracha, for her encouragement during all the stages of this book. Her living example of *emuna* and *bitachon,* her pure character, and her selfless deeds of *chesed,* have been major factors in bringing up our wonderful family in a pure Torah atmosphere. She has truly been a *bracha* to me. May we see only Torah *nachas* all of our lives. It goes without saying that I owe a singular debt of thanks to my in-laws, Mr. and Mrs. Irving Schaffer of Phoenix, Arizona, for bringing up such a special daughter.

It is our prayer that this book should open the hearts of all those who read it and inspire them to ever greater spiritual heights in pure faith and trust in Hashem *Yisborach*. In the merit of our *emuna* and *bitachon* together with Torah and *chesed*, may we be worthy of seeing the *Moshiach* come speedily in our days. Amen.

Rabbi CHAIM P. SCHEINBERG
Rosh Hayeshiva "TORAH-ORE"
and Morah Hora'ah of Kiryat Mattersdorf

הרב חיים פינחס שיינברג
ראש ישיבת "תורה-אור"
ומורה הוראה דקרית מטרסדורף

בס"ד

בואו ונחזיק טובה לידידנו היקר כבוד הרה"ג ר' אליעזר פרקוף, שליט"א, שאני מכירו שזה כבר הרבה שנים מאז שהוא לומד אצלנו והוא מהתלמידים החשובים בישיבתנו תורה אור, וגם הקדיש שנים הרבה להרבצת התורה והיראה בישיבת שערי חיים ע"י שיעוריו על הדף ובהלכה ובשיחותיו התמידים בעניני יראה בתוך כותלי הישיבה, וכבר העמיד תלמידים הרבה ע"י פעולותיו הכבירים לקרב לבבות התלמידים לתורה וליראה ביגיעה רבה ובו"ה זכה לראות את פעולותיו פוריות ומוצלחות.

ועכשו השקיע כחו בדבר חשוב מאד לתרגם לשפה האנגלית את באור המלבי"ם זצוק"ל על איוב ולהמציא לאחינו בני ישראל את דברי קדשו של הנ"ל בשפה המדוברת מקורבה ומובנת להם כדי להחדיר בלבותיהם חיזוק באמונה ובטחון ויראת שמים. ובפרט שהמחבר בעצמו כותב בהקדמתו שאינו מכריע כלל בשום שיטה ביסודות האמונה, ובא רק לתרגם ולעורר ביסודות המקובלות ומוסכמות אצל כל החרדים לדבר ה' שיחי'. ונוסף לזה הראותו את כל זה לגדולים י"ש המבינים היטב בשפה המתורגמת ודעתם שהתרגום נעשה באופן שהוא תועלת וחיזוק ליסודות האמונה והדת בלב אחינו בית ישראל.

ע"כ ידי תכון עמו שטוב עושה והנני לברכו שהשי"ת יצליח דרכו להמשיך בעבודתו בקודש ולקרב לבבות התלמידים ושאר בני עמנו לאהבת תורה ולחיזוק ביראת שמים ואמונה ובטחון ונזכה לגאולה שלמה במהרה בימינו אמן.

ואסיים בברכה להצלחה כעתירת נפש ידידו הדו"ש, פעיה"ק, ירושלים תובב"א, ח' סיון, תשנ"ג.

חיים פינחס שיינברג

רחוב פנים מאירות 2, ירושלים, ת. ד. 6979, טל. 371513־(02), ישראל
2, Panim Meirot St., Jerusalem, P.O.B. 6979, Tel (02)-371513, Israel

Rabbi ZEIDEL EPSTEIN
Panim Meiros 2
Jerusalem, E. Israel

הרב זיידל אפשטיין
פנים מאירות 2
ירושלים 94423

Tel. 02-372471 טל.

עש"ק פ' קרח ער"ח תמוז תשנ"ג.

לכבוד ידידי אהובי הרה"ג שקלו בגבורים, מרביץ תורה לעדרים [illegible]
וכו' מוהר"ר הרב אליעזר הכהן פינקוס שליט"א חד מן ראשי הישיבה ורמי"ם
את הישיבה החשובה ומפורסמת לשם ולתפארת [illegible]
הגאון הצדיק מוהר[illegible] [illegible] [illegible] [illegible]
[illegible] שליט"א.

שמחתי באומרים לי כי [illegible] [illegible] [illegible] ידידי [illegible] [illegible] [illegible]
[illegible] בבניני החסד בהרבצת תורה ויראת שמים טהורה [illegible] [illegible]
[illegible] [illegible] [illegible] הספר [illegible] [illegible] פירוש המלבי"ם [illegible] [illegible]
[illegible] [illegible] [illegible] תלמידיו [illegible] [illegible] [illegible] [illegible]
[illegible] [illegible] [illegible] ויראת שמים [illegible] [illegible] [illegible] [illegible] [illegible]
[illegible] [illegible] [illegible] [illegible] [illegible] [illegible] [illegible] [illegible] [illegible]
[illegible] [illegible] [illegible] [illegible] התורה [illegible] [illegible] רב טוב [illegible] [illegible]
[illegible] [illegible] [illegible] [illegible] [illegible] [illegible] [illegible] [illegible] [illegible]
[illegible] [illegible] [illegible] חיים ושלום [illegible] [illegible] [illegible] [illegible] [illegible]
[illegible] [illegible] תורה [illegible] [illegible] [illegible] [illegible] [illegible] [illegible]
[illegible] [illegible] קרן התורה [illegible] [illegible] [illegible] [illegible] [illegible]
[illegible] [illegible] [illegible] [illegible] [illegible]

[illegible] [illegible] [illegible] [illegible] [illegible]
זיידל אפשטיין [illegible] [illegible] תורה [illegible]
[illegible] [illegible] [illegible]
[illegible] [illegible] [illegible]
ירושלים [illegible] [illegible]

Contents

Foreword

There was once a man who was planning to travel to America. Now in those days, the trip took several months at sea. The boat would stop in France for two weeks to take on supplies, and afterwards, would continue on its way.

The man intended to settle in America, and thus he would have to know English. Moreover, for his two-week stopover in France, he also wanted to know French. Since he would be in France first, he decided to start by learning French and then study English later. Time went by and he only found the time to study French. When the boat docked in France and he disembarked, his knowledge of the language helped him tremendously and he managed to get around almost like a Frenchman, enjoying every minute. Two weeks later, the boat sailed again and continued on its voyage.

When he reached the shores of America, he tried to speak French there too — but no one had any idea what he was talking about, and he couldn't understand them either! Finally he met someone who knew French and he explained his predicament to him. The man replied to him, "What a foolish thing you did! You knew that the stopover in France would be a brief one and that you would spend the rest of your life in America, but nevertheless you went and learned French instead of learning English, the language you will need for a lifetime!"

Man has come to this world for only seventy years, but his main life will be in the Eternal World. There they don't speak the language of this world. And what does Man do? He goes ahead and learns the language of this world, which in the Next World will be useless to him.*

Over the years, in my work at Yeshiva Shaare Chaim, I

* *She'al Avicha v'Yagedcha,* vol. 2, p. 165.

have been constantly involved in speaking with people about *hashkafah* (Jewish philosophy or thought) and its practical application to daily living. One subject which constantly comes up is the problem of the *tzaddik* who suffers. Whether it relates to the Holocaust, or a relative who has undergone tremendous suffering, or personal grief, the question is one that plagues many: Why did this happen to him (or to me)? Rightly or wrongly, people tend to consider themselves to be the *tzaddik*, as it were, and find it difficult to understand the torment they are being afflicted with. The problem can even go so far as to dangerously upset the person's faith. Modern writers have dealt with the topic and some of their conclusions are definitely not in the spirit of traditional Torah *hashkafah*.

What is the root of the problem? Why is this such a perplexing topic? Part of the difficulty is that we are lacking a knowledge of the "whole picture." In our very physical life, we have a difficult time understanding that there is another plane, the spiritual world of *Olam Ha-Ba*, the Next World. Knowledge of this higher plane is the key to understanding the problem of suffering. Like the man in the story, we have mastered only one language. All too often we find long philosophical arguments struggling to come to grips with the topic, and yet ending with spurious conclusions. Only if we master "the language of the Next World" can we begin to deal with the issue in its true light.

But where does one gain this knowledge? A primary source is *Sefer Iyov*, the Book of Job. It is in *Iyov* that we find the main lessons on how to understand Torah *hashkafah* on the *tzaddik* who suffers and the wicked man who prospers. However, its length and complexity, and the fact that the classical commentaries deal with it verse by verse, tend to make it difficult for the modern reader to absorb. Most people today do not even attempt to tackle it. Despite the fact that many students learn the *gemara* in *Bava Basra* (15b-16b; see the Appendix) which discusses *Iyov*, often their understanding remains quite superficial and lacking.

The commentary of the Malbim, in contrast, provides a chapter-by-chapter summary of the entire *sefer*. His commentary is divided into two sections: an overview of each chapter and then a detailed explanation of each verse. (I have limited this work to present his overviews.) Based upon the Rambam's commentary on *Iyov* in the *Guide for the Perplexed*, it provides a magnificent introduction to *Iyov* and to the question of the *tzaddik* who suffers and the *rasha* who prospers — the righteous who suffer and the wicked who prosper. Here, we find a solid Torah outlook on this problem.

The material set off in brackets is my own commentary and/or other information relating to the explanation of the Malbim.

In addition, the Preface, Selected Essays, Epilogue, and Appendix expand and develop the subject even further. It is hoped that this work will provide the English-reading public with a new source of authentic Torah *hashkafah* based upon the classical Jewish works as handed down to us by the *Gedolim* of each generation, all the way back to Moshe *Rabbenu*. We pray that this will serve at least as a beginning lesson in the language of the spiritual world.

One word of caution. The *hashkafos* discussed in this book are very deep, and are fundamental and essential for a proper understanding of the Torah perspective. Although the purpose of this book is to lay a foundation to be studied and thought about, *hashkafah* is a very difficult matter and ultimately must be studied under a competent authority. Moreover, such study is not a dry philosophical exercise, but has serious repercussions on all aspects of one's life. *Hashkafah* provides us with the framework in which we cope with difficulties and tragedies, and with simple halachic questions as well as serious ones. All issues as fundamental as these must ultimately be referred to a proper Torah authority.

Preface

Let us imagine a certain person, a straight and upright individual. Very learned, and a philosopher. Not overindulgent, careful about his health, not wasteful with his money. And principled as well — he doesn't deviate from what he considers right for anything in the world. And most of all, he is God-fearing. He is a righteous person, scrupulous about avoiding anything that has any tinge of wrongdoing.

He has everything a person could ask for: success, security, a loving family. He takes upon himself the responsibility for the spiritual as well as the physical well-being of his family. His children's mental attitudes are a serious matter to him, and he sees to it that they develop a pure outlook on life. He has wealth, property, servants, and social standing. He is considered by everyone in his generation to be one of the greatest men of his community. And he lives up to his reputation impeccably.

Suddenly, he is struck by one disaster after another, without any obvious reason, without apparent justification. Suffering, tormented, he cries out bitterly against Divine *Hashgachah* (Providence). He can find no discernible reason, natural or Divine, to account for his suffering.

How is he to understand this? He worked so hard to be righteous — and now this?

This is a story repeated many times throughout history. Each of us at some point in our life experiences a very difficult ordeal. It doesn't seem to make sense; it doesn't seem fair. We consider ourselves religious, believing individuals, and know that there has to be a reason, but we come to a point where we are incapable of figuring it out. Our search, with the best of our abilities, comes up against what seems like a brick wall. Why did this happen to us? We don't understand it.

The issue has been dealt with by many. According to some of our Sages, *Iyov* was written by Moshe *Rabbenu* to deal specifically with this problem: the righteous who suffer, and the wicked who prosper.

Iyov comprises a discussion of these issues by four great minds. There are different opinions among *Chazal* (*Bava Basra* 15b) as to whether Iyov actually ever existed, but that is presently irrelevant to us. What we are interested in is that in *Iyov* the issues are addressed from four different intellectual viewpoints. If we understand these approaches, then perhaps we can understand better the ways in which we and others handle these issues, and then we can proceed to understand how *da'as Torah* tells us we should handle them.

FAITH AND UNDERSTANDING

Sefer Iyov is a very deep philosophical work which sheds light on these very important and basic issues. The major thrust of the book is the development of a rationale which will help us to come to an understanding of the matter.

However, before we continue, we must remember the fifth and last personality that we are introduced to at the end of the work — Elihu the *Navi* (prophet). As he unravels the truth as to what really transpired behind the scenes, we are introduced to what is perhaps the main lesson of the book, namely, that if we continue merely intellectually, then we will fall into the same trap that Iyov and his three friends fell into. For there would be a dimension missing from the thesis: the basis of all of our thinking must be *emunah*. Ultimately, what is required of us is simple faith. Yes, we are encouraged to use our minds to the fullest to understand. We are charged to approach such problems with the deepest thinking possible. However, the basic underlying foundation of all our understanding must be simple *emunah*.

The question is: What is the ultimate purpose of Man?

What is the "real" life goal that we should be working for? Look at Iyov. He struggled with these issues on perhaps the deepest level ever recorded by Man. He debated the issues with the greatest minds of his generation. And yet they too missed the real dimension: God and all the spiritual worlds. This is a realm with which most of us need direction. But it is quite difficult to come to any concrete understanding of it.

OUR INTELLECT IS LIMITED

At the end of the debate, Iyov and his friends were informed by Elihu the *Navi* of their mistake. Thinking is good, and we should use our minds to the fullest to understand. But we should never forget our limitations. We must rely on our Tradition to teach us the dimensions of which we ourselves will never have direct knowledge. We must approach our study with humility, acknowledging that even the best and deepest of our thinking is but our limited understanding of a vast universe. We are even less than the proverbial mouse trying to understand the battlefield. God has given us a certain capacity for understanding, but this is not the epitome, the zenith of comprehension.

In a similar vein: Rav Simcha Wasserman, *zt"l,* once recalled* walking with his father, Rav Elchonon Wasserman, *zt"l,* and as they crossed a bridge they came to a certain spot (which he remembered quite clearly) and his father stopped, and said in the name of the Chafetz Chaim, *zt"l,* "Our understanding of Torah is small compared to the understanding of the *Gaon* of Vilna, which was deep and extensive. However, even the understanding of the Vilna *Gaon* didn't reach the understanding that the *Rishonim* had. And the understanding of the *Rishonim,* with all their greatness, didn't reach that of the *Ge'onim.* And the *Ge'onim* didn't reach the understanding

* cited in *Kuntres Simchas Elazar,* vol. 2, p. 4.

of the *Amora'im*. And the *Amora'im* didn't reach the understanding of the *Tanna'im*. And the *Nevi'im* understood even more of the Torah, but not as much as Yehoshua, Moshe's disciple. But even the understanding that Yehoshua had of Torah wasn't like the understanding of Moshe *Rabbenu*, who received Torah from Sinai. And all this," Rav Elchonon concluded, in the name of the Chafetz Chaim, "is nothing but a drop in the bucket compared to 'the pure Torah of God.' "

THE RAMBAN'S REQUEST

There is a famous story* about the Ramban and one of his *talmidim*. The *talmid* was ill, and the Ramban saw that he was close to death. "I have a specific question," the Ramban said, "that can only be answered in a certain *heichal* in Gan Eden." (The concept of a *heichal* is obscure in the Gemara and the commentaries. The Gemara says that the soul learns Torah in a *beis midrash* in Heaven [*Berachos* 18b, *Sotah* 7b], and that it is constantly graduating from Heavenly yeshiva to yeshiva [see *Shomer Emunim ma'amar sechar ve-onesh, perek* 4, 5]. It seems that a *heichal* connotes a certain level of attainment and understanding in Gan Eden. More than that is not clear from the standard sources. But the Ramban was reputed to have been very well-versed in Kabbalah, so he definitely knew more.) "Take this amulet," he told his *talmid*. "With it all the gates of all the *heichalos* will be open to you. When you get to this certain *heichal* ask this question that I have, because it pertains to the whole of *Klal Yisrael*." Then he wrote the question down and asked his *talmid* to return to him in a dream and tell him the answer.

The *talmid* died, and for several months nothing happened. But then, one night, as the Ramban was sitting by his window studying Torah, the *talmid* finally appeared. "Every-

* cited in *Yalkut Lekach Tov, Devarim*, vol. 1, p. 282, and *Yalkut Me-Am Lo'ez, Shoftim*, p. 61.

thing was exactly as you told me," he related. "Everywhere I went I showed the amulet you gave me and all the gates opened up for me. I rose through all the *heichalos* just like you said. And when I finally arrived in this *heichal*, I wanted to ask the question that you had prepared for me. But immediately I realized that there really are no questions — everything is so clear, everything is so just. But I cannot explain it to you, for you just won't understand it."

Our job is to emulate as much as possible Avraham *Avinu*, who was instructed, "Go before Me and be *tamim* (pure)" (*Bereshis* 17:1). That was Avraham's greatness — his pure faith. There are many questions, but there are also many answers, even if our limited minds cannot comprehend them.

A LINK IN THE CHAIN

God came to Iyov (chapter 38 and onward) and asked him, "Where were you when I laid the foundations of the Earth? Declare, if you have understanding..." Did you know when "it was changed like clay under the seal?... Did you know that you would be born then, or the number of your days?" Do you know anything of the comings and goings of the world, and of your appearance as an infinitesimal link in the unending chain of the generations?

> ***While Adam was lying in a golem-like state of existence, the Holy One, blessed be He, showed him all the tzaddikim that were to be descended from him. Some were suspended from his head, others from his hair, his forehead, his eyes, his mouth, his ears... At the time when Iyov argued with Him, the Holy One, blessed be He, said to him, "Where were you when I laid the foundations of the Earth?" What does "Where were you?" mean? Rav Shimon ben Lakish said, "God said to Iyov, 'Tell Me your "where" (the roots of your essence —see Etz Yosef),***

from where on Adam you are descended —from his head, or his forehead, or whichever of his limbs. If you know which place, your "where," then you can argue with Me' " [Midrash Rabbah, beginning of Ki Sissa].

THE COUNTRY MAN IN THE BIG-CITY SHUL

My *Rosh Yeshiva, Morenu Maran Ha-Gaon Ha-Rav* Chaim Pinchas Scheinberg, *shlita*, relates that the Chafetz Chaim used to tell a story of how a Jew from the country once spent Shabbos in the big city. In shul on Shabbos morning, during the reading of the Torah, the *gabbai* called up men for *aliyos*, from all different corners of the shul. After the services, the guest went over to the *gabbai* and said, "My dear sir, I enjoyed the davening here very much, but tell me, why did you have to call the *aliyos* from all over? Wouldn't it have been more organized to call the first row this week, the second row next week, and so on? In that way you would be able to call everybody up in an orderly manner and make sure that everybody receives his turn."

The *gabbai* smiled and replied, "*Oy*, you come here for one Shabbos and want to understand everything? If you had been here over a period of several weeks, you would have realized that two weeks ago the man on the first bench had a *yahrtzeit*, and had to have an *aliyah* then. Last week the fellow behind him celebrated his son's bar mitzvah and he had to have an *aliyah*. The man on the third bench has been sick for the last few weeks and would have lost his turn according to your suggestion! And this week the fellow next to him is getting married, so naturally I had to give him an *aliyah* today. If I were to follow your advice, nobody would get his *aliyah* when he needs it and everyone would be unhappy."

So too, teaches the Chafetz Chaim, do we come into this world for a mere 70 or 80 years, and we want to understand everything! But in order to understand it we have to put it into the context of the whole universe, from the beginning of time until the end of days.

THE FARMER AND THE FOOL

A few days before he was murdered by the Nazis, Rav Elchonon Wasserman, *zt"l*, was asked by his *talmidim* if he could explain the horrible ordeal they were going through. He told them the following parable:* A man who understood nothing of agriculture once met an old, experienced farmer and asked him to demonstrate his work to him. The farmer happily agreed, and invited the fellow to go out to the field with him the following morning.

The next morning, as the man gazed upon the beautiful sight of a lush, green field, to his surprise the farmer got into his tractor and proceeded to plow the field and turn over all the earth. "Are you out of your mind?" cried the guest. "This field was so beautiful, and now you've ruined it!" The farmer replied calmly that he would have to wait patiently until he understood what he was doing.

The next day, the farmer took out a sack of beautiful grain and planted it in the earth. "Are you crazy?" asked the guest. "Why are you burying these beautiful seeds?" The farmer asked him to please be patient.

After some time the seeds sprouted in the field and beautiful, full stalks grew. The guest told himself that now he understood everything the farmer had done. But it didn't take long before the farmer came along with a scythe and started cutting down all the stalks. "But what did you work so hard for, if now you come and cut everything down?" The farmer requested that he be patient.

Afterwards, the farmer took the cut stalks, removed the

* cited in *Kuntres Simchas Elazar*, vol. 2, pp. 10-11.

wheat berries from them, and brought them to the mill. The guest stood by, mumbling to himself, "Now he's going to take all his hard work and turn it into dust!"

Afterwards, the farmer gathered his "dust" in a large bowl and brought it to his house. There he took some water, poured it into the "dust," and mixed it together. "What!" cried the guest. "Now you're making mud?"

The farmer sighed, but continued to work, and molded his "mud" into a beautiful loaf. Then he took a match and lit the oven. When the guest saw that, he couldn't control himself and he yelled, "Now you're going to burn up all of your hard work?!" The farmer smiled and put the loaf in the oven. In a few minutes a wonderful aroma filled the kitchen and the farmer's smile widened as he watched the guest's consternation. Soon, the farmer removed the hot, golden bread from the oven and invited his guest to partake of the end result of all his incomprehensible behavior.

"The farmer is a *mashal* (parable) for the *Ribbono shel Olam,*" Rav Elchonon explained. "The foolish guest standing at the side is *Klal Yisrael*. For we see only how God plows, cuts, makes dust and mud, and puts his people into the oven. But God, be He blessed, views the end already from the beginning. He sees the wonderful hot loaf of fragrant bread which will eventually come out of all this."

It is specifically when our intellect doesn't understand, when everything looks bleak and senseless, that we are beckoned to show our greatness. In *Tehillim* (121:1) it says, "I lift my eyes to the mountains. From where will my help come?" The word "from where" in Hebrew is *me-ayin*, literally "from nothing." It is "from nothing," that my help will come. God created the world "from nothing" and He helps and creates the salvation "from nothing."*

* *Or Ha-Musar*, vol. 2, p. 31, citing Rav Avraham Zalmans, *zt"l*.

THE FINE LINES OF FAITH

One who has pure *emunah* and *bitachon* is completely secure in his trust in God (see *Chovos Ha-Levavos*, beginning of *sha'ar Ha-Bitachon*). When he is tried to the edge of his endurance, and he feels his *emunah* bending under the stress, he may begin to harbor the thought that perhaps Divine Justice has been mistakenly turned against him. As he feels he can endure no more, he cries out, like Iyov, "Perhaps a storm wind passed in front of You and You got confused between *Iyov* (איוב) and *Oyev* (אויב, enemy) [a mistake of transposing two letters]." It could be that his trials have not caused him to lose all his faith, to "turn the bowl over and spill out the soup" (*Bava Basra* 16a), and that regarding cosmic events, he is still a firm believer that God runs the world and "everything is in the hands of God." However, the small particulars are attributed, at best, to "pure accident." "Why has this happened to me? I don't deserve it!" is the thought which plagues him. He has been weakened in his firm belief in Divine Providence over the fine details. He feels that the fine line between *Iyov* and *Oyev* has been breached. The implication is, God forbid, that it is impossible for Divine Providence to discern the fine lines.

It was on this very point that God came Himself to Iyov, to demonstrate that there is no difference in His *Hashgachah* between the "macrocosm," the general plan for the universe, and the "microcosm," all the small details. He oversees everything equally, and even the "fine lines" are governed by *Hashgachah Pratis*.

> ***Then Hashem answered Iyov from the storm wind and said ... Now gird your loins like a man, and I will ask you and [you] will answer Me*** [38:1,3]. ***He said to him: I have created a certain number of hairs on each person. For each hair I created its own separate pore in order that two hairs should not draw nourishment from one pore. For if two***

> *hairs drew nourishment from the same pore, one's eyesight would be diminished. Between one pore and the next I did not get confused; would I get confused between Iyov and Oyev?!*
> *The mountain goat is very cruel to its offspring. When the time comes for her to give birth, she climbs to the top of a mountain so that her young should fall to the earth and die.* * *I prepare an eagle to catch the newborn in its wings and put it down safely in front of her. If the eagle were to be early by one second or late by one second the newborn kid would immediately die. I did not get confused between two seconds; would I get confused between Iyov and Oyev?!* [Bava Basra 16a,b].

With this, God illustrated to Iyov that there is no difference to Him between one second and the next, between one hair and the next: each moment of time has its own purpose and there is no space of empty time. Surely in dealing with such an important creation as a human life, it is unthinkable that He would get confused between *Iyov* and *Oyev*. Thus a person should brace himself against any amount of pain, for any amount of time. Every second of torment is given with Divine *Hashgachah*.

Rebbe Aaron Rotte, *zt"l*, in *Shomer Emunim* (*ma'amar* on *Hashgachah Pratis, perek* 18) comments on this *gemara*, "If Hashem has put so much *Hashgachah* on birds and creatures which are impure (*teme'im*), all the more so does He put His *Hashgachah* upon Man, who was created in the image of God. And even more so on the seed of Yisrael, the holy nation whom He called 'dear beloved children,' the seed of Avraham, Yitzchak, and Ya'akov. Most certainly there is no moment that,

* The mountain goat's womb is narrow, and delivery is much more painful to it than to other animals. It hates the young for causing it this pain (Rashi and Metzudas David).

Heaven forbid, Hashem removes His *Hashgachah* from any Jew, down to all the details, and certainly in a general way. So, too, each step any one of us takes, each movement, is watched over by Divine *Hashgachah*, as Iyov said, 'Does He not see all my ways and count all of my steps?' (31:4).

"Man, however, due to his foolishness and his weak faith, causes, Heaven forbid, *Ha-Kadosh Baruch Hu* to hide His face from him. But in all these stages of 'concealment' lies His *Hashgachah*, only that it comes from behind and is concealed. Sometimes He hides Himself this way, and sometimes that way. And sometimes the 'concealment' is in order to confuse the person in serving Hashem, and the person thinks that He is hiding from him, while really He is openly appearing to him. One must dig very deep to find Him, using one's strong *emunah* and *bitachon*, and sometimes through crying out to Hashem. This is because this 'concealment' of *Ha-Kadosh Baruch Hu* was done in order that Man should search for Him. Once he breaks through the 'concealment,' the light of Hashem's countenance opens up to him."

THIS WORLD IS BUT A SERIES OF TESTS

Mesillas Yesharim starts off by saying that the true purpose of life in this world is to be a means of gaining entry to the next. The "real" purpose of our existence is to do all that we can to ensure the greatest amount of reward in the next world. Or more exactly, to attain the highest level of connection to God (I once heard it referred to as "God-awareness"), which is the criterion for enjoyment in the Next World. The more one achieves love of God, the more one's thoughts are preoccupied with developing a relationship with Him. The closer one gets to Him, the higher one's level in the Next World. As Rav Avigdor Miller, *shlita*, put it in one of his *shiurim*: If one has reached a level of 60% in this world, then he should know that in the Next World he will constantly be raised higher and higher, but always at 60%.

In simple terms, this world is a series of tests, some small, some great. How one passes or fails each test or series of tests determines one's *Olam Ha-Ba* — World to Come. Iyov dealt with the issue from a very limited stand, addressing the subject only from a rational and logical viewpoint. Using pure logic, he came to the best conclusion possible. However, pure logic led him to conclusions which can at best be labeled as mistakes, and at worst, *apikorsus* — heresy (see note in chapters 6-7, chapter 42, and Appendix). He was unaware of the whole context: that there was a Satan who had discerned the flaws in his perfected character, and that the whole affair was a test to see if he would correct the flaws or not. He did not deal with the spiritual realm, which works on a different plane. Our job is to gain as much knowledge as we can of how that plane works, and to act accordingly.

Now, let us proceed to study *Iyov*, led by our teacher, the Malbim.

The Malbim on Iyov

BACKGROUND

IYOV 1

Iyov begins with an important prelude which is the key to understanding the whole debate which follows. The point of the whole debate is found here, as we are informed of the root of the entire episode and the truth of what brought about Iyov's suffering and trials. All this, however, was hidden from Iyov and his three friends until the Prophet Elihu, the last debater, uncovers the truth and reveals the secret which we are about to share.

The crux and principle of the debate is the torment which came upon Iyov inexplicably and without any apparent justifiable reason, causing him to cry out bitterly against Divine Providence. Therefore the episode is preceded by a preface which informs us of the makeup and nature of this person who suffers so greatly, to let us know that, indeed, there is no apparent reason of any sort to which to ascribe his torments.

איש היה בארץ עוץ איוב שמו והיה האיש ההוא תם וישר וירא אלקים וסר מרע. ויולדו לו שבעה בנים ושלוש בנות. ויהי מקנהו שבעת אלפי צאן ושלשת אלפי גמלים וחמש מאות צמד בקר וחמש מאות אתונות ועבדה רבה מאד ויהי האיש ההוא גדול מכל בני קדם. [א:א-ג]

There was a man in the land of Utz, his name was Iyov, and that man was sincere and upright, God-fearing and shunning evil. And seven sons and three daughters were born to him. And his livestock consisted of seven thousand sheep, three thousand camels, five hundred yoke of cattle, five hundred she-donkeys, and very much production, and that man was the greatest of all of those in the East [1:1-3].

NO APPARENT CAUSE OF IYOV'S SUFFERING

According to our way of thinking, everything must have a cause. Why should someone suffer? We can imagine several causes for poverty and suffering coming upon a person:

1. Personal causes, due to one's nature or makeup
   a. Natural causes: Being a glutton and a drunkard constantly weakens one's body; one who is not careful with his money because of his bad character can sink to poverty. But we are informed that Iyov was *tam v'yashar* — sincere and upright. "Upright" includes straightness of mind and character, according to one's nature. However, even the upright sometimes stray from the straight path when external causes require such a response, i.e., at a time when being honest will bring about damage or prevent profit. However, a *tam* — innocent and sincere — will stick to his principles without any consideration of personal benefit. He remains as strong as a rock and never wavers.
   b. Divine causes: Sometimes, even though one is by nature sincere and upright, still, suffering or poverty come upon a person as a Divine punishment, if one doesn't fear God properly and isn't keeping His commandments and statutes, or if he is careful only about those mitzvos which he feels are reasonable or make sense. This too did not characterize Iyov, for he was *yireh Elokim v'sar me-ra* — God-fearing and shunned evil.

2. Family

A natural cause for a person's world to crumble can be childlessness, the lack of family. One who has no help or support is destroyed by others seeking to inherit his wealth. Iyov, however, had seven sons, "like olive trees surrounding his table," guarding him from all harm.

3. Poverty

A person's demise is often caused by poverty, for poverty

breeds more poverty and everyone despises a poor man. Iyov, however, was overflowing with wealth. He had herds of cattle and flocks of sheep, fields and vineyards, servants and workers busy at work. All his wealth guaranteed a force quite able to guard him from all injury.

4. Social standing

One without social standing is looked down upon and scorned. He is crushed in public, with no one willing to come to his aid. Iyov, however, was *gadol mi-kol benei Kedem* — in the eyes of the whole East he was considered great and favored, and crowned with a reputation.

והלכו בניו ועשו משתה בית איש יומו ושלחו וקראו לשלשת אחיתיהם לאכל ולשתות עמהם. [א:ד]

And his sons would go and make a feast in each one's house on his day, and they would send and call for their three sisters to eat and drink with them **[1:4].**

5. Familial strife

One's downfall can be caused by his children and other members of his household, when brothers hate each other and plot evil in the home, as happened to Ya'akov as a result of his sons' hatred of their brother Yosef. In contrast, here we read of how the brothers lived together in mutual harmony, for "his sons would go and make a feast in each one's house...and call for their three sisters to eat and drink with them." It was their practice that each son had one day of the seven days of feasting set aside, that on this day they would all eat by him. It was done in such a way that there was no jealousy or animosity among them, nor with the sisters, for they were always invited.

6. Shirking responsibility

We cannot presume that Iyov's suffering came upon him

due to the transgressions of his household or his lack of responsibility in preventing them. It is recounted how he paid attention to his household with the utmost supervision, to sanctify them and purify them from all sin.

ויהי כי הקיפו ימי המשתה וישלח איוב ויקדשם והשכים בבקר והעלה עלות מספר כלם כי אמר איוב אולי חטאו בני וברכו אלקים בלבבם ככה יעשה איוב כל הימים.
[א:ה]

Now it would come about when the cycle of the feasting days would be over that Iyov would send and sanctify them, and he arose early and offered up burnt-offerings according to their total number, for Iyov said, Perhaps my sons have sinned and blasphemed God in their hearts so would Iyov do all the days **[1:5].**

"Now it would come about when the cycle of the feasting days would be over," at the end of the seven days, before the start of the next seven days, "that Iyov would send and sanctify them" to prepare them for the next day when he "offered up burnt-offerings according to their total number." A burnt-offering comes to atone for the thoughts in one's heart, "for Iyov said, 'Perhaps my sons have sinned' " during the feast, " 'and blasphemed God in their hearts.' " Perhaps some corrupt thought rose up in their hearts against God. And he didn't do this just once, but rather, "so would Iyov do all the days."

This introduction removes any speculation that there was some wrongdoing to which we could attribute Iyov's suffering, for there was no reason. It was neither punishment, nor natural, nor of his own free will. Logically, Iyov should have enjoyed sweet success in everything he did. So now we are allowed to become partners to the real secret behind his terrible and apparently unjustified suffering.

THE TESTS

THE PHYSICALITY OF MAN AND THE ESSENCE OF MAN

The Rambam (*Guide for the Perplexed*, section 3, chap. 8) explains that all evil, whether general or specific, is due solely to the fact that we are made up of physical matter. All physical existence must, by its very nature of being a material body, suffer disintegration. But besides the material being of each object, there is another aspect, what the Rambam calls the "form." It is the abstract concept of what that ideal object is, the spiritual essence of each being. For example, there is the "form" of a human being. This "form" is constant, unchanging, never suffering any deterioration. The concept of a human being never changes. However, this form can be damaged incidentally through its connection to the material. The nature of a material body is such that it cannot avoid being affected by disintegration, and therefore it is constantly losing one form and taking on another.

The Rambam explains that all destruction, deterioration, and loss is a result of the material. For example, a person may suffer from an ugly appearance, or malformed limbs, or he sustains weakness which prohibits him from carrying out normal activity, or creates awkward movements, or a total inability to act. This may have originated from his conception or occurred to him afterwards. But it is all purely due to his material destructibility and not due to his essence (the human form). So, too, each living creature must inevitably die or fall sick as a result of its being matter. All human crimes and sins are a result of being physical.

All virtues, however, are a result of one's essence. For example, perception of one's Creator, or the ability to formulate logical reasoning, the way one controls his lusts and his anger, his ability to investigate and decide what he wants, or what he must distance himself from — all these are a result of the human form. But eating and drinking, cohabitation, and most of one's lusts and anger, and other evil characteristics one finds within himself, are a result of his being material.

With this in mind, we come now to understand the parable at the beginning of *Iyov*.

> ויהי היום ויבאו בני האלקים להתיצב על ה׳ ויבוא גם השטן בתוכם. [א:ו]
>
> ***Now the day came about, and the Heavenly powers (angels; literally, children of God) came to stand before God, and the Satan, too, came among them*** [1:6].

THE FORCES OF CREATION

We are accustomed to viewing the universe as having been created, and everything that we see, as a result of that Creation. *Chazal*, however, inform us differently. "He renews in His goodness the act of Creation constantly" (*Shacharis*). God causes and creates all of Existence in an ongoing process, and all of the forces of the universe (literally, children of God) come to stand before Him, for the universe exists in a state of continuous Creation and the forces of Creation have come to take their new orders from the Almighty. Now we are told how even the Satan, the force which causes all disintegration, the source of evil, loss, sin, and all damage, has come among them.

The *Guide for the Perplexed* (section 3, chap. 22) explains that the verse does not state, "...the Heavenly powers and the Satan came to stand before God," for then it would have implied that the existence of both of them was on an equal plane, that Satan shared the same relationship to them. Instead, it states that he "came among them," as if he didn't come in and of himself intentionally to stand before God, for he has no roots in the process of the continuous Creation of Existence, but rather in imperfection and destruction. He merely "comes among them," being that he is merely a condition of the "lower powers," the forces of the material world. For you will never find the existence of material beings without the previously assumed concept of deterioration, constantly throwing off one form and taking on another.

We have a tradition that over each of the powers of Creation is appointed a higher force which is its spiritual root. These are the *benei Elokim*, the angels (literally, the children of God) who have come to stand before Him. They are the angels appointed over all the forces of nature, whose power and influence all come from God. As *Chazal* have stated, "There is no blade of grass that doesn't have appointed to it an angel commanding it, 'Grow!' " (*Bereshis Rabbah* 10:7). The force of disintegration and destruction also has a spiritual power appointed over it: he is the Satan, the Accuser, the angel of death, the force of imperfection. As *Chazal* have stated, "He is the adversary, he is the evil nature of a person (the evil inclination), he is the angel of death" (*Bava Basra* 16a). He has come to prosecute and renew his power to destroy.

ויאמר ה׳ אל השטן מאין תבא ויען השטן את ה׳ ויאמר משוט בארץ ומהתהלך בה. [א:ז]

And God said to the Satan, "From where are you coming?" And the Satan answered God, "From floating around the Earth and from walking on it" [1:7].

THE SATAN — THE FORCE OF DESTRUCTION

"And God said to the Satan..." The story continues now to explain with a parable. God asks the Satan, "From where are you coming?" Disintegration and destruction, which are in the power of the Satan, are not attached to the higher (spiritual) existence, but are attached to the materiality of this world. Therefore he answers, "From floating around the Earth and from walking on it." This comes to tell us two things: 1) Disintegration and destruction exist only on the Earth and not in the Higher (spiritual) Realm. 2) They are found on the Earth (meaning, in material beings) in two forms: a) general, constant disintegration, which is an inseparable part of the nature of the physical in that any compound inevitably separates, and man and animal must inevitably die when their end comes; and b) accidental disintegration, such as when one dies or falls ill from overindulgence in food or cohabitation, or through people killing one another, etc. Thus "From floating around the Earth" refers to the accidental, and "from walking on it" refers to the constant deterioration, for "walking" implies steadiness.

ויאמר ה׳ אל השטן השמת לבך על עבדי איוב כי אין כמהו בארץ איש תם וישר ירא אלקים וסר מרע. [א:ח]

And God said to the Satan, "Have you paid attention to My servant Iyov? For there is none like him on Earth. He is a sincere and upright man, God-fearing and shunning evil" [1:8].

"And God said to the Satan..." A parable is used to explain that since Divine Wisdom saw it necessary that the very distinguished human form be attached to this dark and dusty materiality which brings it to suffer deterioration and destruction, God has also given to the human form the ability to control and rule over the physical, to coerce it to curb its sensual desires and redirect them to the straight and balanced. From this point of view, for the truly spiritual man who completely conquers his material being, who has complete control over his physical lusts, and whose soul rules powerfully over all his faculties, even the force of imperfection which emanates from his material side has no effect upon him. This perfect man is protected by Divine Providence from all mishaps or problems caused by the material and its evil.

Therefore God asks the Satan: "Have you paid attention to My servant Iyov?" He is My servant, and therefore you have no influence over him. "For there is none like him on Earth." He is completely divorced from the material world and the physical. He is a totally spiritual man, "a sincere and upright man, God-fearing and shunning evil."

ויען השטן את ה׳ ויאמר החנם ירא איוב אלקים. [א:ט]

And the Satan answered God and said, "Does Iyov fear God in vain?" [1:9].

THE FLAW

"And the Satan answered..." [This is where the Satan finds an opening, where there is a defect in the perfection.❖] He replies that there is a special condition here. When one serves

---

❖ Rav Yerucham Levovitz of the Mir Yeshiva, *zt"l*, in his work *Da'as Torah* (*Bereshis*, p. 135), writes that a *nisayon* (a trial) is an indication of deficiency in the individual. The verse says, "And it was after these things that God tested Avraham" (*Bereshis* 22:1). The commentators are bothered by what "these things" were that preceded the test. Rashi writes that some of the commentaries explain that the test came after the Satan had spoken. He came and made an accusation against Avraham: "He has made so many feasts, and not once has he offered up anything to

God and subdues his lusts in the hope of reward or out of fear of harm, then this is not considered a spiritual endeavor, but a very physical one. This is like one who gets paid to fast. It isn't a spiritually motivated fast, but rather an expression of how much one loves his physical being. Since he loves his body, or in order to earn money to fulfill his needs, he afflicts his body for a short time in order to gain afterwards. It is not fitting to say that as a result of this affliction he has sanctified himself and divorced himself from the physical and attached himself to lofty spiritual worlds. For it is just the opposite — he is sunken in the love of money so much that he is willing to fast and suffer in order to attain it.

So, too, does the Satan judge Iyov, whose fear of God and shunning of evil are not spiritual accomplishments, because they do not come out of a love of good for its own sake. That would only be the case when one has no expectations of receiving any reward or being saved from any harm that he fears, but rather behaves freely, unrelated to any ultimate reward.

God from them." God replied, "Do you think that he made those feasts for himself? He made them only for his son. Why, if I were to tell him to offer up his son to Me, he wouldn't keep back from doing it."

Rav Yerucham explains that the hidden potential of an individual is brought out into realization by a *nisayon*. *Chazal* explain the word *nisayon* (נסיון) / (נס) (as originating from the word *nes*, meaning the banner or flag of a ship. The banner announces the identification of its bearer.

The cause of a *nisayon* is the accusation of the Satan, who searches for the hidden faults of the individual and lays them before the Heavenly court. Through the *nisayon*, by being tested, the person transforms his potential into reality and in that way annuls the accusations of the Satan. Then the person is finished and complete, and has the ability to endure.

הלא את שכת בעדו ובעד ביתו ובעד כל אשר לו מסביב
מעשה ידיו ברכת ומקנהו פרץ בארץ. [א:י]

"Haven't You protected him, his household, and all that he has around him? You have blessed the work of his hands and his livestock has spread out in the land" [1:10].

"Haven't You protected him..." Here the Satan mentions the two conditions listed above which detract from one's purely spiritual intent. The first is fear of harm: "Haven't You protected him...?" for You have protected and sheltered him so that harm should have no effect on "him, his household, and all that he has around him." This includes protection of Iyov himself, of his children, and of his property. He is afraid of losing this protection, especially since he is aware that according to the "stars" he is "doomed" to suffer evil, as he says, later on, "I feared and it came upon me" (3:25).

The second motive behind Iyov's righteousness was hope of reward: מעשה ידיו ברכת, "You have blessed the work of his hands" — You have sent him a blessing in his business and other dealings. "And his livestock has spread out in the land" — above the natural norm.❖ This is the reward that he receives almost instantly in return for his reverence and righteousness. It is reasonable to assume that his reverence and righteousness may be tainted by the love of reward or fear of harm. It should

---

❖ What is the meaning of "You have blessed the work of his hands"? Rav Shmuel bar Rav Yitzchak said, "Anyone who took money from Iyov was blessed." What is the meaning of "and his livestock has spread out (literally, broken through) in the land"? Rav Yosei bar Chanina said, "The livestock of Iyov broke through the fence (normal bounds) of the world. The normal way of the world is that wolves kill the goats. With the livestock of Iyov, the goats killed the wolves" (*Bava Basra* 15b).

be possible to determine this through a test and a trial.

ואולם שלח נא ידך וגע בכל אשר לו אם לא על פניך יברכך. [א:יא]

"However, stretch forth Your hand and touch all that he has. Will he not blaspheme You to Your face?" [1:11].

"However, stretch forth Your hand..." — and this will be the test. If Iyov's righteousness is for the sake of pure good, and not due to any ulterior motive of reward or punishment, then even if You remove the protection and the blessing from him, with all this he will not waver in his righteousness. But if his righteousness is based on the hope of reward or fear of punishment, then if You "stretch forth Your hand and touch all that he has," when he is put in a situation where there is nothing left for him to fear or to hope for, then "Will he not blaspheme You to Your face?" That is to say, then not only will he no longer be a *tzaddik,* since the motive for his retaining his righteousness is gone, but he will even blaspheme and discredit Your conduct because of Your *Hashgachah* and the way You have turned against him. He thought that through his righteousness he deserved wealth and possessions. But now when he sees everything he had, which he felt he deserved, being taken from him, he will attribute this to wrong conduct [on Your part] and will say that You don't judge righteously. This will be the clear-cut test: If his service to You is motivated by love, then he will not complain. Rather, the bad times will, in his eyes, be equal to the good times.

The Satan specifically says that God should "touch *all* that he has," for if anything should be left over, then the test would not be complete, for then Iyov would still have something more to fear and prevent him from rebelling against God in order that He not take from him this last remnant.

ויאמר ה׳ אל השטן הנה כל אשר לו בידך רק אליו אל
תשלח ידך ויצא השטן מעם פני ה׳. [א:יב]

And God said to the Satan, "Behold, all that he has is in your hands; only upon him do not stretch forth your hand." And the Satan left from before the Presence of God **[1:12].**

THE FIRST TEST — "WITH ALL YOUR MIGHT"

"And God said to the Satan..." It is clear from the parable that Iyov's torments were in reality a form of test, to determine if his heart was really entirely faithful to God, and to see if he would stand firmly righteous even in his poverty. [Many people have faith, but the question is, until what limit.] This was all in order to determine if he served God from true love. His suffering was not due to any previous transgression; he was pure and had no tinge of sin, as God testified about him that he was a sincere and upright man. However, all this was unknown to the three friends who debated with him until Elihu the Buzite revealed the truth at the end of the debates.

The parable goes on to relate that first the Satan was not permitted to test Iyov personally, but only in regard to his external possessions and his children, as is stated, הנה כל אשר לו בידך רק אליו אל תשלח ידך "Behold, all that he has is in your hands; only upon him do not stretch forth your hand." The Rambam explains in the *Guide for the Perplexed* (section 3, chap. 22) that "There are those who do not lose themselves over the loss of monetary possessions. However, the loss of their children causes them so much emotional pain that they can die. There are also those who can bear the pain of losing their children, but their own pain is too much to bear.

[In the *Shema* prayer we say the words בכל נפשך ובכל מאדך, "...with all your soul and all your might." The Gemara understands "might" as "money," and in *Berachos* 61b comments that some love themselves more than their money, and others love their money more than themselves. The first test of Iyov was בכל מאדך, "with all your might" — love God with all your possessions, all your wealth, all your children. The second test was to see if he loved God with all his soul.]

Therefore, the Satan was first given permission to destroy his property and children.

ויצא השטן מעם פני ה', "And the Satan left from before the Presence of God." Destruction and imperfection do not come directly from God. He is the Creator Who establishes and sustains all of Existence. Rather, they come from nonexistence: when God removes His power from a place, allowing the force of concealment to take effect (see *Yeshayahu* 45:7, "...Who forms light and creates darkness").

ויהי היום ובניו ובנתיו אכלים ושתים יין בבית אחיהם הבכור. [א:יג]

Now the day came about that his sons and daughters were dining and drinking wine at the home of their firstborn brother [1:13].

"Now the day came about..." We are given a detailed explanation that all this was not due to any previous sin of Iyov's, or of his children. For it was on the day, ובניו ובנתיו אכלים ושתים בבית אחיהם הבכור, "that his sons and daughters were dining and drinking wine at the home of their firstborn brother." This was the day when the cycle of feasting ended and on that day they brought up burnt-offerings to atone for all their sins.

THE SATAN ARRANGES THE MOST TREMENDOUS IMPACT POSSIBLE AGAINST IYOV

ומלאך בא אל איוב ויאמר הבקר היו חרשות והאתנות רעות על ידיהם. ותפל שבא ותקחם ואת הנערים הכו לפי חרב ואמלטה רק אני לבדי להגיד לך. [א:יד-טו]

And a messenger came to Iyov and said, "The cattle were plowing and the she-donkeys were grazing beside them, and Sheva fell upon them and took them, and they slew the youths by the sword, and only I alone escaped to tell you" [1:14-15].

"And a messenger came..." The *Guide* writes (section 3, chap. 12) that all evil which comes upon a person fits into one of three categories: 1) evil which comes from the nature of existence and decay, i.e., evil which develops because of changes in the physical elements, caused by damage from the air, or from lightning, or geological shifts, etc.; 2) evil which comes about through Man, one group against the other; 3) evil which occurs to each person as a result of his own actions, i.e., illness which results from an overly lustful desire for food and drink, and sex, and overindulging in them or partaking of them haphazardly, or partaking of foods devoid of quality. Here he says that this time the Satan brought upon Iyov the first two categories of evil. First the marauders of Sheva attacked (evil perpetrated by Man). And then a natural element of evil occured: a tremendous fire (see *Metzudas Tzion*). This was repeated again with attack by the Kasdim, and the whirlwind.

Moreover, in each of these evils were mixed elements of two other categories. The "evils perpetrated by Man" were due to either the desire for money and gain, which resulted in the attack by Sheva who came to take plunder and spoil, out of love of money; or to love victory and control, which cause one people or nation to wage war against another. This was the motivation of the Kasdim who attacked on three fronts in a form of battle strategy.

So, too, "the evils of the elements" occur either purely accidentally — like the tremendous fire which fell from heaven — or as a result of the normal course of nature — like the wind which came from across the desert. Moreover, the messenger tells Iyov how Sheva didn't come during the night or in an ambush, but rather at a time when the cattle were plowing and the donkeys were grazing, right in the middle of the day. This was so that one couldn't say that the shepherds were not there to stand up against them: instead, they fought them and were smitten by the sword.

עוד זה מדבר וזה בא ויאמר אש אלקים נפלה מן השמים ותבער בצאן ובנערים ותאכלם ואמלטה רק אני לבדי להגיד לך. עוד זה מדבר וזה בא ויאמר כשדים שמו שלשה ראשים ויפשטו על הגמלים ויקחום ואת הנערים הכו לפי חרב ואמלטה רק אני לבדי להגיד לך. [א:טז-יז]

While this one was still talking, another one came and said, "A tremendous fire fell from heaven and burned the flocks and the youths and consumed them, and only I alone escaped to tell you." And while this one was still talking, yet another one came and said, "The Kasdim formed three bands, spread out on the camels and took them, and slew the youths by the sword, and only I alone escaped to tell you" **[1:16-17].**

"While this one was still talking..." The evils came one right after the other, as Iyov said, "I was not at ease, neither did I have quiet, and I did not rest, and trouble came" (3:25). It was as if the messenger had escaped just to tell him the evil tidings, and then, as *Chazal* said (see Rashi, verse 19) he immediately died. Then the second one informed him that the tremendous fire had fallen and devoured the flocks, and then a third messenger told him that the Kasdim had spread out on the camels. Thus the order was that first the cattle and donkeys were lost, then the flocks, and afterwards the camels.

At the beginning of the book it says, "And seven sons were born to him...and his...cattle..." The author lists the sons, the flocks, the camels, and afterwards the cattle and the donkeys.

It is clear that in relating his wealth and possessions, the more important ones were listed first. But when his possessions were lost, the least important were lost first, until finally his sons were lost. If this is the case, would it not have been better that the order be: the cattle and donkeys, then the camels, and after them the flocks, and last the loss of the children? Why did the flocks precede the camels?

I have already explained that the tragedies were divided into groups. One tragedy came about through Man, and one through the elements; then again through Man, and afterwards through the element of wind. If the camels had been lost through the Kasdim before the flocks, there would have been the two tragedies through the hand of Man immediately following each other. And also the two evils of the elements. It would not have not been so startling if the Sheva and Kasdim came at one time, or the fire and windstorm. But at the time of the attack of the Sheva there were no Kasdim yet; and only afterwards the fire came down and devoured the flocks. Also, the wind didn't come together with the fire. This added up to give the news a tremendous impact.

עד זה מדבר וזה בא ויאמר בניך ובנותיך אכלים ושתים
יין בבית אחיהם הבכור. [א:יח]

As this one finished talking, another one came and said, "Your sons and daughters were dining and drinking wine at the home of their firstborn brother" [1:18].

עד זה מדבר, "As this one finished talking..." The first three messengers informed him of the loss of his possessions, which were all in one category. Therefore each one came even before the previous speaker had finished his words, as it says, "While this one was still talking." The fourth, however, informed him of the loss of the children, which was a new test (see above, verse 12) and a separate category, and therefore he came *after* the third had finished his statement. That is why it says עד — after, until, "this one finished talking."

והנה רוח גדולה באה מעבר המדבר ויגע בארבע פנות הבית ויפל על הנערים וימותו ואמלטה רק אני לבדי להגיד לך. [א:יט]

"And behold, a big wind came from the other side of the desert, and struck the four corners of the house and it fell upon the youths, and they died, and only I alone escaped to tell you" [1:19].

"And behold, a big wind..." This too was unusual, for the wind came from the other side of the desert. As *Chazal* said, it was an easterly wind, and when it approached the house, it broke into four separate winds which encircled it.

ויקם איוב ויקרע את מעלו ויגז את ראשו ויפל ארצה וישתחו. ויאמר ערם יצתי מבטן אמי וערם אשוב שמה ה׳ נתן וה׳ לקח יהי שם ה׳ מברך. [א:כ-כא]

And Iyov stood up and rent his garment, tore the hair from his head, and fell to the ground and prostrated himself (prayed). And he said, "Naked did I come from my mother's womb, and naked shall I return there. God gave and God took away, let the Name of God be blessed" [1:20-21].

IYOV PASSES THE FIRST TEST

"And Iyov stood up," to stand while making the *berachah*. "And rent his garment" — on the loss of his children (according to Halachah). And "tore the hair from his head" — on the loss of the possessions, for the prohibition against tearing one's hair out as a sign of mourning applies only in the case of a death ("Do not make yourselves bald over the dead" [*Devarim* 14:1]), but over the loss of physical objects there is no such prohibition.

ויאמר ערם יצתי, "Naked did I come..." He had room to complain against God in one of two fashions: 1) If the possessions which were now taken from him were inseparable from his body (like one of his limbs), then even though God had created them and given them to him, still, since they were a part of himself from the beginning of his conception, he would have considered it a crime for God to take them from him. But this is not the case with these possessions: his property and his children. They are external possessions not attached to his own person. They did not originate from the beginning when he was first formed, for he was born without these possessions: ערם יצתי מבטן אמי, "Naked did I come from my mother's womb," without these possessions. Nor are they destined to be part of him, for: וערם אשוב שמה, "And naked shall I return there" — to the womb of the mother of Mankind, the Earth, who is the mother of all life.

2) But here, too, even considering these possessions not to be an intrinsic part of him, there is room to complain, for if he acquired them through his own ability and power, then they should have been considered his, being that he brought them into existence. However, since, ה׳ נתן, "God gave" them, וה׳ לקח, "and God took [them] away," therefore there is no room for complaint. And so, "Let the Name of God be blessed."

Moreover, he said that just as God gave with the attribute of *Rachamim* (Mercy) [Iyov used the four-letter Name of God, implying Divine Mercy, not the name *Elokim*, which implies Divine Retribution], so too did He take with mercy. For certainly this evil is for some good purpose. Perhaps He took the children and the possessions as an atonement so that Iyov personally should remain in life and health. Therefore he blessed the evil in the same way one blesses the good.

[For the moment Iyov has passed the test. He has accepted the loss of all his children and possessions. Everything is for the good. He is accepting everything that God has done to him. The Malbim makes no mention of anything wrong here. As a matter of fact, Iyov's words are the words of a *tzaddik*. But if we follow the lines of the Satan's charges above, perhaps we can make out the beginnings of a flaw developing. The four-letter Name implies the attribute of Divine Mercy, as opposed to Divine Retribution. As God gave these possessions with mercy, so too did he take them. This seeming evil must be for some beneficial end. He has taken the children and the possessions in atonement in order to allow Iyov himself to remain alive and well. Therefore Iyov blessed the bad in the same way we bless the good. Perhaps we can infer that Iyov is only willing to accept the bad as long as there is some personal benefit to be derived from it. To accept the bad purely out of love of God seems beyond him. The Satan has found a crack in Iyov's perfection.]

בכל זאת לא חטא איוב ולא נתן תפלה לאלקים. [א:כב]

Despite this, Iyov did not sin, and did not attribute a blemish to God [1:22].

If there had been any rotten roots of a complaint simmering in Iyov's heart, then his remarks would have taken a different vein. He had one of two paths he could have followed. Either he could have concluded that no wrongdoing can come from God the Righteous One, so therefore evil must come from elsewhere, from "nature" and the Heavenly order. In so doing, he would have been denying *Hashgachah* (Divine Providence), saying that God does not oversee what is happening. This would have opened the gate to sin, for if there is no Divine Providence, then there is no reward or punishment. (And without reward, then what was the use of his righteousness?)

[This line of reasoning is exactly what Iyov used later on. Note that unfortunately this is sometimes the conclusion of those who have experienced tremendous suffering (such as the Holocaust). God the Merciful could not have allowed such a thing to take place. Therefore, there is no God, only blind nature. That being the case, there is no purpose in being religious, and everything is permitted.]

Or he could have consented that there is Divine *Hashgachah;* but that would have forced him into criticism of God's ways: to say that He doesn't rule with justice, and that His ways are bland (תפל) and without taste.

[This path would have allowed him to retain belief in God but would force him to denounce His ways, because He is not Just.]

But, איוב לא חטא, "Iyov did not sin." Iyov has so far passed the test. He has not criticized. He still retains his faith. He is still one who shuns evil, as before. ולא נתן תפלה לאלקים, "And did not attribute a blemish to God," by denigrating His ways. He has concluded that there has been no wrongdoing [on God's part] in His taking from him external possessions which were given as gifts and taken from him for his own good. This loss is not evil, but merely the prevention of extra good.

THE SECOND TEST — "WITH ALL YOUR SOUL"

IYOV 2

Now the parable continues. Having withstood the first test and having not given in to despair over the loss of his possessions and his children, Iyov is now tested with the second and final test — physical torment and pain.

ויהי היום ויבאו בני האלקים להתיצב על ה' ויבוא גם השטן בתכם להתיצב על ה' . [ב:א]

And the day came when the Heavenly powers came to stand before God, and the Satan, too, came among them to stand before God [2:1].

Previously (1:6) the Satan came among the other heavenly powers. He didn't come on his own. Now he comes on a special mission, for he has a special request to make.

[The Malbim has noted here the extra statement that the Satan has come "to stand before God." This implies that he has come for his own personal request.]

The very existence of the material world naturally implies deterioration and destruction (*hefsed*). Whether through the natural elements or through the evil which men perpetrate against each other, there is destruction. Only through the protection of Divine intervention is Man guarded from the elements. For the first test, all that the Satan had to do was to ask God to remove from Iyov that Divine Providence granted to *tzaddikim*, and the results were the natural outcome of this removal. The first time the Satan came, he came among the powers of nature; there was no need to request special intervention of Divine power. Let "nature" take its course. Now, however, he has a special request.

Illness which has its origin in excess cannot by nature afflict the righteous who guard their health through moderation. צדיק אוכל לשובע נפשו, "The righteous eat to satiation of the spirit" (*Mishlei* 13:25). Nature dictates that such a man remains healthy and does not become afflicted with boils and ailments. Thus the second test required special Divine intervention. It was not sufficient merely to remove Divine Providence; the very nature of the world had to be changed in order to afflict Iyov. Now the Satan comes separate from the other powers: he requests special Divine intervention into the laws of nature in order to bring about this second test.

ויאמר ה׳ אל השטן השמת לבך אל עבדי איוב כי אין כמהו בארץ איש תם וישר ירא אלקים וסר מרע ועדנו מחזיק בתמתו ותסיתני בו לבלעו חנם. [ב:ג]

And God said to the Satan, "Have you paid attention to My servant Iyov? For there is none like him on Earth. He is a sincere and upright man, God-fearing and shunning evil. And he still maintains

his sincerity, and you enticed Me against him for nothing" [2:3].

"Have you paid attention to My servant Iyov?" God knew that the Satan had come to ask for special Divine intervention against Iyov. So He tells him straight out that even this unique form of damage can have no effect upon Iyov, for he is a God-fearing person and his very nature obligates that he should not fall sick and suffer. Therefore, he told the Satan, "Even removing My *Hashgachah* from him and abandoning him to your hand, to lose his possessions and his children, was unjust, seeing that he withstood the test."

"And he still maintains his sincerity." This proves that he serves Me out of love, and not from expectation of reward or fear of punishment. Therefore, your inciting Me against him was for nothing.

ויען השטן את ה׳ ויאמר עור בעד עור וכל אשר לאיש יתן בעד נפשו. אולם שלח נא ידך וגע אל עצמו ואל בשרו אם לא אל פניך יברכך. [ב:ד-ה]

And the Satan replied to God, "Skin for skin, and whatever a person has, he will give for his life. However, stretch forth Your hand now and touch his bones and his flesh; will he not blaspheme You to Your face?" [2:4-5].

"And the Satan replied to God," Yes, Iyov passed his first test, but it was incomplete. We have not yet proven that he serves You from love. All we have proven is that his faith is not shaken by losing his possessions and his children because his self is more dear to him than his might. Even now he still won't sin, out of fear of being punished directly.

עור בעד עור, "Skin for skin" — a person is clothed in two sorts of clothing: his garments and his own skin. A person will relinquish his "clothing" (i.e., all his personal possessions) in order to save his own skin. If you were to threaten him that if he does not give you all of his clothing, you will rip his skin off, he would definitely comply and part with this "external skin." וכל אשר לאיש יתן בעד נפשו, "And whatever a person has, he will give for his life" — but more than that, he will even give up his own skin in order to save his life. He would rather have all of his skin ripped off than have his life taken. Even if the Satan is given the ability to afflict his skin with the most painful disease, still it is not the true test. At least his life has not been threatened. He can console himself that at least he is not suffering a fatal ailment. This is the only true test: אולם שלח נא ידך וגע אל עצמו ואל בשרו אם לא אל פניך יברכך, "However, stretch forth Your hand now and touch his bones and his flesh; will he not blaspheme You to Your face?" Attack not only his skin, but Iyov himself beset, and threaten his life until all hope is gone. Then he will have nothing with which to console himself or to hope for. Let us see if then he will scorn the Divine plan, says the Satan.

ויאמר ה׳ אל השטן הנו בידך אך את נפשו שמר. [ב:ו]

And God said to the Satan, "He is in your hand. Just [be sure to] preserve his life" [2:6].

Iyov's whole self was given over to the Satan, but with a condition: his life was not to be touched. *Chazal* observe, "The pain of the Satan was greater than the pain of Iyov. For this was like telling someone to break the barrel but not to spill a drop of wine" (Rashi, based on the Gemara *Bava Basra* 16a). The whole essence of the Satan is destruction; for him to stand up against this, his natural power, was more difficult than to stand against the power of life. For the Satan it is easier to destroy life than to preserve it.

> ויצא השטן מאת פני ה׳ ויך את איוב בשחין רע מכף רגלו ועד קדקדו. ויקח לו חרש להתגרד בו והוא ישב בתוך האפר. ותאמר לו אשתו עדך מחזיק בתמתך ברך אלקים ומת. ויאמר אליה כדבר אחת הנבלות תדברי גם את הטוב נקבל מאת האלקים ואת הרע לא נקבל בכל זאת לא חטא איוב בשפתיו. [ב:ז-י]
>
> ***And the Satan left from the Presence of God, and he smote Iyov with terrible boils from the sole of his foot to the top of his head. And he took himself a piece of pottery to scratch himself with, and he sat down amidst the ashes. And his wife said to him, "Do you still hold on to your sincerity? Blaspheme (literally, bless) God and die!" And he said to her, "You talk as one of the disgraceful women talks. Shall we also accept the good from God, and not accept the evil?" Despite all this, Iyov did not sin with his lips*** [2:7-10].

"And he took himself a piece of pottery to scratch himself with, and he sat down amidst the ashes." The Midrash comments that his top half was full of dry boils and he had to scratch them. His lower half had moist boils and he had to sit in ashes to draw out the pus. Each affliction's remedy irritated the other.

Now Iyov is brought to the ultimate trial. His life is over, he is doomed to die, and meanwhile he must suffer unearthly torment. In this second test he does not repeat the path he followed previously. Before, he blessed the evil as he would the good: יהי שם ה׳ מברך, "Let the Name of God be blessed." Here, however, he does not bless at all. His heart is not wholly committed, as it was previously.

This brings him incidentally to another kind of test: his wife. ותאמר לו אשתו עדך מחזיק בתמתך ברך אלקים ומת, "And his wife said to him, 'Do you still hold on to your sincerity? Bless (literally) God and die!' " In a glorious show of sarcasm, his wife fuels the fire for the ensuing debate. When you bless God and show your loyalty, she says, He only showers upon you more suffering. So bless him some more so that He should kill you! His wife has shown her true colors.

IYOV'S PHILOSOPHY TAKES FORM: THE BAD OUTWEIGHS THE GOOD

But Iyov holds firm. ויאמר אליה כדבר אחת הנבלות תדברי גם את הטוב נקבל מאת האלקים ואת הרע לא נקבל, "And he said to her, 'You talk as one of the disgraceful women talks. Shall we also accept the good from God, and not accept the evil?' " Superficially, this seems to be the answer of a true God-fearing *tzaddik*. And so have the commentaries explained. However, upon closer examination, his words reveal an apostasy lurking in the depths of his heart. "Shall we also accept the good from God, and not accept the evil?" גם, "Also" — of course there is good in the world, he is saying, but it is mixed with evil, with much evil, with an abundance of evil. For the evil outweighs the good.

Iyov's later philosophy has already taken form. He thinks that God cannot give the good alone, and one who wants to accept the good must by necessity also accept the evil. This is like one who wants to drink a lot of wine or eat a lot of sweet honey — he must not complain if the wine makes him drunk or the honey gives him a stomachache. On the contrary, what he received was good. So, too, if you want to accept God's good — life and existence — one must accept the evil which is greater than and overpowers the good, which is relatively scarce. According to Iyov, one is justified in saying that basically we receive mostly evil, and along with it also some good. Man, upon entering existence, enters a vast sea of evils and worries and tribulations which will overtake him during his short life span. This is essentially what he was born for. Along with this he gets also some good — this very short life.

Thus in the small word גם, "also," we find revealed the roots of Iyov's complaint. This is the bitter, rotten weed that has embedded itself in his heart and mind. He cries out against the Divine ways which have created Man for his Evil, an evil that outweighs the good. This is the basis for the ensuing debate. However, at present it is hidden, and only hinted at in the word גם, "also" even though this is what is in his heart. בכל זאת לא חטא איוב בשפתיו, "Despite all this, Iyov did not sin with his lips" — but in his heart he sinned (Rashi, based on Gemara *Bava Basra* 16a).❖

Now the stage is set for the debate. As the three friends of Iyov learn of his calamity and come to console him, they are taken aback by the enormity of his suffering. For seven days silence reigns, as they all mourn what has befallen their friend. Finally, Iyov speaks.

❖ Compare Iyov's attitude with that of Rabbi Akiva, who taught that one should be in the habit of saying, כל מה דעביד רחמנא לטב עביד "Everything that the Merciful One does is for the good" (*Berachos* 60b). He understood that *everything* is for the good, because God is a Merciful One, and no bad can come from the source of Divine Mercy. Not only that, but one should get in the habit of saying it, repeating it over and over to himself. Our intellect is not always able to dominate our emotions. Therefore, in order to make sure that even the heart understands this, one must make a habit of saying it, in order to consistently and fully believe it. It was in this way that R. Akiva prepared himself for his own final test. See the Epilogue for a fuller discussion.

THE DEBATE

Part One: The Righteous Who Suffer

IYOV 3

The *Sefer Ha-Ikkarim* (*perek* 4, *ma'amar* 4) states that in the medieval understanding of the universe, there were two schools of thought. The first, the philosophical school, believed that the heavenly forces and the stars influence this, the lower world. Through the continuous change in the heavenly picture, they act upon the elements, combining them and conditioning them until the form of nature that we see is produced. The result is that some people are wise, and some are not; some are suited for Divine prophecy, and some are not. Here the determinism ends. Nature does not determine anything else, i.e., poverty, affluence, marital success, social standing, or relationships with others. In these, everyone has an equal chance. The philosophers felt that it would be false to say that the stars (i.e., nature) have an influence outside of their defined realm.

The second school was that of the astrologers, who believed that everything that happens to Man is predetermined in the stars. They prove this from the ability of astrologers to predict events in fine detail: how many years one will live, whether he will be rich or poor, have children or not, etc. We find this opinion mentioned in the Gemara (*Shabbos* 156a).❖

Iyov was of the second school: Everything is predetermined by the stars and heavenly elements.

❖ In modern terms, if we translate the "power of the stars" into the "forces of nature," we find similar schools of thought in modern scientific philosophy. The schools of scientific or psychological behaviorism, which claim that Man is a function of his innate instincts, inherited genetic structure, or childhood experiences and psychological traumas, have equally stripped Man of his ability to use his free will.

This is the premise Iyov sets down at the beginning of his speech, when he curses the night of his conception and the day of his birth, for they were clouded over (3:3-10). If in Heaven it was ordained that he should be unsuccessful all of his life, then it would have been better not to have been born at all. Why should he have been forced to exist just for pain and suffering (3:10-14)?

Even though Man perceives the loss of his existence as a misfortune, this is only true once one has come into existence! Experiencing loss at any level — from loss of one's wealth to loss of life — is a result of one's awareness that he exists. If he had never come to exist at all, then the "nonexistent" would be equal to that which "was" and is no longer. In this sense it is not really possible to measure the amount of "loss." If one loses his existence without ever having reached greatness, it is equal to one's losing his existence without starting at even the lowest plane; for there is no difference between nothing and nothing (3:14-17).

In this vein, Iyov develops an argument similar to that of the Arab philosopher Alrazi, quoted by the Rambam in the *Guide* (section 3, chap. 13), who claimed that evil outweighs good. If you will compare a person's moments of pleasure in tranquil times with his strife, tribulations, torments, worries, and troubles, then you will find that the existence of Man is mere vengeance and a terrible evil. Look at the allegories and songs of the nations — is it not rare to find something good? They are mostly constant tragedy. It is along these lines of argument that Iyov develops his position (3:17-20).

But even if one will deny this and claim that the pleasant light of success is shining in his eyes, and that he has tasted the sweetness of honey, and therefore he wishes for long, eternal existence — still, there remains the gnawing question: Why should he have been brought into this existence only to await death (3:20)?

Iyov: The Only Answer is that Everything is Predetermined

Imagine a person, poverty-stricken and destitute, longing only for death and an end to his misery. His fortune decides differently and starts to shine upon him and give him hope. Suddenly he finds a hidden treasure and enormous wealth. And now as he finally turns his hopes toward life and goodness, death finally catches up with him (3:21). Is it not obvious that a person's course is set by the dictates of "nature," whether good or evil? It is impossible to say that Man enjoys freedom of action. Free will and achievement are of no use, for all the fine details of one's actions have already been predetermined by the biddings and influences of "nature." One has no ability to do good or evil outside of this (3:22-24). The proof? Isn't it obvious? Just look at me, says Iyov.

Here was a perfectly righteous man. It is impossible to attribute the great suffering which befell him to punishment for some sinful actions. So, too, is it impossible to attribute this to pure accident. Observe the unnatural sequence of events that caused the loss of everything he had. All the different elements (a storm, fire, bandits) attacked suddenly and at the same moment — definitive proof that the heavens are warring against him. The only explanation is that "nature" has decreed upon him that at this moment his fortune should turn (3:26). Moreover, his constant fear of such future harm can be attributed to his natural sense of predetermined bad fortune (3:25).

How does a believing man fit all this into the Divine plan? It is impossible to attribute to God any imperfection, any lack of knowledge, or to say that He has done an injustice. The injustice has been done by "nature," Iyov believes. It was not a Divine punishment, for how can you punish Man if he has no free will?

[Here Iyov sets down his "philosophy." He has full *emunah,* absolute faith in God. God is perfect and can do no evil. But being that we see so much evil in the world, Iyov is drawn to the conclusion that there is a force called "nature," or more accurately, "the stars," the "system," which predetermines everything that is to occur in one's lifetime.

Iyov has fallen victim to the inherent contradictions in his situation. God is good, but this behavior toward me is not good. Therefore, in order to avoid the contradiction, there must be something else causing me this suffering. He is forced to the necessary conclusion. So here, right at the outset, do we find the difference between Iyov and Avraham *Avinu*. Both were tested with contradictions, but Avraham acted completely differently:

THE *NISAYON* OF AVRAHAM: NOT TO QUESTION THE CONTRADICTIONS

Rav Yerucham of the Mir, *zt"l* (in *Da'as Torah, Bereshis*, p. 140), asks why the *Akedah* was considered only Avraham's test. Yitzchak was the one who was being asked to give up his life! Wasn't it also his test? We could even say that Yitzchak's courage was greater than Avraham's, for it was his life which was at stake.

We must conclude that the greatness of this *nisayon* was not that Avraham was willing to sacrifice his only son, but rather his steadfastness in light of the contradictions. Yesterday God told him, "In Yitzchak will be called your descendants," and today He says to him, "Offer him up as an offering," and Avraham accepts it wholeheartedly, with no second thoughts....

This is the intent of the Midrash, that the Satan came to Avraham *Avinu* while he was on his way to the *Akedah*. (We think that Avraham *Avinu* had no *yetzer ha-ra* and no internal battle within him. This is not the case. Even Avraham had to deal with the Satan, and he had to fight him hard in order to win. See the Epilogue for a fuller discussion.)

The Satan argued that Avraham would be accused of murder and of having never spoken in God's name. It is even possible that there was logic to the Satan's claims and Avraham knew this. But his sole answer was, "I accept that." He told the Satan, "It isn't my job to involve myself with hidden things, and the contradictions don't concern me. I will not doubt God's ways. Whatever passes over me, I am only interested in God's Will." This was the greatness of Avraham *Avinu*: his living faith. He walked before God in sincerity and innocence. He feared God, and this is what enabled him to stand up to each *nisayon*, especially this last and most difficult one.]

Elifaz: Free Will

Elifaz argues the side of Torah: Man has free will, and the power of the stars ("nature") has no power over anything dependent upon Man's free will. Man has the freedom and the ability to act or to refrain from action, for good or for bad. The constellations ("nature") go about in their orbits but are unable to act upon this "lowly world" (5:7). A person's path is not predetermined by the stars, but is etched out according to one's own choosing, for good or for evil. Do we not see that anger and sensual lusts kill the fool who chooses to engage in them (5:2)? Man was created for toil; diligence is of primary importance, and endeavor is necessary for success (5:7). What of apparent sudden success which comes with no effort or toil, as if one has reached his heart's desire without any of the chain of intermediate steps normally leading there? This is false success, which will be unable to endure in either his or his children's hands. In contrast is true success, arrived at through one's hard efforts. This is the seed which will definitely sprout and bear fruit (5:3-7). IYOV 4,5

There was a fear which constantly weighed down upon Iyov (see 3:25). Iyov attributed it to a sense of foreboding emanating from his "fate," but this was a mistake. It was in fact due to his sins. This is the true cause of one's rise or fall. הלא יראתך כסלתך תקותך ותם דרכיך, "Your fear was your foolishness, [this was] your hope and the sincerity of your ways" (4:6) — meaning, "You should have feared your foolishness, while your sincere ways were your hope."

THE BALANCE BETWEEN FREE WILL AND DETERMINISM

The *Sefer Ha-Ikkarim* (*perek* 5, *ma'amar* 4) explains that it is impossible for human behavior to be completely predetermined, as is believed by the astrologers. To assert this is to deny the principle of choice of possibilities that is obvious to all Mankind, and which is a basic principle of the Torah. However, the opinion of the philosophers — that everything must be the result of human choice and pure free will, and that achievement is solely the result of effort — is also an impossibility. Haven't we all seen people making great efforts to accomplish something, making all the possible preparations needed to achieve a goal — and then not only is the goal not reached, but the very preparations themselves bring about the opposite of what was wanted. This is what happened to Yosef's brothers. They attempted to sell him as a slave in order to prevent him from ruling over them, and this itself was the cause that brought him to power. We also see the opposite, people who achieve a certain good with no work at all, as did Sha'ul, who became king with absolutely no effort on his part.

Thus we see that there are two categories of human action. 1) Some actions are completely a matter of choice. They have the nature of the possible within them, and they belong to the realm of diligence and effort. A person is praised or scorned based only upon them: commandments and prohibitions, reward and punishment, pertain to them. 2) Some actions, however, are purely predetermined, such as those decreed by God to happen no matter what, like the incident of Yosef.

THE ROLE OF DIVINE PROVIDENCE — *HASHGACHAH PRATIS*

There are some actions, however, that are mixed: partially determined, and partially a matter of free will. For example, a person plants, and the crop sprouts. A person digs, and finds a treasure. Without the effort of planting, the crop will not grow, but equally important is the influence of the rain and wind, and the proper seasons (or — in the second example — the circumstances which laid the treasure there). The actions which are predetermined — whether partially or completely — are not dictated by "nature" but by *Hashgachah* and Divine Will (5:8).

Elifaz proceeds with proofs of *Hashgachah*, from rain (5:9-12) and from those incidents in which the weak are rescued from the strong, even though by nature the stronger should have overpowered the weak and destroyed him (5:12-17). Moreover, sometimes something bad occurs to a person through Divine *Hashgachah* in order to save him from something even worse. Imagine, for example, a person who plans to take a trip, but before he starts out he injures his foot. Or someone who plans to go on a sea voyage, but falls ill before the journey. And then bandits attacked, or the ship sank in the ocean. We see that a little bit of bad can sometimes be, in reality, God's protection from some greater evil (5:17-23). With *tzaddikim*, this *Hashgachah* permeates all the details of their actions (5:8), protecting them from all possible harm (5:23). Even those things which are proclaimed to be dependent upon *mazal* (fortune) as in *Chazal*'s statement that חיי בני ומזוני לא בזכותא תליא מילתא אלא במזלא תליא מילתא "life, children, and livelihood (literally, food) are not dependent upon merit but upon *mazal*" (*Moed Katan* 28a) come upon a person according to *Hashgachah*. Everything is a result of *Hashgachah* and cannot be attributed to blind "fate" (5:24-27).

In this way, Elifaz rejects Iyov's accusations and "proofs" denying Divine *Hashgachah* because of the evil that befalls the righteous. Why call it evil? Elifaz argues. Perhaps this can really be for their good (5:17-23).

SUFFERING AS AN ATONEMENT

Nevertheless, this was all insufficient and merely a product of Elifaz's logic. Therefore, he did not rely solely on this (5:27). Elifaz's main line of thought on this question is elaborated upon in chapter 4. The truth was revealed to him in a prophecy: the evil which befalls the righteous is due to some sin. As *Chazal* have stated, there is no suffering without some transgression (*Shabbos* 55a). Even though at first glance Iyov seems innocent, still, no one can really say that he has been completely pure at heart. Man owes the Almighty so much for all that He has done for him, and Man is so lowly in comparison, that it is impossible for a person to stand up before the One On High and claim that he has completely fulfilled his obligations. Therefore God brings upon him suffering, not for his evil, but for his good, to cleanse him and heal him of the ills he has caused to his soul before it is irreparably damaged, and before he brings upon himself a greater and more permanent punishment, such as loss of his soul's eternity, or premature death (4:12-21). This medicine is relatively lighter than being completely cut off from the Eternal.

From all this we see that, yes, the righteous will suffer, but they will not be destroyed (4:7-12). As far as Iyov's suffering, this merely proves that the *tzaddik* suffers, not that the *tzaddik* is lost (4:7,12). There is no proof that the world has been given over to blind "nature." This distress obviously has come upon Iyov for some sin by which he did not fulfill his obligations to the Almighty. The suffering is not destruction, but construction (4:7-12,20-27). Elifaz then proceeds to chastise Iyov for his lack of perfection, as demonstrated by his complaining and his denial of Divine *Hashgachah* the moment that suffering descended upon him. This implies that all Iyov's fear of God was really nothing but a desire for reward or fear of punishment. The truly God-fearing man will never buckle in such a way in times of Divine punishment (4:2,7).

Iyov's Rebuttal

Iyov holds firm to his conviction, maintaining that the control of the world is in the hands of "nature" (literally, the constellations). There is no accounting of a person's actions. Good or bad, all one's actions are forced upon him by his "fate," and he has no ability to change. Therefore, there is no difference between the *tzaddik* and the *rasha* — the righteous and the evil man. This he proves from all that had happened to himself. Here was a *tzaddik* apparently perishing in spite of his being righteous and faithful. Elifaz tried to counter this by explaining Iyov's suffering as being merely a temporary punishment for some slight sin, in order to cleanse him from some worse punishment, or eternal destruction. But one look at the suffering inflicted upon Iyov will prove the opposite. Here definitely is a *tzaddik* who is suffering not temporary torment, but permanent loss, as Iyov faces no hope of survival from his afflictions; he is on his deathbed (6:4-13). Iyov asks his friend: How dare you try to console me that these torments are merely a cleansing of my light sins, a mere gesture to save me from an eternal destruction of the soul, and that I will eventually return to live after this downfall? Do you not see that there is no hope left but sweet death to free me from this terrible agony (ibid., also 7:11-17)? However, if you dare to convict me of committing a sin so terrible that it deserves death, then tell me, what is my sin, what is my transgression (6:28-30)! You brought as proof of my crime my not standing up to the test but immediately complaining as soon as suffering afflicted me. But don't you think that these charges against me are minuscule compared to the immensity of my suffering (6:2-5)?

MAN'S PURPOSE — PERFECTION

Iyov now starts developing his argument philosophically in an attempt to destroy Elifaz's views and assumptions. Elifaz alleged that it is possible that a *tzaddik* will be tormented in order to be cleansed, and thereby saved from being punished by death for his sins. Against this Iyov lays down a very valid assertion. It is obvious that every living creature was created by God for some specific purpose. True, there are some creatures whose purpose is certainly not obvious, and one can only say that their very existence is their purpose. Still, we see most of creation toiling, acting, and being acted upon, as if running to achieve their particular purpose in the world. Man, then, as the very zenith of Creation, obviously must seek to perfect his goal during the course of his existence. What are the means which will bring him to his perfection?

There are two schools of thought on this matter. There are those who maintain that the means to a person's perfection are finite; if he accomplishes them all, then it can be said that he has attained perfection. Others say that the means are in and of themselves infinite, and it is only the person who is limited. A person has to toil for his whole life and his perfection depends upon this constant toil, whether he completes the actions or not.

We find a similar argument in the Gemara *Sanhedrin* (111a):*

> לכן הרחיבה שאול נפשה ופערה פיה לבלי חק (ישעיה ה׳:יד]. אמר ריש לקיש מי שלא קיים אפילו חוק אחד יורד לגיהנם (רש״י — חוק אחד: מלשמרו נידון בגיהנם). אמר ליה ר׳ יוחנן לא ניחא למרייהו דאמרת להו הכי (רש״י — אין הקב״ה רוצה שתהא דן את ישראל כל כך לכף חובה) אלא מי שמשייר אפילו חוק אחד.

"Therefore Hell has enlarged herself, and opened her mouth without measure" [*Yeshayahu* 5:14]. [The Hebrew word *chok* means both statute and measure. The Gemara interprets this

* The Malbim quotes a slightly different text than that found in our Gemaras. I have quoted the standard version of the text as it more clearly represents the two opinions presented.

as meaning that Hell opens her mouth for those who are without a statute.] Reish Lakish said, "This refers to one who leaves over even one statute [and fails to fulfill it. He will be lowered down into Gehinnom. — Rashi] R. Yochanan answered him, "Their Master does not want you to talk this way to them. [He doesn't want you to judge Yisrael so unfavorably. — Rashi] Rather, say that even if he only learned (other texts: fulfilled) just one statute [he will not fall into Gehinnom]."

Reish Lakish held that the means toward perfection entail the complete fulfillment of the whole Torah without exception. (The commandments of the Torah are finite, and it is our job to accomplish them all. Therefore, if a person left out even one mitzvah in his lifetime, he has not reached the perfection required of him.) On the other hand, according to R. Yochanan's understanding, it is sufficient to fulfill just one statute. [Torah is infinite, and so] perfection is dependent only upon one's doing all he can during his lifetime. Putting this into our frame of reference, R. Yochanan would say that Man must constantly labor in Torah and mitzvos for his whole life. In this way, he can reach perfection regardless of whether he lives a long life or dies young, and regardless of whether he has the opportunity to fulfill all of the six hundred and thirteen mitzvos or not. If, for reasons beyond his control, he is prevented from fulfilling them, and is able to fulfill only a few of them, still he has acquired perfection. Thus we understand that "perfection" is not quantitative, but rather is dependent upon one's constant striving for it throughout his whole life — whether it be a long life or a short one.

[The Ein Ya'akov in the *Anaf Ya'akov* explains, according to the *Sefer Ha-Ikkarim* (*perek* 29, *ma'amar* 3), that the argument here is whether the Torah grants perfection in its entirety or even partially. Reish Lakish is of the opinion that all the mitzvos and admonitions of the Torah are necessary for the acquisition of human perfection. If one of the mitzvos is lacking, then it is impossible to achieve perfection. Therefore, one who leaves over even one statute unfulfilled, must descend into Gehinnom to purify himself from his deficiency. The *Etz Yosef* explains that there are 248 limbs in a person, equivalent to the 248 positive mitzvos, and 365 tendons, equivalent to the 365 negative commandments. A person has to perfect and purify his whole body with the performance of the mitzvos. Therefore, Reish Lakish held that one who leaves over even only one statute has failed to purify the limb connected to that mitzvah and therefore will have to undergo purification in Gehinnom. R. Yochanan's view, however, is that the performance of only one mitzvah has within it the power to acquire human perfection. Perfecting and purifying the one limb connected to that statute spreads the perfection to the whole individual, and as a result, he will not have to descend to Gehinnom.

Perhaps we can understand R. Yochanan according to the Rambam. The *mishnah* at the end of *Makkos* states, "*Ha-Kadosh Baruch Hu* wanted to give merit to Yisrael; therefore He increased for them Torah and mitzvos." The Rambam in his *perush* on the Mishnah explains that since there are so many mitzvos, it is impossible that a person in his lifetime wouldn't do at least one of them properly and perfectly. By performing that mitzvah, he gains eternal life. Similarly, R. Yochanan held that in order to achieve eternity it is sufficient for a person to do even one mitzvah in its entirety (assuming that this one mitzvah was all that he was able to accomplish in his situation). This is a special gift that God gave Man. Even one mitzvah properly done will gain him entry into *Olam Ha-Ba*. (Heard from Rav Avraham Pincus, *shlita*.)]

The other opinion, that of Reish Lakish, is that one must complete his obligations. He must fulfill all the mitzvos, and only then will he have attained perfection. If some are lacking, even through no fault of his own, still he has not perfected himself.

Either way, Elifaz is not justified in arguing that a *tzaddik*'s torments are an atonement for some slight transgression which he committed, thereby failing to complete his service to God — the service God is worthy of receiving. But this cannot be, for these sufferings will completely distract him from his work. The correction is self-destructive. Imagine a servant of the king who — out of laziness — didn't finish his job and as a result was imprisoned by the king in order that he atone for his crime. But the king has now made certain that the job will not be accomplished, as long as he remains in prison! So, too, how could God be benefiting the *tzaddik* who has not accomplished all he is capable of doing, by sending him grief which just forces him into negligence and cessation of his work (7:1-11)!

NOT BEING ABLE TO SERVE GOD IS LIKE DEATH

As to Elifaz's claim that suffering now will save him from premature death and eternal loss, Iyov replies that he has already died. His torments have halted the holy service in life for which he was created, and as long as he remains ill it is as if he were dead. What difference does it make if he dies at the end of his life, or is dead in the middle of his life, he asks. That portion of time during which he would be able to perfect himself is gone, an eternal loss, as if it never existed. [This is what *Chazal* meant when they said (*Berachos* 5), "What are torments of love? Those that do not disturb one's Torah study or *tefillah*." For having one's holy work disturbed through suffering is considered a terrible evil, and is compared to death.] Isn't it better to die at the end of one's days rather than in the middle (7:6-8)?

IYOV DENIES THE ETERNITY OF THE SOUL

Elifaz hinted that there does exist eternal life: מבלי משים לנצח יאבדו, "they perish to eternity without giving a thought" (4:20). Iyov rejects this. Just as he denied Divine Providence and free will, and attributed everything to "nature," so too does he deny the eternity of the soul and future reward (7:8-9).

[Iyov here is developing a philosophy that definitely appears to be *apikorsus* (heresy). He denies free will, and the concept of life after death and the eternity of the soul (literally, resurrection of the dead) (see *Bava Basra* 16a). Rava in the *gemara* is of the opinion that Iyov not only sinned, but blasphemed: " 'And with all this Iyov did not sin with his lips' (2:10). Rava said, 'With his lips he didn't sin, but he sinned in his heart.' ...Rava said, 'Iyov wanted to turn the pot upside down (and spill out the food)' [to uproot all respect of the Almighty by his cursing and blaspheming — Rashi]." There are also other harsh statements against Iyov in that same *gemara*: "Rav said, 'Throw dirt into Iyov's mouth.' " (See the Appendix for a full rendition of the *gemara*.) Yet, he was introduced to us as a very righteous person. And at the end of the work God calls him "My servant Iyov."

Rava himself (who just accused Iyov) learned from this contradiction a very great principle: "Rava said, 'We learn from this that a person cannot be held accountable for what he says in a time of distress.' " Iyov remained a *tzaddik*. But under the duress of his torment he made statements which under normal circumstances would be considered heretical.

The Malbim takes a different path and at the end of the debate (chapter 42), when God Himself comes and demonstrates to Iyov how Divine Providence oversees everything, Iyov reveals that he had been a *tzaddik* all along and that his "philosophy" had been merely for the sake of argument. He had played the role of a so-called "devil's advocate" in order to clarify to his friends their fallacy in thinking that Iyov's torment proved that he was a *rasha*. He was only arguing that there appears to be no Divine Justice. The Gemara in *Sotah* 27b (see the Appendix) also seems to be of the opinion that Iyov remained a *tzaddik*.

The Gemara in *Bava Basra* 15b, however, brings another opinion — that Iyov did indeed sin. He had been tested and failed: "There was a *chassid* among the nations and his name was Iyov. His sole purpose in coming into this world was in order to receive his reward (in the Next World). *Ha-Kadosh Baruch Hu* brought afflictions upon him and he started cursing and blaspheming. So *Ha-Kadosh Baruch Hu* doubled his reward in this world in order to drive him out of the next."

Morenu Ha-Gaon Ha-Rav Chaim Dov Altusky, *shlita,* once explained this dispute between the two opinions regarding Iyov. According to Rava, Iyov was absolved of his heretical statements because he was under duress. Duress is relative. A person's duress is dependent upon his mental ability to pull himself up out of his pain and keep a clear mind. The *gemara* which stated that Iyov lost his *Olam Ha-Ba* seems to hold the opinion that Iyov was on such a high spiritual level that he should not have been overcome with grief to such an extent that he lost himself. Rava, on the other hand, understood that the torment was so unbearable that even a saintly person like Iyov could not withstand it.

However, the *gemara* which stated that Iyov lost his *Olam Ha-Ba* is still difficult to understand. How does it explain God's statement at the end of the book calling him "My servant Iyov"? How could Iyov be "My servant" after having failed miserably, to the extent that he lost his portion in the Next World? It could be that the *gemara* holds that indeed his previous righteousness had been lost and he had forfeited his portion in *Olam Ha-Ba*. His position as "My servant Iyov" is thus based only on his future actions.]

As for Elifaz's statement that this answer came to him through prophecy, Iyov retorts that if this is true, then would it not have been better for God to speak to Iyov directly and give *him* the prophecy, revealing the truth to him and quieting his aggravation? Why should the spirit of prophecy have left him and gone over to Elifaz? He is surely no more worthy than Iyov (6:13-14).

IYOV DENIES *HASHGACHAH PRATIS*

Besides this, Iyov continues, how can one imagine that the Almighty, so high and exalted, would pay special attention to lowly Man — especially such attention, so constant and personal, that the number of sufferings, and their coming and going, should all be directly from God. Moreover, how can one say that a person's sins would cause this special *Hashgachah* to bring him a certain amount of suffering, and yet at the same bring him a certain amount of suffering, and yet at the same time continue to protect his life, as if there were some need for him to remain alive? How does this reduce his sin? How does it benefit his search for perfection? How is this at all constructive? The idea is philosophically untenable (7:17-21). This is the gist of Iyov's rebuttal, besides his complaints that his friends have turned against him, and besides his complaints against his pain.

Bildad: Would God Corrupt Justice?

IYOV 8

Bildad, the second of Iyov's friends, now takes up the debate and chooses a different approach. Like Elifaz, he believes in *Hashgachah* and free will. He also is violently opposed to the concept of predetermined fate. But since Iyov turned a deaf ear to Elifaz's arguments, Bildad decides to topple Iyov's logic with one mighty blow: Would God corrupt justice (8:3)?

GOD CANNOT BE UNJUST

A condition of the Divine is perfection, and its converse, the absence of imperfection. Such a terrible injustice as has been perpetrated, however, constitutes such imperfection. Iyov also agreed to this tenet, and built all of his proofs upon it. But he viewed it from his personal experiences alone: of course it is logically impossible that the Almighty would do an injustice. However, it appears that the realm of the individual is not regulated according to law and justice. For as we see, there is no distinction between *tzaddik* and *rasha*. Everyone is equal, the righteous and the sinner; all are under the rule of the accidents of time and their constant fluctuations. Since this causes evil to befall the *tzaddik* for no reason, this, in and of itself, is an injustice. But it is impossible to attribute this behavior to God. Heaven forbid that we attribute any miscarriage of justice to the Almighty. Therefore, Iyov deduced that this conduct emanates not from God but from a blind ruler — "nature" (literally, the constellations) — who does not distinguish between one who serves God and one who does not.

THE CONCEPT OF "BLIND NATURE" IS A CONTRADICTION OF GOD'S PERFECTION

Bildad determines just the opposite by taking a broader and all-inclusive point of view. True, he says, injustice cannot be attributed to God because it is an imperfection. However, being that He is perfect, we must attribute to Him total ability. To say that God has handed over the rule of the world to a blind governor who does not distinguish between good and evil is just such an unacceptable injustice. Even though it may solve the specific problem to say that the imperfections are not based in God Himself but rather come from the governor of "nature" who rules over the realm of the individual, still, how can we justify God for the original design in the first place? Isn't this itself an injustice, handing over the world to "blind nature"? There is no satisfactory answer to this. The only alternative would be to say that He has no ability to personally oversee the justice of the world, which is another impossibility: Divinity implies total ability.

To this argument Bildad says, הא-ל יעות משפט, "Would God corrupt justice?" (8:3). How could the Omnipotent pervert Justice? The alternative would be to say that he is so disgusted or angry with these lowly creatures that he has forsaken them and has no desire to oversee them (see the Rambam in the *Guide*, section 3, chap. 16). But this also is a contradiction to justice. We must assume that the course of the individual's life is governed by God's direct guidance, *Hashgachah Pratis*. What appears to us as the bitter lot of the righteous who suffer is an error in our perception, for in reality everything is perfectly organized according to law and justice.

TORMENTS OF LOVE

However, we still haven't addressed fully the basic problem of the evils which afflict the *tzaddik*. For this, Bildad takes a different path, which he claims he has as a tradition from his forefathers (8:8-10). Sometimes God will inflict pain upon the *tzaddik* who has no previous sins, he explains, in order to benefit him in the end and recompense him for this suffering with a reward many times greater. Thus evils are just a temporary exchange which will eventually lead the *tzaddik* to attain the good (8:6-7). Just as when the gardener finds a flower growing amidst barren rocks, and he rips it out and replants it in a rich and watered spot, this uprooting is not destructive, but beneficial in order to ultimately enhance its growth. However, not all plants are equally suitable for replanting. Those which are used to growing in very moist surroundings by their nature fail to take root once they have been uprooted, and likewise they are the first to wither when their source of water dries up. So, too, is Man. The *rasha*, used to his luxuries and indulgences, will not be ripped from his place, but will be taken from this world before his time. It is better not to live too long and not to be a *rasha*. The *tzaddik*, on the other hand, is sometimes ripped from his place, from his possessions, and suffers physical torments, only for his benefit, to be replanted in a stronger location, where he will enjoy peace and tranquillity, see the fruits of his labors, have a long life and Heavenly success (8:11-20). Therefore, Bildad advises Iyov to gird himself with strength and put his trust and hope in God. Then instead of suffering, he will accept his portion and in the end he will prosper (8:17,21-23).

[Rav Eliyahu Dessler, *zt"l*, in *Michtav Me-Eliyahu* (vol. 2, p. 225), discusses the concept as developed by the Maharal:

There are forms of suffering that come as a punishment due to some transgression, in order to instruct the person to do *teshuvah*. There are other types of suffering that come to allow the person to serve God perfectly by giving him the opportunity to not harbor any thoughts against God's ways. Also, they come to give him the chance to reach a level of accepting torment with love and joy. For example, when one endures suffering from birth, it is a sign that it is not a punishment (unless it is coming for a transgression in a previous lifetime [*gilgul*]). Therefore it must be that his purpose in this world is to accept the suffering with love.

The concept of "torments of love" (*yissurim shel ahavah*) requires much clarification. How is it possible that "the Holy One, blessed be He, will bring suffering upon a person out of love," asks the Maharal. We also find the *gemara* in *Berachos* 5a which says, "Anyone whom *Ha-Kadosh Baruch Hu* is interested in, He will crush with suffering." This is very difficult to understand.

The Gemara continues there: "If a person sees that suffering is coming upon him, he should look into his actions. If he looked at himself and found no transgression, he should assume that it has come for *bittul Torah* (laxity in the study of the Torah). If he didn't find even this transgression, then they are most certainly torments of love."

The Maharal (*Nesiv Ha-Yissurim, perek* 1) explains that sometimes a *tzaddik* should be on a higher spiritual plane than he is: due to some side of him which is spiritually imperfect, he experiences some attachment to the physical and thus cannot attain his true level. Then suffering comes to cleanse his soul and remove the impurity of the lowly material until he is completely pure. Therefore, such sufferings are called "torments of love" because Hashem loves him and wants him. In order to bring him closer to Him, God cleanses his physical blemishes until he is finally worthy of attaching himself to the spiritual. But this happens only when he accepts the sufferings with love, knowing that they will bring him to a high plane, close to Hashem. But if he doesn't accept them with love, then they cannot bring him closer to God — so how can they then be considered "torments of love"?

(See also the Epilogue, "Three Wonderful Gifts," for a similar discussion by *Morenu Ha-Gaon Ha-Rav* Zeidel Epstein, *shlita*.)]

Iyov Answers Bildad

IYOV 9,10

Holding firm to his position, poor Iyov tries to remain a pillar of iron: the moving force in this world which pours out scorn on the noble, and whose tribute to the blameless is mockery, cannot be the eyes of God. His Throne is clean from these accusations. No wrongdoing can originate from Him. The culprits are the messengers of "nature" into whose hands the whole world has been given. Iyov's rebuttal is divided into three parts.

I. PESSIMISM DERIVES FROM EGOTISM

Iyov begins by answering Bildad's first premise: that it would be considered either a crime or a blemish in the perfection of God the Omnipotent and Righteous to think that He handed over direction of the world to evil servants. It is befitting that we should find in God no iniquity, but only perfection. Thus Bildad questioned, "Would God corrupt justice?" On this Iyov answers with a philosophy we find mentioned in the *Guide* (section 3, chap. 12). The pessimists claim that the evils of the world outnumber the good. The Rambam answers that this is due to their viewing Existence egotistically. Such fools think that the universe was created only for them, and that nothing else exists. Therefore, when something occurs which is contrary to their desires, they automatically deduce that all Existence is evil. If only they would examine Existence and understand their minuscule part in it, it would become clear to them that it is a kind of mass insanity that brings people to such pessimism. They would no longer say that it is a law of nature, but rather that it affects only a few individuals. Man must not be mistaken and think that the universe is for him alone. The universe exists out of the Will of the Creator, and the human race is but the most minuscule part relative to the entirety.

THE MATERIAL WORLD IS BY NATURE IMPERFECT

The Rambam explains that there are three kinds of evil which afflict Man. 1) Evil that is a result of Man's material makeup, that is, arising from the fact that he is made of material. This is the reason people suffer physical deformities, for example. 2) Evil that is due to environmental changes, such as lightning, geological disturbances, etc. 3) Evil that is due to Man's actions against his fellowman.

Divine Wisdom has determined that Existence must be accompanied by imperfections, whatever they may be, and without them the continuation of the species would not be ensured.

[This world was created as a passageway to the next. Therefore, it had to be created imperfect, to allow room for achievement. For if the world had been created perfect, we would not be able to accomplish things and there would be no room for improvement. The Ramchal (Rav Moshe Chayim Luzzatto, *zt"l*), in *Derech Hashem* (section 1, chaps. 2-3),* develops the concept, as we find in the following selected quotations:

"God alone is true perfection, free of all deficiency... Since God desired to bestow good, a partial good would not be sufficient. The good that He bestows would have to be the ultimate good that His creation could accept. But since God alone is the only true good, therefore His wisdom decreed that the nature of this true benefaction be His giving created beings the opportunity to attach themselves to Him to the greatest degree possible for them."

"Therefore, even though created beings cannot emulate God's perfection in their own right [for by definition the fact that they were created is automatically a lack of perfection], the fact that they can be attached to God allows them to share in His perfection, since they can be considered part of God's perfection as a result of their association with Him. They can thus derive pleasure from that true good to the greatest degree possible for them."

* Jerusalem and New York: Feldheim Publishers, 1977.

"...God's wisdom, however, decreed that for such good to be perfect, the one enjoying it must be its master. He must be one who has earned it for himself, and not one associated with it incidentally... God therefore arranged and decreed the creation of concepts of both perfection and deficiency, as well as a creature with equal access to both. This creature would then be given the means to earn perfection and avoid deficiency... When this creature earns perfection, he is worthy of experiencing his Creator by virtue of his resembling Him."

"...In order for all this to be possible, various different concepts of perfection and deficiency must exist. This creature must then be placed in an environment with access to them all, and thus have the ability to earn perfection and avoid deficiency."

"...In order that this goal be best achieved, the Highest Wisdom decreed that Man should consist of two opposites. These are his pure spiritual soul, and his unenlightened body. Each one is drawn toward its nature, so that the body inclines toward the material, while the soul leans toward the spiritual. The two are then in a constant state of battle. If the soul prevails, it not only elevates itself, but elevates the body as well, and the individual thereby attains his destined perfection. If he allows the physical to prevail, on the other hand, then besides lowering his body, he also debases his soul. Such an individual makes himself unworthy of perfection, and thus divorces himself from God."]

One who wishes to be flesh and blood and yet still not suffer the consequences of the material, is trying to grab on to two opposites. If you do not accept imperfection, you cannot exist as a human being. The principle set down by Galinus [Galen] was very true: Whatever exists, of whatever material, can only be as good as the material it is made of... [This can be seen in the human race.] Whatever imperfections are inherent in the parents are naturally passed on to the offspring. Still, all in all, evils are but minor compared to the general picture and the human race as a whole.

IYOV'S VIEW OF THE WORLD: GOD HANDED THE WORLD OVER TO NATURE, AND NATURE FOLLOWS ITS LAWS

Iyov uses this as an introduction to proceed to a more vast topic, to develop his view of the entire universe. Scientists have determined that even the stars fall into the category of things that suffer material loss and imperfection; they are not a separate class of material, as had once been thought. There is no different material that the celestial bodies are made of. They are all composed of the same materials as is our Earth. Therefore they suffer the same rules of loss and ultimate disintegration. This is clearly stated by the Prophets: כי שמים כעשן נמלחו והארץ כבגד תבלה, "For the heavens will one day dissipate like smoke, and the Earth will disintegrate like a piece of cloth" (*Yeshayahu* 51:6).

Moreover, the scientists have determined that our sun, queen of the heavens, together with the family of planets circling around her, are like nothing compared to the billions of other suns spread around at a distance so unimaginable that they appear to us only as points of light floating in the sky. This vast number of worlds which are also comprised of material are doomed to disintegration. If there should come a time when the sun and moon and the whole family of planets should finally vanish together with all their inhabitants, this would not be considered absolutely evil or the fault of the Creator of all Existence, since in His wisdom He willed to create this universe of material existence which includes a vast multitude of worlds of which the sun and planets are but a minuscule part. If all this eventually should disintegrate, this would merely be a result of the nature of the material of the entire universe.

IYOV'S VIEW: EVIL IS ONLY RELATIVE TO THE WHOLE PICTURE

Let us take this logic one step further. If such destruction occurred only on one small part of the solar system — the planet Earth — how could it be considered evil in comparison to the existence of the entire universe, of which the Earth is but one drop in the sea. And even more so, if this did not wipe out the entire Earth, but only a section of it, i.e., if an earthquake caused a mountain to sink and tens of thousands of people die... Relative to the entire universe this is not an evil. This is only "nature" running its course. The Earth cannot be made up of material elements and *not* suffer events such as earthquakes and eruptions due to the internal gases, fires, or subterranean water which are locked deep inside her and which are a necessary part of her very makeup. The evil which this sometimes causes is null and void in comparison to the general good. The Earth could not exist any other way (unless the universe were purely spiritual or comprised of some new category of material).

Now, if this evil afflicts only one individual — like Iyov — it cannot even be imagined to be anything bad. Therefore, Iyov the philosopher says that he has no complaints against the general principles of Divine Justice. In his opinion, it is not a flaw in the perfection of the Creator to create Existence, for Existence in general is good. This is what His wisdom and His Will desired; we cannot consider this a misdeed if, by necessity, some disintegration and loss occur to one individual of the human race, or even to the entire race itself. This is all only a result of the laws of nature which can exist no other way.

[Iyov has touched upon a very important point. As we mentioned in the Preface, each individual act must be understood in its relation to the whole. Everything that happens to the individual is a result of his place in history, from the beginning to the end of time. So what looks like an injustice in the very narrow framework of his "world" is in reality a deep benefit to him in relation to the whole picture. This is, however, where Iyov strays from the truth.

IYOV'S DENIAL OF *HASHGACHAH PRATIS*

Iyov takes this argument one step further: Therefore, he says, when an individual suffers, it is minuscule in the macrocosmic outlook. No! Each individual is a universe unto himself. God, the Source of all good, would never inflict suffering upon anyone unjustly. The concept of *Hashgachah Pratis* dictates that He oversees every minute detail of everyone's life and makes sure that each detail fits into the total plan. There is no such thing as a person suffering merely because the total picture dictates it. If the situation requires that the total picture requires such an outcome, still it must also perfectly fit that individual's personal *Hashgachah*. Like the Chafetz Chaim's *mashal* about the country man in the big-city shul (see the Preface), we would have to understand everything that happened in the world from the beginning of Creation until the end of time to understand how everything fits in perfectly. For the moment, however, until that time arrives, we will have to suffice with pure faith, and believe that: הצור תמים פעלו כי כל דרכיו משפט, אל אמונה ואין עול צדיק וישר הוא, "He is the Rock, His work is perfect, for all His ways are justice, He is the God of faith with no injustice, He is righteous and straight" (*Devarim* 32:4).]

Thus Iyov rejects Bildad's premise of "Would God corrupt justice?" The basic premise is that God is pure and good, with no imperfections or injustice. If we assume, like Bildad, that the order of the universe is under the personal direction of Divine Providence, then we find no peace of mind. We would then be plagued by the question as to why He takes no notice to protect the innocent from evil. This forces Iyov to conclude that He handed over the governing of the world to "nature," and that therefore it cannot be considered a crime that innocent people suffer unjustly. God only overlooks the general running of the universe, seeing that it should be the best possible for the general sake. Any evil which affects the individual vanishes in significance in relation to the general good (9:2-13).

[Iyov's argument is quite logical, but pure logic can distort the truth. The truth, as revealed at the beginning of the book, is that God oversees everything with a very precise *Hashgachah*. Iyov knows this. He has always been a very righteous man and full of deep faith. However, his *emunah* has been shaken by the apparent injustice being perpetrated upon him. His logical mind cannot accept the obvious inconsistencies. He is forced to redevelop his thinking in order to retain some semblance of *emunah*: God is just. So where is the injustice coming from? It must be that the world has been handed over to "blind nature." By concentrating on *Hashgachah Klalis* — general *Hashgachah* — he has automatically eradicated his problem. Everything must be viewed in relation to the general picture, and therefore his suffering cannot be considered unjust. However, he has, in the process, been forced to disregard the concept of *Hashgachah Pratis* — personal, detailed Divine Providence. He has been driven by his philosophy to deny God's personal intervention in the individual's welfare.

Iyov's argument is a prime example of a very common way of thinking. Those who believe in God and yet also believe in the "laws of nature" are faced with a dilemma, as Bildad has pointed out. God, by definition, is just, but the laws of nature are not. To reconcile this, Iyov has taken this world view to its logical conclusion and rationalized his way out of the problem: If it is a "law" that "nature" must of necessity cause injustice, then it cannot be considered unjust; it is merely a logical consequence of what must be (i.e., the "law"). This, of course, is false logic. Injustice is injustice and cannot be swept away by redefining one's terms. God is just and oversees the world with a very fine, detailed *Hashgachah*. What appears to us as injustice appears so because of our inability to see the whole picture. If we could see all the many pieces of the "jigsaw puzzle" of the universe, from the beginning until the end of time, there would no longer be any questions.

But Iyov has shed some light on this "philosophy." It is not a view independent of itself, but rather an alternative of what Iyov really wants to believe. With this, Iyov has strayed from pure *emunah*. Man's logic is by definition limited. We are directly aware only of the physical. But by centering on the physical nature of things, Iyov has completely ignored the spiritual. This is his fatal error. He took purely empirical facts and used pure reason to reach the logical conclusion. True, if we concentrate on the physical, Man is but a tiny drop in the sea of the universe. But if we consider the spiritual, then each individual is an entire universe in himself. Iyov's mistake throughout the debate is to ignore the spiritual and focus on the physical, the empirical.

There are those who sometimes hold similar ideas. How many have strayed from pure *emunah* because of the problems which plague them! With the insight into our own minds that Iyov gives us, perhaps we can learn to see through our false logic and return to the pure faith of our Fathers.]

II. REWARD FOR SUFFERING

The second point that Iyov reflects upon is Bildad's assertion that the *tzaddik* will be made to suffer in order to ultimately receive an even greater reward. However, Bildad fails to explain what exactly this reward would be. So now Iyov investigates all the different possibilities. Such reward in return for suffering can be imagined in five ways. Basically, it must be either a result of a direct relationship between the evil and the reward, or as a result of an incidental relationship. Each of these in turn can be imagined in one of two ways. In the case of a direct relationship, the relationship is natural, meaning, that just as every living creature can reach its potential only through hard work and pain, so too the *tzaddik* can reach his potential only through suffering. [In this way the reward would be the natural outcome of one's suffering.] On the other hand, we could say that the person is rewarded in return for the suffering. Then according to the measure of his suffering, God will grant him, in return, a portion of reward. In this case the relationship is not a natural one.

In the case of an indirect and incidental relationship, the suffering causes the reward by causing one to turn to God with *tefillah*, praying for His mercy. This will influence Him to pay the *tzaddik* back for his good deeds. Or it could be a test, and if the *tzaddik* bears it and does not complain, he will be rewarded bountifully. Thus, so far, we have four possible approaches. We can also imagine this "evil" to be merely a protection from harm. For if God in His wisdom sees that the nature of the *tzaddik* is going to lead him to some future transgression, He will preempt it by bringing suffering upon him to humble his heart and subdue his nature. Then God will joyously turn to lavish upon him wonderful good. These are five ways to understand reward as a result of suffering.

Now Iyov, the philosopher, proceeds to answer each possibility. The first is that reward is the natural consequence of one's work and pain. This draws Iyov's protest, for his suffering had no natural connection to any good that could be caused by it. True, when an animal toils for its prey, the food comes at the same moment and as a direct result of his toil: cause and effect. Work leads to bread. But how can a reward be a result of suffering to which it has no natural connection (9:25-26)?

[Iyov continues to relate only to the empirical — what he does not see does not exist. Perhaps there *is* a natural connection, unseen by the physical eye?]

The second approach is that the reward is in return for and in direct proportion to the suffering. This leads us to a basic contradiction. How can you tell me to strengthen my heart and accept the pain joyfully? asks Iyov. For this contradicts what you told me, that the pleasure which comes afterwards is in proportional balance. If I become strong and remove the grief from my heart, then the length of my suffering must be increased to the proper amount which has been measured out for me, in order to balance the reward. Instead, it would be better to increase my pain now and in that way shorten the time of torment (9:27-28).

[Again Iyov errs. His shortsightedness cannot distinguish between suffering and accepting the suffering with joy. Although the person's physical being suffers, he has the choice of either concentrating on the torment and suffering, or concentrating on the spiritual and using his mental faculties to accept and even be happy with his anguish. The reward is for the effort the person makes to live in the spiritual dimension rather than in the physical.]

As for the third approach, that suffering is a means of causing one to increase *tefillah* and beseech mercy, Iyov questions how this could be acceptable to an intelligent mind. Here is someone who is afflicted unjustly and who can justify himself to his afflicter, claiming that he has done no wrong to rightfully deserve such treatment. How, then, dare you tell him not to demand justice, but rather to plead for mercy? That he should not claim innocence but rather plead forgiveness, as if he were guilty? If the Judge pays no attention to his righteousness, why should He pay any more attention to his prayers and supplications? A philosopher will not willingly accept that God will accept his *tefillos*, for if so, then that would assume a change in God's position, from unwilling to willing. He is not a human being who repents and changes his mind (9:13-22). This is the meaning of the verse: אם קראתי ויענני לא אאמין כי יאזין קולי, "If I call, and He answers me, I will not believe that He would hearken to my voice" (9:16).

[A third mistake. Iyov equates his intellect with God's. He has decided that he can argue his case better than can God. And as far as praying for mercy, this does not bring about a change of God's mind, so to speak, but rather a change in the person, a humbling of oneself before God's infinite wisdom and an ability to live with more awareness of God's benevolent *Hashgachah Pratis*. This change in the person arouses a change in the way God responds to him. Or perhaps the suffering was itself His means to bring the person to turn to God to pray and renew his connection to the Almighty.]

The fourth way is to understand the whole ordeal as a test. But if the person dies as a result of the test, where is the reward and redemption which come from withstanding the ordeal (9:23)? [Iyov here is referring to himself — he sees himself as if he were dead, for he has no hope of recovering from his affliction. Therefore, he asks, what is the use of standing up to the test?]

[Again Iyov demonstrates that he denies the existence of the spiritual world, and thus death in this world is the ultimate end.]

And as for the fifth way, if the purpose of the suffering is to prevent him from future sin, where is there Divine integrity in being punished lest one sin in the future? Since when does the punishment precede the crime (9:29-32)?

[Iyov has touched upon a very deep and fundamental concept. In a similar vein, the *Sho'el u'Meshiv* (quoted in *Yated Ne'eman "musaf"* parashas *Ki Setzei* 5751) comments:

כי יהיה לאיש בן סורר ומורה איננו שמע בקול אביו ובקול אמו ויסרו אתו ולא ישמע אליהם. (דברים כא:יח)

"When a person has a rebellious son who doesn't heed the voice of his father or mother, and even when they chastise him he doesn't listen to them..." (*Devarim* 21:18).

Rashi tells us that this rebellious son is put to death because of what he is eventually going to do. The Torah delved deep into his mind and declared that eventually he will devour all of his father's money, and when he is overcome by his lustful habits and doesn't have any more means to fulfill them, he will take to going out on the road and stealing. The Torah states that he should die while he still has a clean slate and hasn't done anything wrong, rather than wait and die as a criminal.

The commentaries say that this contradicts a very important principle regarding the way in which Heaven judges us. Concerning Yishmael, it says that God looked upon him, באשר הוא שם, "according to the way he was at that moment" (lit., "for what he was there") (*Bereshis* 21:17). Rashi quotes the Midrash, which explains that Heaven looked upon his actions at that very moment, and not at his future actions. This raises a very important question regarding the rebellious son: How can he be judged according to his future actions? This appears to violate the principle of "according to what he was there."

In my opinion, the question in fact doesn't even arise. Why is it that a person is judged only according to the way he is at the present time? Doesn't God know the future and what the person will do? But that raises the classic questions about predetermination and free will. So we must say that God "limits" His knowledge. For if He didn't, Man would be compelled in his actions. That is the reason God judges only according to what he is at present. This creates a situation in which Man is not compelled, but rather has free will. That being the case, it is impossible to judge someone according to the future.

In regard to the rebellious son, however, when it says that the Torah delved into the depths of his mind and saw the future, this does not refer to the fact that God knows with His infinite wisdom what the future is. Rather, it means that the Torah evaluated his character, that given everything about his nature right now, he definitely would act in a certain way in the future. If so, it is certainly possible to judge him on his later actions, because this is not an absolute binding of his free will. Rather, his present actions already have the kernel and roots of his future actions. With Yishmael, however, the question was whether or not to judge him according to the absolute future when his descendants would persecute the Jews during the first Exile. This would have contradicted the concept of free will and so he was judged "according to what he was there." (For a further discussion of this topic, see *Ohr Yisrael* by Rav Yisrael Salanter, *zt"l*, at the end of *Igeres* 30 where he discusses the Rambam's paradox on free will.)]

III. THE PARADOX: GOD'S FOREKNOWLEDGE AND MAN'S FREE WILL

Now Iyov opens a new front against the opinions of his friends. They have affirmed that God is aware of everything in the world and all the details of men's lives, including their future actions. Still, Man is free to act as he chooses, and [God's] foreknowledge of the future plays no role in Man's actions. This, Iyov maintains, is an open contradiction. Since God is perfect, it is impossible to attribute to Him any form of ignorance. He must know everything. A condition of His being One is that there cannot be any change in His knowledge, meaning that it is impossible that He should gain some new information that He didn't know already. Therefore He must know the future, and it follows that Man does not have free will. His actions must be limited by "nature" either for good or for bad, and God knows in advance all that is preordained that one must do. This reasoning gives Iyov an opening to complain: Since he is forced to act in a preordained fashion and his good or bad actions have been fixed by previously determined limitations, why then should he be forced to suffer and bear responsibility for his actions? Since God knew that Iyov would sin, this very knowledge compelled him. Therefore, Iyov felt he had a right to complain to God: You have forced me to be a *rasha* and I had no choice!

Moreover, he asks an ancient philosophical question against those who claim that God knows all details and fluctuations of this world. How is this possible, since these details can be comprehended only through material senses and conceptualization? Being that God has no material being, how can He perceive these details? Secondly, these details exist within time. How can God perceive the time-bound, being that He is above time? He has no movement or rest. As Iyov said, העיני בשר לך הכימי אנוש ימיך, "Do You have eyes of flesh, or do You see as a man sees? Are Your days like the days of a mortal, or are Your years like the days of a man?" (10:4-5).

This line of reasoning also includes many other philosophical questions. According to all this, then, His perfection has been decreased, for perfection depends upon the knowledge of the perceiver and if we say, as above, that God has no knowledge through material senses, or within time, then God's knowledge is limited. Moreover, conceptualization of new ideas implies a change in the knower, for as he gains knowledge, he becomes more perfect. But we know that God is One, meaning, never changing. So how can God Who is One be connected with the material world which is pure variety and lack of unity? All this is included in his previous two questions.

[Iyov has again been forced into a position by pure logic. He has come up against the classical paradox of God's knowledge of the future versus Man's free will. He then is forced to conclude that God's infinite knowledge necessitates that Man has no free will. This subject is also discussed later on in Tzofar's answer to Iyov (chap. 11). This ancient logical analysis is discussed in the *Guide* (section 3, chaps. 18-20) where the Rambam explains that we cannot use logic to understand God's thinking. There is no comparison of our limited thought processes to His infinite wisdom. It is also discussed in the *Mishneh Torah*:

"All of existence outside of the Creator, from the highest life form to the smallest insect buried deep in the belly of the Earth, exists from the force of God's reality. And since He knows Himself and recognizes His own greatness and His Glory and His Truth, He therefore knows everything. Nothing is hidden from Him. *Ha-Kadosh Baruch Hu* understands His own reality and knows it exactly for what it is. He doesn't 'know' with an external knowledge the way we know, for we and our knowledge are not one and the same. But the Creator, He and His knowledge, and His Being are One, from all directions and corners, from any approach: it is pure unity. He is the Knower, He is the Known, He is the Knowledge itself, everything is One. This is something that the mouth has no ability to describe, nor the ear to hear, nor Man's heart to understand clearly... Therefore He does not perceive His creations nor know them through the same means of 'knowing' that we have, the way we know, but rather He knows them for what they are in themselves. Since He knows Himself, He knows everything, for everything depends upon Him for its existence.

(Rambam: *Yesodei Torah*, chap. 2, *halachos* 9, 10)

"You may claim that if God knows everything that will be, then before a person is born He knows if he will be a *tzaddik* or a *rasha*. Now, if He knows that he will be a *tzaddik*, it is then impossible for that person *not* to be a *tzaddik*. If you say that He can know that he will be a *tzaddik*, and yet it is still possible for him to be a *rasha*, then it must be that God didn't know the future clearly. [Both options are equally unacceptable.] You should know that the answer to this question is greater than the Earth, wider than the sea, and many basic great tenets and high mountains are dependent upon it. However, know and understand what I am about to tell you. We have already explained in chapter 2 of *Yesodei Torah* that God's knowledge is not an idea separate from Himself, like Man whose self and knowledge are two separate entities. Rather, He and His knowledge are one and the same. This is something that Man's intellect cannot conceive clearly. Just as it is not within the ability of a person to fathom and to grasp the true reality of the Creator — as it says, לא יראני האדם וחי, לא מחשבותי מחשבותיכם ולא דרכיכם דרכי, 'Man cannot see Me and live' — so too a person cannot fathom the Mind of the Creator. This is what the *Navi* meant when he said, 'My thoughts are not your thoughts, and your ways are not My ways.' Therefore, we do not have the ability to understand how God can know everything about all creatures and their actions. But what we do know without a doubt is that a person's actions are in the hand of that person, and God does not force him or decree upon him to act. Not only do we know this as a tradition of faith, but there are many logical proofs for it as well. Therefore we have been told by the Prophets that Man is judged for his actions according to whether they are good or bad. This is a basic premise upon which all prophecy is based."

(Rambam, *Hilchos Teshuvah*, chap. 5, *halachah* 5)

In short, we can summarize that the Rambam wishes to answer the paradox by saying that God's wisdom is far beyond our comprehension and therefore we cannot fathom how His knowledge is no contradiction to free will. Rav Chaim Dov Altusky, *shlita,* explained that the paradox between Man's free will and God's knowledge of the future is based upon our concept of time. We are within time and so understand it sequentially, moment after moment. God, however, not only is above time, but He created it. There is no past or future; everything is present. This is because He retains for Himself the situation of before the creation of time. Being that He created "the beginning" (*Bereshis*), there is no "beginning" as far as His essence is concerned. He can look at all of time and see everything all at once. And yet, this doesn't obligate one's actions. Rav Altusky used the analogy of watching someone from across the street. Even though I know exactly what he is doing, he has full freedom of action. God is, so to speak, across the street, watching all of time at once.

Rav Eliyahu Dessler, *zt"l*, developed this one step further. First, he said, we have to determine whether we are discussing His knowledge regarding us, or His knowledge regarding Himself. His knowledge regarding us means His knowledge inasmuch as He shows it to us through His running of the world. In this, certainly, He doesn't show us His knowledge itself, for this is above time. Rather, what characterizes the way He runs the world is His judging Man באשר הוא שם, "according to the way he is at that moment" (*Bereshis* 21:17). Whenever He judges a person, He doesn't take into consideration that person's future free will, whether for his benefit or censure. Even later on, when the future actions come under the scrutiny of Divine Judgment, it is merely within the category of cause and effect, of one mitzvah causing another, or one *averah* causing another. One's present ability to choose out of free will causes the rise or decline of his spiritual level, but always within the realm of "according to the way he is at that moment." This is the key to the future — the root of the future already exists in the present choice. In one's present situation is found everything that is likely to result from it, according to the laws of cause and effect. (See above, chapter 10, in the note discussing *Sho'el u'Meshiv*.) It is according to this outlook that Man is judged regarding his needs and possessions in this world (unless it is a case in which the person changes the development through *teshuvah* — this would be a new situation, above the realm of nature).

However, if we are discussing God's knowledge itself, this is what seemingly contradicts our free will. This knowledge is what the Rambam was referring to when he said it is a category of knowledge by itself, unlike our concept of knowledge and with no correlation in all of Creation. It is impossible to try to ask a question from what is within Creation to what is outside of Creation (*Michtav Me-Eliyahu*, vol. III, p. 262).

RA'AVAD'S COMMENTARY ON THE ABOVE RAMBAM

"The author [the Rambam] has not chosen to follow the custom of wise men: that one does not start a topic and not know how to finish it. He has started with deep questions and left the subject as a question, and so has fallen back on faith. It would have been better to leave the matter to the innocence of the innocent and not arouse their hearts (to the question) and left their minds in doubt. Perhaps a time will come and their minds will start questioning this. Even though there is no final answer to this, still it is better to rely on a partial answer, and say: If the righteousness or wickedness of a person were dependent upon the decree of the Creator, then we would say that His knowledge creates a predetermination. Then the question would be very difficult indeed. But now that the Creator has released such governing from His hand and given it over to Man himself, His knowledge of the future does not predetermine, but is rather like the knowledge of the astrologers who know through some other power what will be the path of this person. It is a known fact that the Creator has given over to the stars ("nature") all incidents of Man, large or small. However, He has given Man an intelligence to pull himself out from under the governing of the stars. This intelligence is the power given to Man to choose good or evil. The Creator knows the strength of the stars (of "nature") and whether each person's intellect is strong enough to accomplish this or not. This is His knowledge, but it is not predetermination. However, all this is still not sufficient."

In summary, the Ra'avad wishes to answer the Rambam's paradox by saying that God willingly limited His knowledge in order to allow Man a realm in which he has free will. Along similar lines, Rav Avigdor Miller comments: "The existence of free will is the greatest miracle after the Creation of the universe. The Creator, by especial miracle, left a space in which He allows Man to act and move of his own free will. Outside this space, everything is decreed and preordained; but in this area, men have the freedom to choose to act according to their own wishes. No object, or force, or being in all the entire universe has any impulse or will of its own choice—except Man. Then Man, in a sense, is a partner with God in the universe. His share, however small, is his very own to administer as he chooses" (הרה״ג Rav Avigdor Miller, *shlita*, in *Rejoice O Youth!* sec. 606-607).]

DETERMINISM

All this proves that Man's actions are predetermined. Predeterminism sweeps all of our questions away. Of course God knows the future, but only in a general aspect. From the beginning of time, He understood all the interactions of all the elements and what would result in the future according to the laws of nature. His perception is not a direct perception through material senses, but rather a knowledge of the basic makings of all matter, their order and limitations from the beginning of time. He doesn't understand them due to any new changes that arise with time, but rather because they are fixed in their nature; the changes are a predetermined result from the beginning. Also, we cannot say that He becomes more perfect as He gains more knowledge, but rather the opposite: that His knowledge is what obligates their existence. In addition, one cannot ask how His knowledge can constantly increase, indefinitely, because the intelligent order which obligates Existence makes it finite and unified.

According to all this, it is impossible to find in Existence any realm of possibilities dependent upon Man's free will. That would only bring back all of our questions. Rather, all of Man's actions are fixed, predetermined and set, from the beginning of time. God knows everything with a basic, all-encompassing knowledge which never changes, never increases, never adds anything new, not with the increase in the creatures of the universe, nor with events which (according to our conception) depend upon time and free will. He knows everything through understanding the very essence which connects all causes and all results until the end of this chain of cause and effect. This is the basic theme of Iyov's reply in chapter 10.

All this permits Iyov to complain. Possibility and free will are not in Man's hands, and being a *tzaddik* or a *rasha* has nothing to do with him, but rather is due to the eternal laws which dictate one's actions and movements. This being the case, how can a person be reprimanded for any transgression which he was essentially forced to do? And if you claim that this suffering is not a punishment, but rather a purging to cleanse the world of evil, the way we exterminate snakes and scorpions even though they do not willfully cause damage but are driven by their natures, then he asks: If God knew from the moment of his birth that this person would sin and perpetrate evil, why then did He create him and give him life? Would it not have been better *not* to have been created? And if with the knowledge that he would definitely sin in the future, still He granted him the right to exist even before he obtained existence and while still a nothing, then it is definitely proper to continue the existence which he has already acquired; nothing new has transpired which has caused him to be lost, which God was not previously aware of. This is Iyov's question. The answer is to be given in Tzofar's rebuttal.

Tzofar

IYOV 11

Iyov's two friends have agreed to his premise that if God is watching over the world, then it is an impossibility that there should be a *tzaddik* who suffers unjustly. What they argued, however, each according to his viewpoint, was that, really, there is no such thing as a *tzaddik* suffering unjustly. [Elifaz viewed suffering as an atonement for one's transgressions, and therefore Iyov's suffering as proof that he was not a *tzaddik*. Bildad, on the other hand, took the viewpoint that sometimes a *tzaddik* will suffer "torments of love" in order to increase his reward in the Next World.] Now Tzofar comes and challenges this basic premise. He asserts that even though God watches over the world, still it is possible to find a *tzaddik* suffering, and that this is not unjust at all.

SUBJECTIVE OR ABSOLUTE PERCEPTION

Perception can be divided into two categories: 1) perception of something for what it is absolutely, and 2) perception of something according to our senses. We know that it is impossible to perceive something absolutely, according to what it is in and of itself; we can perceive it only according to how it influences our senses. All information comes to a person and his intellect through the senses, and from this the intellect must connect the new information with previous information. The conditions of the senses receiving the information are not necessarily the conditions of absolute reality. Therefore, we cannot judge things according to what they really are, but rather only according to how their external surface affects our senses, and affects the conditions according to which the senses relay the information to the intellect in time, space, and the other conditions of the senses. One cannot say that these are the conditions of the object itself. Consequently it is impossible to have a clear idea, for we can only perceive the externalities of the thing according to how it affects our senses. Only an intellect completely divorced of the material aspect of the world can perceive a thing directly. He will see things differently from the way we see them through the faculties of our senses. Therefore, even if according to the perception of the external senses it may seem to be an injustice that a *tzaddik* suffers, this will not be an injustice to the pure intellect divorced from the physical, which perceives the true reality of things. This refers to both the concept of the *tzaddik* and the subject of "suffering."

WHO IS A *TZADDIK*?

According to what we perceive, we consider one who is doing good and avoiding evil to be a *tzaddik*. Nevertheless, he is a *tzaddik* only according to our human perception; he may be in reality very wicked (a *rasha*). We can perceive only his external appearance, which is just a superficial garment surrounding the real person — the soul, hiding within the body. We can know nothing about whether or not the soul actually has characteristics of a *tzaddik* or a *rasha*, since the senses cannot perceive the soul, which is the real essence of the person. It may very well be that he is a *tzaddik* according to the actions of the body, and yet he may still be a *rasha* according to the perfection necessary for his soul within.

This makes most sense according to those opinions of *Chazal* that see the events in *Iyov* as taking place before the Torah was given; thus the righteousness of Iyov was only moral ethics in Man's interrelationships. Aren't there many obligations and corrections necessary in order to perfect the soul, which cannot be known by pure intellect? Nor can a person fulfill them all through following rules of right and wrong, which are themselves based on purely physical grounds. This will not perfect the soul according to its full potential, which is hidden from Man's knowledge. It may very well be that he is a *rasha* merely from the fact that he has not fulfilled his soul's potential. This is understandable especially according to the Ralbag, who wrote that righteousness and wickedness are measured according to the person's unique capabilities. For Man was created to do the utmost according to his personal ability.

According to this, it is possible to find people whom we consider good because they are apparently doing good actions, while in reality they fall very short of the good actions they are really capable of doing. For this they are deserving of strict punishment, for a small sin is deserving of being considered large if the person has the capability for more.

In light of this, we cannot complain that the evils which befall the *tzaddikim* are not fair, for we have no way of measuring each individual's unique true potential. Therefore, we cannot really know who is a *tzaddik* and who is a *rasha*.

Moreover, it is impossible to discern the amount of good

or evil which each person deserves for his rebellion or righteousness, to claim that he is being treated unfairly. The amount of good or evil which each person deserves should be relative to his personal ability or lack of ability. One act can have varying possible rewards, depending upon the level of the one who does the action.❖ The greater the individual, the less the reward, and inversely, the punishment for evil actions is that much greater. All this is included in Tzofar's statement, מעוניך (ויגד לך) תעלומות חכמה כי כפלים לתושיה ודע כי ישה לך אלוה, "Would He tell you mysteries of wisdom, for the wisdom is double. And know that God obligates you to pay for your iniquity" (11:6).

[Elifaz had argued that Iyov really did sin in some way and therefore his punishment was deserving. Tzofar now argues that we really cannot know whether a person is a *tzaddik* or a sinner for we cannot know the real truth of that person. This concept, that the reality of the individual is not unquestionably apparent to us, has important repercussions. We find in *Chazal* that a person is judged in different ways depending upon how his actions are viewed, either with *middas ha-din*, the aspect of Divine Retribution, or with *middas ha-rachamim*, the aspect of

---

❖ Rav Chayim Volozhin, *zt"l*, discusses a similar concept in *Nefesh Ha-Chayim* (*sha'ar* 1, *perek* 12). The *pasuk* says, היוצר יחד לבם המבין אל כל מעשיהם, "Who has formed all of their hearts together, Who understands all of their actions" (*Tehillim* 33:15). It would have been more exact to write, המבין כל מעשיהם, "Who understands all of their actions." Instead the *pasuk* says, המבין אל כל מעשיהם, "Who understands *into* all of their actions." David *Ha-Melech* was telling us that God formed each individual. Therefore He understands how each action affects the whole universe. A person is not judged on the action alone. He is judged on everything that is affected by it. The greater a person is, the greater is the effect he has on the world and therefore his responsibility is that much greater.

Divine Mercy. The Chafetz Chaim, in his classic work *Shemiras Ha-Lashon* (*sha'ar Ha-Tevunah, perek* 4), after discussing the obligation to judge one's fellow favorably, elaborates:

"Now, according to the amount that a person trains himself in this character trait, so, too, relative to this will he decrease the transgression of *lashon ha-ra* (speaking bad about people). How much ought a person to strengthen himself in the character trait of judging everybody favorably, for through this trait of judging favorably (or the opposite, Heaven forbid) it will be easier for the person to gain for himself the title *tzaddik* (or *rasha*) forever. It is a known fact that the liabilities and merits of a person are dependent upon the amount of mitzvos or transgressions he has 'in his hand,' as *Chazal* have said in several places that if he has a majority of mitzvos then he is in the category of a *tzaddik*, and if he has a majority of transgressions then he is in the category of a *rasha*. *Chazal* have stated (in the Gemara *Rosh Hashanah* 16b) that 'three books are opened on the Day of Judgment (meaning the Great Day of Judgment after the resurrection of the dead, as Rashi explains there). Pure *tzaddikim* are recorded and sealed immediately for eternal life. Pure *resha'im* (the purely wicked) are recorded and sealed to go to Gehinnom, as it says... The middle ones...' Now, as to the merits that a person has, it is known that even if they are as plentiful as the sand, if the Holy One, blessed be He, will act toward him with the attribute of pure Justice, then nothing will be left in his hand except for the tiniest amount. How many mitzvos did he *not* perform perfectly in all their details and aspects? And even those that he fulfilled according to law may not have been done out of love, with the fear and joy appropriate for performing a mitzvah. The principle is that if the Holy One, blessed be He, scrutinizes, Heaven forbid, every detail of one's performance of mitzvos, then the majority of them will be found to be flawed, and the mitzvos remaining to him will consist of a minuscule amount relative to his liabilities. This person would therefore be labeled a *rasha* forever. However, if the Holy One, blessed be He, acts toward him with the attribute of Mercy, then virtue will be found in his favor in all of his dealings, and his merits will remain intact. Moreover, even if his actions are counted and it is found that he has a majority of transgressions, if the Holy One, blessed be He, acts toward him with the attribute of pure Mercy, then their number will be lessened. For certainly, there will be found a way to cover over many of his transgressions, i.e., he did it unintentionally, or some other explanation. The principle is that if the Holy One, blessed be He, wishes to find virtues for a person, it will not be difficult for Him. And therefore, if some of one's transgressions are decreased, then the balance will weigh in favor of the side of merit and one will gain for himself the name *tzaddik* forever.]

TRUE SUFFERING AND TRUE REWARD

Now to the question of the suffering and destruction of the *tzaddik*. We view it as a loss when the physical body is destroyed. But this is only because we have no conception of the real person, only of that which we can perceive. The reality is that it is only the external person who is destroyed, while the real person, his internal soul, is being rewarded a fierce and glorious joy. The external pain felt by the senses is no proof of internal torment of the inner soul. *Chazal* have explained that true reward and punishment are not the good and evil we experience. For it is only proper that the reward and punishment which are meted out to a person should be those which affect the true aspect of the individual. The best good is success of the soul — for that is the real person — not success and enjoyment of the body. Eating and feeling exist only because the person is an animal, not because he is Man. So too human evil stems from a lack of spiritual perfection, which is true success.

This explains the concepts of reward and punishment as spiritual success or the lack of it. Therefore, the good and evil which are meted out to the "real Man" are orderly and fair. Even if the physical body is destroyed, still the soul lives on eternally, and receives its reward after death (11:15-19).

GOD'S KNOWLEDGE IS BEYOND OUR UNDERSTANDING

Iyov argued in chapter 10 that Man has no freedom of action, for if he did, it would be impossible for God to know everything that will take place in the future, in all its detail. Tzofar takes issue with this, and his reply is similar to the Rambam's: We should not compare our understanding with that of God. Just as His plane of existence is so much above ours, so too is His understanding far removed from ours. This must be, for His knowledge is He Himself. Just as we cannot conceive of Him Himself, neither can we conceive of His knowledge. The philosophers explain that the term "knowledge" is applied to both God and ourselves in name only. That is, just because the same word is used, it does not mean we can compare one to the other.❖

The Rambam in his *Guide* (section 3, chap. 20) explains that God's knowledge differs from ours in five ways: 1) One idea encompasses all the different ideas; 2) He can understand that which doesn't exist yet; 3) His knowledge encompasses the infinite; 4) God's knowledge of future events doesn't obligate their happening. There is still the possibility of the opposite occurring, so that even though He has knowledge of the future, there still remains the potential of different possibilities and free will; 5) God's knowledge doesn't change as new events develop, since He knew about them before they happened. And even though there has transpired a change in

---

❖ See the *Guide for the Perplexed* (section 3, chaps. 18-20), where the Rambam explains that we cannot use logic to understand God's thinking. There is no comparison of our limited thought processes to His infinite wisdom. This is also discussed in the *Mishneh Torah,* cited above. (See, in the discussion on chap. 10, the note: "The Paradox: God's Foreknowledge and Man's Free Will.")

something, which changes the previous idea of the different possibilities to the actuality of what has happened, still this does not constitute any change in His knowledge, for He knew the future already in the beginning.

All these things are beyond the grasp of our intellect. This is because the term "knowledge" in the sense of human knowledge is not the same as His Divine "knowledge." We cannot even conceive of the way He understands, just as we cannot fathom His actual being. The very nature of this knowledge necessitates that it be unimaginable and inconceivable to us. We have already discussed how we perceive things only through the senses, and thus cannot understand perception by means of a pure intellect completely devoid of materiality, and how it can perceive the absolute reality of things, devoid of time limitations. That is a perception of a different nature. Even more so we cannot conceive of God's infinite understanding (11:7-9). This is what Tzofar meant when he asked, החקר אלוה תמצא וכו׳, "Can you conceive the analysis of God? Can you conceive of the limit of the Almighty?" (11:7).

From this, Tzofar concludes that God knows all the future, and nevertheless Man has free will and full potential over his actions. Therefore a person cannot question the paradox of knowledge versus free will at all, and ask: "If God knows that a person will sin, therefore he must have been forced to sin, so how can he be punished?" For this is simply something we cannot fathom (11:10-11).

Besides all this, it is impossible to deny that Man has free will. This is obvious if only from the intuition that everyone feels within himself, that whatever he wants and chooses to do, he has the possibility to do and no power is stopping him (11:13).

Now, if you should ask, Why did God create Man in such a fashion? Why did He not create him in a way that he could understand things for what they actually are, and comprehend everything from beginning to end without the means of the senses, and therefore not be confused by all these questions? Tzofar answers that this is similar to asking, Why didn't God give the donkey the power of reason, to be like Man? The answer is simple. If so, he would no longer be a donkey. So, too, God desired the existence of Man, which is intellect attached to materiality. If Man's intellect were not limited to the sensual, he would be devoid of all material and therefore would not be a human being but some higher creature (11:12).

[See the *Sefer Ruach Chayim* on *Pirkei Avos* by Rav Chayim Volozhin, *perek* 1, *mishnah* 1: "Moshe received the Torah from Sinai...," in the note by his son: *Chazal* state (*Shabbos* 84b) that when Moshe went up to Heaven to receive the Torah, *malachei ha-shares* (the ministering angels) said to him, "What is a man born of woman doing here?", meaning that Man's intellect, combined with his materiality, constitutes only potential and not actuality. What is he doing among us, who are pure, actual intellect?

Ha-Kadosh Baruch Hu answered them, "He has come to receive the Torah." Yes, he has come to receive the Torah which will enable him to influence his material nature and raise his intellect to an actuality greater than yours. They said to Him, "This treasure which has been hidden from before the world was created — You wish to give it to flesh and blood?" The Torah has been hidden in the highest realm of Heaven, where Man's intellect cannot fathom it; it precedes everything, and Man was created after everything. Man [claim the angels] is not relevant to it at all. Instead, give Your Glory up in the Heavens to the angels, who are above time. So God said to Moshe, "Answer them!" And he answered, "But I am afraid they will burn me with the breath of their mouths." *Malachim* are composed of fire, which is closer to the very being of Torah, which is fire written on fire, and *malachim* are also fire, pure spiritual intellect. This is breath which has no sin attached to it, and which has no material form. Man can only fulfill the Torah in the material realm.

So God said to Moshe, "Grab onto My Throne of Glory and answer them." When a person humbles himself and, so to speak, sacrifices his inclination, it is as if he has given the greatest honor to God. The main means of humbling oneself is through the Torah. By bettering one's character through Torah, one is increasing God's honor. So, "Grab onto My Throne of Glory and answer them," meaning, "because of your attachment to My Throne through your efforts on behalf of My honor, this increases the Heavenly influences upon the world." Therefore, Moshe has more relevance to the Torah than do the angels.]

Iyov's Rebuttal To Tzofar

TO KNOW ONESELF

IYOV 12-14

Tzofar's view was that our knowledge comes through the senses which perceive only the externality of things (objects) the way they act on the senses. And so one cannot know the reality of the object the way it is, in and of itself. According to this, one can imagine that even if according to the perception of the senses one is a *tzaddik*, in reality he may be wicked and liable for destruction or punishment due to the real internal nature of his soul. On this Iyov had a good laugh. Is there a bigger joke than this? That a person can appear a *tzaddik* in all of his actions and seem to be free of any blemish or hypocrisy, and yet not know himself, not know who he really is? That in reality he may be wicked and a sinner, and will soon receive his due? How is it possible that God created a person in such an evil and bitter situation as this, which is open to mockery and laughter? So much so that the tranquil thoughts one has, secure in his piety, are really a mockery on his head: What a fool! He doesn't even know himself. He cannot have any faith in life, for he may be a sinner, terribly negligent, and not even realize it (12:3-4).

[Iyov resembles most of humanity in that he doesn't understand a basic principle of the spiritual realm: The measuring rod of Judgment in the Next World is completely different than what we are used to here. משפטיך תהום רבה, "Your Judgments are a great abyss (tremendously deep)." Ya'akov *Avinu* was terribly afraid that God would not protect him even though he had received a Divine promise. He feared that perhaps he had sinned with his thoughts (*Bereshis* 32:8-11, and Ibn Ezra on *pasuk* 9) and that therefore he and his family would be wiped out by Esav! The Gemara in *Berachos* 28b relates that R. Yochanan ben Zakkai cried on his deathbed because he did not know which way he was going, even though the Gemara in *Sukkah* 28a considers him to be among the greatest of *tzaddikim* and Torah scholars. We really cannot comprehend the depth of the Heavenly Judgment; we cannot know who we really are. (See the above note from the Chafetz Chaim.)]

IYOV, AN EMPIRICIST: ALL OF MANKIND RELIES ON THEIR EXERIENCES AS REALITY, AND THEY CANNOT ALL BE MISTAKEN

The main thrust of Tzofar's argument was that Man has no clear perception or knowledge of the true reality of things, which may be the opposite of what he views it to be. Iyov argued that, on the contrary, the knowledge that a person gains through experience and by means of the senses is a clear and real knowledge. Have we not seen that that which one perceives through the senses is the same as what humanity has perceived throughout all the generations? Listen to the ancient and ongoing tradition that all of humanity's perceptions and knowledge are the same as yours. This proves that one's knowledge is clear and true, that the nature and reality of things must be exactly as one perceives them to be, because it is impossible that imagination should wildly mislead the whole human race (12:11-12 and 13:1-2).

IYOV: GOD'S THINKING IS NOT DIFFERENT FROM OURS

Tzofar's basic premise was that God could know all the details of one's decisions together with complete knowledge of the future, and yet with all this, that there could still remain a realm of possibility and human free will. For His knowledge is not of the same nature as our knowledge. He perceives the actual object simply and directly, independent of the conditions of time, place, and the senses, while we are not even able to imagine this knowledge, just as a blind man cannot imagine sight. The difference between our knowledge and His is like the difference between the perception of civilized man and that of the beast, or wild primitives. Iyov's opinion is similar to that of the Ralbag in his *Milchamos* (*ma'amar* 3, *perek* 3), where he disputes the opinion of the Rambam in the *Guide*. The Ralbag claims that there really is no difference between God's knowledge and ours, except that what God knows is more complete and perfect than what we know. It is more accurate in its delineation and clarity, but it is not different, or the opposite of our knowledge, in the way that the *Guide* claims.

Therefore Iyov brings back all the proofs from chapter 10: that it is impossible that God knows all the details of one's future choice and that there should still remain the concept of possibility and Man's free will, for these are contradictory. Iyov again reiterates that one must conclude that Man's actions are predetermined, and he can thus do only what God knew from the beginning that he would do, being forced by "nature" to act in a certain way. Man is like the rest of the creatures in the animal world, which do not have free will but act merely on instinct and are compelled in their actions (12:7-13).

God governs and compels the actions of Man the way He compels all of nature. Just as the element of water sometimes floods the world and sometimes dries up, it is nonetheless always governed by the laws of nature. So, too, are the actions of Man against his fellowman (12:14-16).

GOD PLAYS WITH KINGS AND PAWNS

Iyov then brings more examples demonstrating that Man is compelled in his actions. Look at the conduct of nations and peoples, he says. Sometimes their wise men and leaders go wild, taking a foolish course which brings about the whole nation's downfall. It seems apparent that a supernatural force is corrupting their wisdom and guiding them to their foolish thinking (12:17 - end of chapter).

Now Iyov cries out bitterly that he has been coerced in his actions and therefore will receive no reward for his righteousness. He is a victim of pure accident and the evil which was engraved upon his fortune. It would have been better had God allowed him freedom of action in order to receive his reward, to perform faithfully as a worker, rather than to toil for vanity and naught (14:5). Man's days are few and evil. The nature he was born with forces him to be inclined toward impurity and destructive action. He is constantly battling with his evil inclination. Still, at least he should be allowed enough freedom to act like a day laborer (14:1-5).❖

Tzofar had laid down that Man's main success and reward come after death, when he then, hopefully, can live spiritually in eternal bliss. Iyov spent some time mocking this, for his philosophy denied the supernatural life and spiritual reward (14:7 - end of chapter).

Still, even though he took the time to rebut Tzofar's view, he muttered throughout all of chapter 13 against his three friends who waged battle against him. Their words belie their hearts, he said, and they themselves know that their arguments are empty. They come merely out of a desire to triumph over him, like the hypocrites who speak deceit while their thoughts are quite distant. Again he asks them to let him know his sin and the extent of his transgressions.

❖ See in the Appendix the essays by Rav Yerucham Levovitz, *zt"l*, "Iyov's Complaint that It Is Impossible to Fight One's Nature," and "The World Has Been Handed over to an Evil Power."

This ends the first debate about the sufferings of a *tzaddik*. Now Iyov opens a new front which has not been discussed yet: the wicked who prosper. ישליו אהלים לשודדים, "The tents of robbers are peaceful, and those who provoke God are secure..." (12:6). The answer to this question cannot be deduced from any of the opinions thus far stated. For the *rasha*'s wickedness is obvious to all. It is impossible to call him a hidden *tzaddik*, for we see that he is a bandit and angers God as he perpetrates evil deeds out of pure spite. And yet he enjoys a peaceful existence, free from fear, with no Divine rod being directed against him. Now the debate opens on the subject of the *rasha* who prospers, and each of the participants answers according to his viewpoint.

Part Two: The Wicked Who Prosper

IYOV 15

Iyov has now posed his second question, that of the wicked who prosper. The previous answers are insufficient to handle this question, so the debaters return to a second round.

Elifaz: The Wicked Live In Constant Fear

Elifaz answers that the prosperity of the wicked is prosperity in appearance only; it is not real. Even if you see him succeeding, amassing wealth, power, and possessions, the wicked man nevertheless lives in constant fear. He always feels like a hunted man. And it is as if poverty, destitution, and all the evils of time have caught up with him, so much so that he has no heart to enjoy his wealth. He suffers from constant anxiety, worry, and confusion. This is God's punishment for perpetrating evil right in front of His eyes, in order to anger Him. Therefore, He unsettles the heart and thoughts of the wicked with fear and trembling. For real success is tranquillity of the spirit, peace of the soul, and joy of the heart. "It is better to have dry bread in peace than a house full of meat with quarreling" (*Mishlei* 17:1).

This is a description of what actually happened to Iyov, as he said, פחד פחדתי ויאתני, "I felt a terrible fear." This constant fear which haunted him is a sign of the *rasha*'s end, for in the end, he will be cut off, he and his offspring, and all that is his, which is exactly what has happened to Iyov. This is the essence of Elifaz's view.

First, however, Elifaz chastises Iyov again for denying the reward of the soul in the Next World. Even if one wants to deny the physical resurrection of the dead, still he cannot deny the eternity of the soul. All true happiness and success depend upon this (15:11,13).

Secondly, he again criticizes him for denying free will and holding firm in his belief that Man is coerced in his actions. Anyone with understanding intuitively feels himself free to choose, he maintains, with no external forces compelling him in his actions (15:18-19).

TEMPORARY PHYSICAL SUFFERING FREES THE SOUL FROM ETERNAL TORMENT

And since Man is free to act, there is of course an accounting. And being that it is impossible not to commit some sin which will necessitate his punishment, therefore God punishes him with temporary suffering in this world in order that he not lose his eternal soul. This is the same answer that Elifaz gave in the first rebuttal. Only there he did not explain explicitly that punishment comes in order to save one's soul from being severed from its spiritual reward. He merely said that suffering comes upon a person temporarily in order that he not be lost eternally through premature physical death. On this Iyov had countered that there is no difference between dying now and dying later (for the time spent suffering is like death), as discussed in chapter 7. Now, Elifaz explains that there is a reward for the soul, and the spiritual life is eternal life. Therefore, it is better to suffer, or even to die a temporary death, rather than suffer eternal loss (15:14-17).

Besides all this, instead of accusing Iyov of committing the minor sin of serving Him not out of love, now Elifaz presents Iyov as totally wicked because he denies all facets of faith. It is obvious from what Iyov has said that his statements were not the rantings of a tormented man, who cannot be criticized for words spoken under duress. No, says Elifaz; his thesis was too organized and was expressed wisely. Obviously he had thought about it for a long time, even while all was still well (15:2,7).

Besides this, he laughs at Iyov's foolishness in complaining about Man's creation, as if he were the first man ever created in the world. How many generations have already passed who lived their lives and enjoyed their labors! And all of them praised God for His kindness. Is Iyov going to out-vote the whole world (15:7-11)? Does the clay tell the potter what to make? He is a creation with no hands.

Iyov

IYOV 16,17

Iyov waits to answer Elifaz and Bildad on the success of the *rasha* and for the moment doesn't argue. He is waiting for all three debaters and then he will answer with one all-encompassing rebuttal which will destroy all of their arguments, in chapter 21.

Also, as for Elifaz's repetition of his first address, in which he related his view on the suffering of a *tzaddik* (15:15-17), Iyov does not answer him here either, for he has already answered him previously and doesn't want to merely tire him with too many words, for this is not the way of wise men (16:2-5). Likewise, he doesn't answer his statement about free will, in order not to repeat something already stated.

He does proceed, however, to answer Elifaz on two

points. 1) Elifaz had proceeded to accuse him of being totally evil, and concluded that he deserved the judgment of a *rasha* and the punishment that goes with it. Everything he mentioned about the *rasha*'s fear and his downfall was like pointing an accusing finger at Iyov, to whom all of this had indeed happened. This causes Iyov to cry out and protest (16:7-21).

2) Elifaz continued his premise by saying that the main reward is the soul's enduring after death (המעט ממך תנחומות אל...כי תשיב אל אל רוחך, "Are God's consolations little for you...for you will return your soul to God?" [15:11,13].) Iyov found a lot to disagree with on this, since the concept of the soul is a hidden concept and most people cannot comprehend this mystery, seeing only what is tangible: that the *tzaddik* is being tormented and is suffering. No one is able to guarantee that there is any other life after death. These things are hidden from the perception of the eye. Even the mind cannot conceive of it (כי לבם צפנת משכל, "For You have hidden their hearts from understanding..." [17:4]). All of Mankind only consider the visible and tangible life. And when they see the *tzaddik* suffering, some will pervert the matter and prove from this that he was a *rasha*, as happened in Iyov's case. And some will maintain that he is a *tzaddik* and criticize the Divine *Hashgachah*. Therefore the whole chapter deals with how the suffering of the *tzaddikim* and success of the *resha'im* bring Man to denial, criticism, and desolation of wisdom. It is the destruction of all order. It would have been better to give the *tzaddik* according to his righteousness, and the *rasha* according to his evil, here in this world, in order that Man should see and learn a lesson.

BILDAD

MAN: THE SPIRITUAL BEING

IYOV 18

Bildad begins by being upset at Iyov's revelation that he doesn't believe in, or at least is doubtful about, the eternity of the soul after death. If such is the case, he asserts, then Man is no better than an animal. They both face the same death and they both share the same spirit. Why then did God create Man in His image, blowing into his nostrils the spirit of life, which thinks and understands? The human form is, according to this, of absolutely no purpose except to add insult to injury by allowing Man to realize that he is destined for ruin. Since we see that God planted within him priceless spiritual powers which do not exist in the rest of the living creatures, does this not prove that these are the essence of Man, and that his soul does not die with his animal body, but rather lives eternally?

["The essence of Man is his soul, which rises above, before the King of kings, the Holy One, blessed be He, to face Judgment. The body, created from a putrid drop, and which will eventually return to dust, is of little importance, as Iyov claimed: 'What is this Man born of woman, whose days are so short.' The physical body is what led Iyov astray to deny reward and punishment, because since it is naturally inclined to sin, it can have no Judgment. He also denies the concept of the resurrection of the dead, as *Chazal* tell us (*Bava Basra* 16), just as the philosophers claimed that it is impossible that from clumps of dirt should blossom the seed of Man.

"However, they said this because the light of God's Torah never shone upon them. When the light of our Torah was revealed to us, we gained proximity to the concept that the day that God created Man, He gave him a soul. Man's soul comes from Above, from the Divine. All of Man's life is generated by the soul. As the Ramban said (in *Parashas Bechukosai*), in answer to the Rambam's question as to why the Torah makes no mention of spiritual reward, physical reward in this world proves the virtue of our Holy Torah. In the spiritual Next World it is quite understandable that the soul should attach itself to its source. However, it is a marvel that even in this world, fulfilling the Torah generates good; by occupying ourselves with it, the heavens give off rain and the Earth gives its bounty. And the soul, even when it is below in Man's body, is still attached to its roots Above. However, with the first Man's sin, the level of his soul was diminished.... But Man's free will has the ability to change his physical materiality into something spiritual. And, Heaven forbid, the opposite happens as well, that if he blemishes the Spirit, his being returns to its physicality as mere flesh.... Those men who change their physical flesh into spirituality are called *ba'alei nefesh* (spiritual beings). Unfortunately, due to our many transgressions, men who are truly spiritual are very few. But if one really merits it, the spirit descends into his body.... As the *pasuk* relates, 'Indeed, it is a spirit in man, and the breath of the Almighty permits them to understand' (*Iyov* 32:8).... This creates a strong incentive to fulfill Torah and mitzvos. For a person shouldn't imagine that he has no need to involve himself in loftiness. On this the Tanna states, 'Consider things and you will not come into the grip of sin: know from where you came, to where you are going, and in front of Whom you are destined to give an accounting...' (*Pirkei Avos* 3:1). In other words, you should know that you will have to give an accounting. Why? [If the body is so lowly how can one deserve an accounting?] Because the soul is the essence, and therefore by force of your spirituality you have the ability to rise higher and higher. As *Chazal* state (in Tanna de'vei Eliyahu Rabba, chap. 25). 'A person should always say to himself: When will my actions reach those of our forefathers, Avraham, Yitzchak, and Ya'akov?' (Rav Chayim Volozhin, *zt"l, Ruach Chayim, perek* 3, *mishnah* 1)]

TRUE SUCCESS IS SPIRITUAL SUCCESS

With this Bildad introduces his new thesis to explain the success of the wicked: it is due to their being Man. This, in and of itself, is the success of the soul, for just by being "Man" one is separated from the animal. True success definitely is not physical success, since the human body is basically the same as the animal body. Therefore, the *rasha*'s success in attaining material possessions in this world, which are only physical pleasure, cannot be the true success. The opposite is the case. The punishment of the *rasha* is that he will not leave behind any legacy. His spiritual soul will be cut off and destroyed; it will not bask in the light of the true life of eternal bliss. Neither will he leave behind any legacy in the form of offspring, for even his children will be cut off and his name and any vestige of his memory will disappear from the face of the earth. That is the worst and most terrifying form of punishment imaginable.

In contrast is the *tzaddik*. He will enjoy eternal remembrance in this world, and life even in death, as his soul lives on in eternal bliss. There in the Next World, he will enjoy all of his reward in return for all the suffering he endured in this world.

This completes Bildad's thesis that the suffering of the *tzaddik* is a form of exchange. All of Iyov's attempts to upset and topple this view were based on the supposition that the exchange is experienced in this world: that one would receive a good reward in this world in return for all that he suffered. His arguments vanish if the reward is a spiritual, eternal reward to his immortal soul, giving it eternal bliss in return for the temporary suffering. The different aspects of Divine Judgment will be justified as it becomes apparent that it is one unified plan, and all of Iyov's replies will dissipate like a cloud of smoke in the wind.

Iyov continues to wait, and doesn't answer Bildad. He is waiting to reply to his three friends together. However, he does say that they are causing him pain with their bitter, sharp, and degrading criticism. Even if he had spoken improperly, still a person cannot be criticized for having spoken so out of suffering. He sees that they all have turned into his enemies and are pursuing him mercilessly. He hands judgment over to the future generations who will justify him in his debate. And he hands his case to Heaven against them for hunting a man as afflicted with illness as he, and so fatally broken in spirit. He tells of his pain and torment and warns that they should fear Divine punishment for having afflicted him with verbal torment instead of giving him their friendship.

Tzofar

IYOV 20

The debater from Na'amah now departs from the philosophical position he presented previously. At that time he addressed philosophically the question of the *tzaddik* who suffers, explaining that there is a difference between knowledge of things according to what they are in and of themselves, and recognition by means of the senses, through which all of Man's knowledge passes. Man can only sense the externality of things and it is impossible for him to judge their true reality. With this ideology, he would have been able to address the second question — the prosperity of the wicked — in the same way, by saying that we don't know for sure what is good and what is bad according to true reality, according to the spiritual soul, etc.

Instead, he comments that Iyov already has had a good laugh at his ideology. Tzofar's philosophy will be found pleasing only to those who are occupied with logic and deep thought. So for the moment, he leaves this path and apologizes that for the time being he cannot state his true opinion for he knows that Iyov will only embarrass and make fun of him. Thus he answers that even if in this generation we find that the wicked prosper, still, in previous times they were disgraced, humbled, and hunted. Even now preparations are being made for their true justice. They will die a terrible and miserable death. And all their wealth and possessions will disappear, through the hands of those they have oppressed. Their very greatness will increase the severity of their downfall. The higher up one is, the harder will he fall, breaking his neck and being destroyed forever. Even during his lifetime he will not enjoy his wealth, for God will not allow him to partake of it. All those he oppressed are continually lying in wait to prey upon him. It would be better if he had not been wicked and not enjoyed a long life.

Iyov: The Tzaddik, Like the Rasha, Goes Down to the Grave

Now that his three friends have expressed their opinions on the question of the prosperity and tranquillity of the wicked, Iyov comes with his rebuttal to answer all of their views in one fell swoop. In their answers he has been the main target of their arrows. He is evil in their eyes, and therefore the evils which have overtaken him answer the question of the success of the wicked: they can look forward to no future, just as Iyov's success did not last.

To all this he answers them firmly. His original question was general, encompassing all of humanity. Their answers are insufficient to explain the many wicked who do enjoy a successful life (21:4-6). How can Elifaz claim that *resha'im* are filled with constant fear and cannot be secure in their success, when we find *resha'im* quite secure and enjoying tranquillity (9-11)? And Bildad's answer, that their whole lot and section of humanity will be cut off, is also insufficient, for we find *resha'im* alive and well and quite successful (8). Their estates exist for long periods of time (20-29). And as to his claim that their souls will be cut off and receive their punishment in the eternal world, who knows about this punishment, hidden from everyone's eyes? Death? She spreads her wings over all flesh without distinction; the *tzaddik* like the *rasha* goes down to the grave. Who knows if there is awareness and an accounting in the Hell to where they go (30-34)? As for the answer of Tzofar, that the *rasha* dies suddenly and falls down to Hell alive, just the opposite is the case; this is a mark of success, to die without pain, and this is what Iyov longs for (12,13). Is this justice and righteousness that the *tzaddik* who suffered such torment should die with a bitter taste, and the *rasha* should die in the midst of his peace and tranquillity? And that both of them should be lowered down equally into the grave, the *tzaddik* next to the *rasha* (22-26)? And even if his children should be cut off after his death, the *rasha* is no longer around to feel this punishment anyway. It would be more fitting that he himself be punished, and that he suffer for a long time in order that he recognize it as God's punishment (17-22). Having shown their answers to be insufficient, Iyov has upset all their arguments.

Elifaz

IYOV 22

We have waged a double debate with six rebuttals, on both the question of the suffering of the *tzaddik* and the success of the wicked, and Iyov the philosopher has been victorious over them all with his answers. So Elifaz again gathers his strength and readies his arrows for opening a new battlefront. He now presents a well-formulated opinion on both questions, lucid and well-thought-out.

IN ORDER TO HAVE FREE WILL

It was God's specially and wisely devised plan not to reward the *tzaddikim* or punish the *resha'im* immediately in this world, in order that their Divine service be pure, and not motivated by a desire for reward or fear of punishment. Service to God is most desirable if the person performs good for the sake of good itself, and in order to fulfill the statute of the Higher Lawmaker, and only for the sake of His Great Name. However, if he does his service for a reward or out of fear of retribution, then he is not truly serving God, but rather he is serving himself. This is not the service desired by God. Therefore, if the judgment on evil actions were quick in coming, and He meted out the *rasha*'s punishment immediately, no one would have any desire to do evil, out of fear of the consequences. And everyone would try to do good, knowing that the reward would be immediately forthcoming. Thus, no action would be for the sake of God. And there would no longer be any concept of reward and punishment, since everyone would be compelled in their actions out of fear of the punishment or hope of reward. There would be no concept of free will or tests, which were God's purpose in creating Man.

But God wanted a situation in which the evil inclination would be able to tempt Man, and in which he would have the freedom to do as he pleases, and yet with all this, the strength to refrain and turn away from evil out of respect for God and His commandments. Because of this, Man was given knowledge of the world, but knowledge that did not include the ability to discern Divine actions, neither the reward of the *tzaddikim*, nor the punishment of the wicked. Thus we find evildoers succeeding, the *resha'im* being praised in the very city where they perpetrate their evil. The Divine Hand is hidden from the eyes of most of humanity. Man's heretical impulse perverts reason, making him deny Providence and claim, "The world is merely following its natural course; everything is determined by normal cause and effect and the laws of nature. God's Glory is high above the heavens and He has no interest in us, the lowly creatures," and other such heresy. All of these heretics bring proof from the evil in the order of things, that the *tzaddikim* are oppressed and the *resha'im* successful.

This itself is the trial and the test to distinguish between one who serves God truly and purely and one who does not serve Him for His sake. The one who serves Him not for the sake of any reward is a *tzaddik* who will live in his faith and never be swayed from his convictions. He will be paid in that world which was especially created for reward. There he will enjoy a pure, eternal spiritual reward, for he has been tested and found perfect. Judgment awaits the scoffer also, in the world of the soul. God will bring him to judgment even for his hidden acts, for He is a God of faithfulness. All He does is just and all His actions are steadfast.

With this, Elifaz reinforces his previous position on two

points. He reiterates the reason he gave for the suffering of *tzaddikim* — that it is to punish them in this world for the light transgressions they committed, in order to reward them in the Next World. And he also recounts what he said about the success of the *resha'im* — that, all things considered, their success is not perfect, for their hearts are filled with fear of the punishment awaiting them. Even though, for the most part, it will come only later, in the Next World, still their hearts forebode what awaits them. In this Elifaz justifies scolding Iyov originally, in his first rebuttal, when he said, יראתך כסלתך, "Your fear was your foolishness" (4:6). The most desirable Divine service is that which is performed without hope of reward or fear of punishment, and in this Iyov sinned. Your stumbling confirms my speculation, says Elifaz. Therefore God has poured out His wrath upon Iyov. All of Iyov's previous rebuttals are answered by this argument, that everything that happened was necessary in order for him to act with free will. It is up to each reasonable person to understand what his service should be: pure and for the sake of God, performed out of pure love only.

Iyov

IYOV 23,24

Elifaz's position is twofold: First, it provides an answer to the problem of the torments of a *tzaddik*. His suffering comes about because he does not serve God with a whole heart, purely for His sake, but rather for ulterior motives, in the hope of reward or out of fear of punishment. Therefore God must purify him with suffering, to humble him and test him in order to grant him ultimate good in the Next World. Second, it includes an answer to the problem of the success of the wicked. This prosperity comes about in order to allow Man to have free will, to choose to do good or not. If the punishment were to come immediately, Man would be afraid to do evil and there would be no choice. Moreover, one's service to God would not be for Heaven's sake.

On both these points, Iyov delivers a powerful blow with two arguments. First he says, How is it possible that God should torture him with such terrible torments, just because his heart may have harbored the motivation of expecting some reward? Even so, did he not guard his duty to God's mitzvos and judgments? He has done nothing so bad to be deserving of such a terrible punishment (23:6-7). Moreover, if he were only able to argue with God, Who knows the truth, then he could prove that he served Him with no ulterior motive, but purely for His sake. True, occasionally it entered his mind that he is dependent upon God for attaining all of his needs and all of his dealings. Still, with all of this, he immediately reflected and returned to his service for the sake of His Great Name, with no other motive. From all this, Iyov proves that his righteousness was predetermined and fixed from the outset by God's preknowledge, and therefore he is not going to receive reward for it. He has been abandoned to the accidents of nature and the torment of the fortune of his birth (23:10-17).

In his reply to Elifaz's second point (chapter 24), Iyov upsets his explanation of the tranquillity of the *resha'im*. Here he shows that there are wicked people who destroy civilization and disturb the tranquillity of humanity, and yet God makes no effort to destroy them and remove their evil, to prevent them from destroying the world. If there is Divine Providence, Iyov asks, would it not be more proper to protect Mankind from these destroyers of civilization? Moreover, savages like these dwell in the deserts and on islands in the sea far from civilization, and from there they venture out from time to time to plunder and murder and capture many slaves. If God would only wipe them out in their hiding places, then no one would even know and concepts of Divine service and free will would not be damaged. Thus it would be fitting that God's Providence eradicate them from under His sky. With this, Iyov again demonstrates that God does not watch over the details of Man's existence. [See chapter 35 for Elihu's answer.] Rather, everything is dependent upon fortune. With this Iyov cries out bitterly, asking why he was not "cut off before the darkness." It would have been better for him never to have existed (23:16-17).

Bildad

REWARD AND PUNISHMENT IN THE GENERAL SCHEME

IYOV 25

Now Bildad as well attempts to defend his stand on both points he had made, in the face of Iyov's arguments: 1) that the sufferings of the *tzaddikim* are a form of exchange, and 2) that the *resha'im* enjoy success because the major part of their punishment will be meted out in the Next World, where their soul and any remnant of them will be totally executed. On both counts Iyov was victorious in his arguments. So now Bildad girds himself with strength to batter down the gates with the following defense: Everything is governed by Divine Providence, and God, the Great Benefactor, will definitely pay the *tzaddik* for his righteousness and the *rasha* for his wickedness. Still, with all this, in order to retain the general laws of nature, sometimes He must refrain from benefiting or punishing the individual immediately, because it does not fit into the overall plan. For example, rain comes through God's Will, for benefit and goodness, to cause the grass and crops to grow. Yet it keeps raining even when the *tzaddik* is walking at that moment on that path and suffers discomfort from the rain. Would you say that He should stop the rain for the *tzaddik*? Light is for everyone's benefit. Yet the *rasha* uses it to see his way to the place where he plans to perpetrate acts of murder and oppression.

Darkness, which was made to give rest to the weary, also helps the thief to sneak into houses under its cover. And with all this, no one thinks that God should change the course of nature away from the benefit of the general populace just because of one individual. The general nature encompasses everything and is watched over wisely, competently, and according to the general good. Even though sometimes it accidentally generates bad for the *tzaddik* or good for the *rasha*, still He doesn't change the general plan of nature for the single individual. All this, however, does not detract from any of the reward coming to the *tzaddik* or any punishment to the *rasha*. It is just that their reward or punishment is given in special ways that do not disturb nature, whether in this world or the next.

[Bildad seems to be suggesting that God will bring suffering to the *tzaddik* even if he is not deserving of it, if only because that is what is demanded by the General Scheme. With this Bildad seems to have strayed here from pure *emunah*. God is described by the *pasuk*, הצור תמים פעלו כי כל דרכיו משפט אל אמונה ואין עול צדיק וישר הוא, "He is the Rock, His works are perfect, for all His ways are justice, He is the God of faith with no injustice, He is righteous and straight" (*Devarim* 32:4). Everything He does is completely perfect. Like the Chafetz Chaim's *mashal* of the big-city shul, we would have to understand the whole chain of events of the entire universe from beginning to end to understand. However, such is the rule of *Hashgachah Pratis*. God oversees every detail of every individual's life. There is nothing that happens to the individual "by accident." (See *Chovos Ha-Levovos, Sha'ar Ha-Bitachon*, chap. 3.) But perhaps we can understand Bildad along these lines: Nothing is an accident and no bad can happen to the *tzaddik* without Divine *Hashgachah*. But God will arrange that any punishment or discomfort which is coming to the *tzaddik* will fit into the general *Hashgachah* in order not to disturb the general plan.]

GOD WILL NOT CHANGE THE GENERAL PLAN OF NATURE

Therefore we can very well picture that the *tzaddik* could be tormented if he was born into bad fortune and his *mazal* obligates hardships and problems. God will not change general nature for him. As He said to Elazar ben Pedas, "Do you want Me to destroy the whole world for you?"❖ Still, the *tzaddik* will receive his just reward both for his righteousness and for suffering innocently. There is another world, completely spiritual, which is not ruled by the nature of this world nor by its *mazal*. There, he shall bask in the light of life.

❖ R. Elazar ben Pedas was extremely poverty-stricken. Once he let blood [an ancient medical remedy], but he didn't have anything to eat afterwards. He took a piece of garlic and put it in his mouth. He fainted and fell into a deep slumber. The *Rabbanim* came to ask him a question [but he had fainted]... When he woke up, they asked him [what he had seen]. He told them that God had been sitting with him. "So I asked Him, 'How much longer must I suffer in this world?' He answered me, 'Elazar, My son, do you want Me to destroy the world, back to the beginning of time? Perhaps you will be born in a time [conducive] of *parnassah*.' I said before Him, 'All this and *perhaps*?!' " (*Ta'anis* 25a).

We may be able to understand this *gemara* according to what we discussed in the Preface. Everything is planned according to a very fine *Hashgachah Pratis* which connects every detail from the beginning until the end of time. Everything fits in perfectly. R. Elazar ben Pedas had a certain nature to his soul that, for some reason understood only by God, required a life of poverty. This specific nature of his soul was a result of the *Hashgachah Pratis* of the whole universe. In order to change R. Elazar's relationship to the universe, God would have to start Creation all over again from the beginning and then perhaps its relation would be different. But perhaps not, because again there would be created a soul that, due to its relationship to the universe, would have to suffer poverty. Perhaps we can understand this according to the work *Derech Hashem* 2:3:8 (quoted in the Epilogue) which states

This complements what Bildad expressed in his first debate: that the torments of the *tzaddik* are a form of exchange and that he will, in the future, receive his reward for his suffering. Then, however, he did not explain himself fully, and therefore Iyov threw his words back at him: If this exchange is due to God's wanting to torture the *tzaddik* in order to benefit him afterwards, then, "Not your sting and not your honey." But what Bildad meant was that if the fortune of the *tzaddik* and the nature of his locale, and the "stars" of his birth, and all of the factors which influence his makeup, obligate that he should suffer, or that he should be destitute, or sick, or hungry, then God will not change the general plan of nature for him. However, He will repay him good in the future for the evil he suffered due to his bad fortune. With this, Bildad justified his simile about the plant that the gardener uprooted from its place in order to replant it elsewhere so that it should grow and thrive better. So, too, God uproots the *tzaddik* from this land of troubles where he would only grieve and suffer privation, and He replants him in the land of the living, in the spiritual world where he will be satiated by the purity of his soul. There it is like a garden overflowing with fruit and abundance. So, too, in the case of the *rasha* whose fortune determines that he should be wealthy and successful and healthy, God will not change the general plan of nature in order to punish him. Instead, He will leave this world to its nature, as

---

that there is a class of *tzaddikim* whose role is to protect their whole generation. By their suffering they somehow "bring about the chain of events leading to Mankind's ultimate perfection." R. Elazar was so important to the world that even if it would be reverted back to the original Creation, his suffering would still have played an intrinsic role in bringing about the ultimate perfection. That was R. Elazar's role in the world.

Chazal have said עולם כמנהגו נוהג ושוטים שקלקליו עתידים ליתן את הדין, "The world continues in its course, and the fools who ruin it will eventually give an accounting" (*Avodah Zarah* 54b). The *rasha* will receive his punishment in the Eternal World, as was explained in Bildad's second rebuttal. Therefore, there is no question as to why he succeeds in this world: it is because his fortune caused it. His punishment will be doubled according to the amount of good he received as well as according to his evil.

Iyov's Final Rebuttal

IYOV 26 In this, the last rebuttal, Iyov replies with three separate speeches.

In the first speech Iyov answers Bildad. First he shows him that he has in reality strengthened and fortified Iyov's own position: that nature rules the world and designates the fortune of the individual, whether toward favor or toward the "rod," toward success and pleasure or toward poverty and affliction. Nevertheless, Bildad's position differs from Iyov's in its claim that still there exists Divine Providence in all details, and that the stars do not have the power to draw Man's actions away from free will; and that therefore there is reward and punishment for good or evil people. Even so, he has agreed that the driving force of Providence cannot change the driving force of nature.❖ We can still picture the *tzaddik* receiving the same as the *rasha*, and vice versa. For God will not change nature just because of the actions of the *tzaddik*. Therefore the question of the suffering of the *tzaddik* and the success of the *rasha* remains in full force. Bildad had answered that

---

❖ See the Appendix, "Iyov's Complaint," and "The World Has Been Handed over to an Evil Power," in the essays of Rav Yerucham Levovitz, *zt"l*.

they will receive their respective reward and punishment after death. But Iyov cannot accept this, as he has already stated two or three times, for he sees no proof of this afterlife which is hidden from the eyes of all flesh (2,4).

Moreover, Iyov disproves Bildad's principle that it is impossible for God to punish the wicked in this world since this is contrary to the order of nature and the system of the stars. He shows him that even he must agree that the celestial dominion over this world is limited to that which is directly influenced by the movements of the stars and related only to them. This was the philosophy mentioned by the *Sefer Ha-Ikkarim* which was cited in our introduction to Iyov's first speech. According to this there remains much room for the punishment of the *resha'im* by things not determined by the celestial movements. He explains with a simile based on the nature of air and water. Water originally was created with the nature to cover the whole Earth, all around, as it was at the beginning of Creation. The forces which gathered the water into specific pools on the surface of the Earth came about purely through God's Will, and are not dependent upon the nature of water itself. If so, the fact that the water gathered in pools and seas is against its very nature and is not dependent upon the laws of nature. Thus God could destroy the *resha'im* with water, as he did in the generation of the Flood. Or similarly, he could punish them through the lower elements, in ways which are not logically dependent upon the "celestial system" according to the philosophers. However, we do not find God doing this. With this, Iyov proves his view that nature must govern even over areas which have no logical relevance to it, and even over Man's actions and will, such as is the view of the astrologers. This is Iyov's opinion.

In his second speech, Iyov notes that his friends have ceased to argue with him, finding themselves with no answer. He goes on to justify his disagreement with their viewpoints and unwillingness to accept something that his heart could not consent to. This would have been tantamount to deception, which is hated in God's eyes. It is far better to speak out and say what one feels in one's heart is the truth, even if it is heresy and touches on atheism, than to speak flattery with one's mouth, to say the opposite of what is in one's heart — even though one might even use this heresy as a basis to destroy and abandon his faith (27:2-11).

[Again Iyov has shown how he has strayed from pure Faith. Yes, if there are questions in one's heart he should speak out and clarify them. But he must also be humble enough to realize that his intellect is limited and easily influenced by his materiality. Even if he cannot presently agree to it, he should continue and try to influence his heart to accept it. We are commanded to develop a firm belief in God and not to be swayed by the passions of our hearts. ("Do not follow the desires of your heart and your eyes which lead you astray" (*Bemidbar* 15:39). "Of your heart" — this refers to heresy (*Berachos* 12b). We should always try to follow the advice of *Chazal,* that "The external influences the internal."* If a person acts like a *tzaddik,* he eventually comes to think like a *tzaddik.* (See also *Kovetz Ma'amarim* by Rav Elchonon Wasserman, *zt"l, "Ma'amar al Emunah."*)]

On this point, Iyov attacks his friends for saying one thing and knowing in their hearts that the opposite is true. Their claim that the punishment of the *rasha* is the death of his children and the disappearance of his wealth after his death is pure vanity. For who cares about one's household after he dies? At least he whiled away his days and years in peace and joy. It would have been more fitting that he himself be afflicted (27:12 - end of chapter). On this, Iyov bemoans the fact (chapter 28) that God has hidden wisdom from those seeking to understand, so that there is no one who can attain Divine wisdom and knowledge of the way He runs His world, understanding its secrets and mysteries. It has come to the point that all those who delve into this subject are forced to say that knowledge

* See *Mesillas Yesharim,* end of chap. 7; *Sefer Ha-Chinnuch,* mitzvah 216.

of the ways and order of the world can be attained only after death, when the soul relieves itself of materiality. It must be something which is hidden from Man, clothed in body and form. Instead of what should have been — opening men's eyes and showing them the logic and wisdom of His ways — instead, He hid and concealed from them basic knowledge and told them to console themselves with fear of God, to have faith in their hearts, and not to probe Divine actions. He gave them foolishness instead of wisdom, unawareness instead of understanding!

IYOV 29-31

In the third speech he continues his discourse in three fiery statements. In the first (chapter 29), he describes in detail the fortune, honor, and glory he once enjoyed. In the second (chapter 30), he lays out, in contrast to this, his terrible lot, his poverty and disgrace, and his present torment. In the third (chapter 31), he passes all of his actions under the scrutiny of criticism and proves that there is no transgression that he has perpetrated in any way or fashion. He was pure in all his ways and righteous in all his actions. He has been beaten and tortured, though he is innocent. This ends both Iyov's and his friends' speeches, and the debate comes to a close.

The Prophet Elihu

IYOV 32-34

Now that Iyov has finished speaking and his three friends have ceased their replies, having been defeated on all their arguments, a mighty warrior takes to the battlefield. He is a wise man, full of the word of God. He batters down the gates of his opponents and wages war to bring to light the real truth. With the spirit of God upon him, and his heart open to the Divine holy secrets and pure knowledge, he presents a full analysis of all these questions. Finally, at the end of his discussion, he divulges the Divine secret about the Heavenly messengers coming to gather around the Lord of all the Earth and the Satan among them, as was related at the beginning of this book. All this was known to Elihu, for God's secrets are revealed to those who fear Him.

REASON DICTATES THAT GOD DOES NO WRONG

Already at the outset of the debate, Elihu's anger rages against both sides. He is angry at Iyov for trying to justify himself against God. Yes, he knew himself to be a *tzaddik* and he could find no reason for his torment. But nevertheless, he should not have come to a conclusion about the "reality" of the conceived based on the "reality" of the conceiver. We cannot attribute to God any lack of knowledge or ability or desire, and this is something which is true in and of itself, just as true as God's existence. The same powers of intellect that teach us that there exists an unlimited Being Who, with His unlimited wisdom, ability, and desire, brought all Existence into being also teach us that this Being is the perfection of perfection. It is impossible to attribute to Him any imperfection. He rules and oversees with unlimited wisdom, desire, and ability. Even if Iyov were sure that the suffering had come upon him for no fault of his own, and that all the evidence indicates that this is a sign that He governs unjustly, still the tools of reason overrule the power of the senses and appearance. The senses can sometimes trick us in their judgment — for example, the astronomer has determined with his scientific tools that the sun is many times larger than the Earth, and his tools overrule the senses which see the sun as a small dish. He can prove that the senses are mistaken, and he can determine the source of the mistake. So, too, it is proper to ignore what appears as real, according to one's own experience, in face of the general truth determined by the power of general reasoning.

Next Elihu turns his indignation to Iyov's three companions. Neither is it fitting for a philosopher to completely ignore what is obvious, even if logic points to the contrary. It would have been better to try to find a middle path which reconciles reason with the senses, and which reconciles the truth, which is buried naturally in the mind, with the apparent reality. They should not have accused Iyov, who is a *tzaddik* in all his ways, and has no imperfections.

THE BASIC TRUTHS

After this introduction, Elihu replies in four sections. In the first he explains the reason he has remained quiet until now. He had previously thought that the basis of knowledge is that which is learned through the senses and experience, and therefore he had been diffident to these elderly debaters. They had in their long lives passed through many different sorts of trials and experiences. Their hearts had accumulated knowledge and wisdom. However, now he has become a bit wiser and realizes that really the basic truths are implanted in the souls of each individual. (This is similar to the opinion of Plato, who held that there are truths naturally inherited by the person, from the original concept called Idea.) They are based neither on the tangible nor on the empirical, but rather they are a holy adornment from the dawn of one's existence, the womb. They are a Divine gift which the soul brought down from its Heavenly roots. Among them are the truths firmly established in each individual: that there is a Higher Being — the Creator, Who oversees everything, rewards and punishes, is good and merciful — and that the soul is Divine and eternal, etc. It is from these basic truths that one has knowledge about God (for He cannot be perceived through even a lifetime of experience, but only through a spirit which He puts into Man).

Elihu considers himself coming in God's name, for he has been bestowed with Divine Wisdom, and his soul has its roots in the Divine in Heaven. He has been appointed to take God's position and argue on His behalf against Iyov.

GOD DOES NOT ASK THE IMPOSSIBLE

Being that the Divine within Elihu is covered in flesh just like Iyov's, Iyov should not be afraid of him. He can lay out all his complaints without fear or terror. Elihu informs him that God does not require the impossible from Man. He will not ask of a person to rise up to the Divine plane in order to worship Him, for that would be beyond one's human abilities. Rather, God lowers Himself down to the level of Man, as if He were not greater or higher than he is. He has already lifted Man up to the level of the Divine in giving him of His wisdom and knowledge of the truth, in order that belief should be firmly established in his soul, as if he were one of the Heavenly creatures. And yet God has lowered Himself down from His Divinity to Man's level, only wanting to be worshiped and perceived according to Man's limited and restricted abilities. He does not ask more than this.

Iyov, on the other hand, thought that God was looking to condemn and accuse, and that one would be punished for things beyond his grasp or his free will. Furthermore, Elihu makes it clear that Iyov has wasted his time complaining that God has hidden self-knowledge from Man, and does not inform people of the transgressions and corruptions for which they will receive the rod of their rebelliousness. For has Man not already been enlightened from Heaven, in the form of dreams and visions? Truthful dreams are His method of opening men's ears to inform them of their crimes and what is in store for them. Illness and suffering are also used as a means of informing them. All these are ways through which God speaks to Man, to bring him back from his evil path so that he should live.

In Elihu's second address, he argues with Iyov on two counts. Firstly, Iyov used the suffering of the *tzaddik* as the cornerstone of his proof that the justice meted out to the individual does not originate from God the Just. Instead, He handed control over to the heavenly order (nature). The basis of this argument was that it is impossible to attach to God any injustice or inability. Since unwarranted affliction of a *tzaddik* is such an injustice or demonstration of such inability, then this cannot originate from God, but rather from the ruler that He appointed to control the world: the laws of nature, which do not discriminate between *tzaddik* and *rasha*. This cannot be called an injustice, since it is a necessary feature of the course of nature in this world of existence and disintegration that individuals be lost from existence. And even if the whole planet Earth should vanish, this would not be evil, in relation to the universe at large. For the Earth is but a grain of sand, relatively speaking, as was explained at length in the introduction to Iyov's fifth speech.

ELIHU REVEALS IYOV'S FALSE LOGIC

On this, Elihu answers Iyov with a parable. This is similar to one who wants to defend a king who has unjustly committed a crime against one of the benefactors of the people. He states in defense of the king that he didn't mean to harm this benefactor specifically, but rather it was a result of his governing all of his people in such a way that it is bad to all of them, for they are all like ants in his eyes. They are his slaves and possessions, to do with as he pleases. So, too, how can you justify God on the crime perpetrated against one individual (meaning Iyov) merely by saying that this is really a general crime against all of humanity and all of Creation, everywhere and always? It is because they are all considered like the fish in the sea, like the swarms of crawling creatures. And thus Iyov claimed that God had handed over all of Creation to a sinister, blind, ruling agent, who hates justice. On this Elihu counters, does this vindicate God from the claim that He perpetrates so much evil? Iyov's question remains unanswered: Why did He hand the world over to such an evil ruler?

Why does He not personally interfere to pay the individual justly, according to his actions? Is this beyond His ability? Does He maybe suffer from envy, or lust? Or perhaps He is simply sinister!

[Those who relegate *Hashgachah* to nature do a similar injustice to God. Being forced by what appears to be injustice to individuals, they claim that He does not watch over individuals, and therefore He is unjust to all Mankind in the name of blind nature.]

IT IS NOT UP TO US TO TEACH GOD

Now Elihu turns to Iyov's second complaint, which is: Where is God's judgment?! Why does He not punish the wicked immediately and openly so that all can see? On this Elihu answers that God has prepared judgment for the mockers. He knows their deeds, and there is no cover of darkness in which they can hide from His punishment. However, it is not Man's place to ask questions like: Why does He punish them in hidden ways and not openly? It is not up to us to teach God how and in what ways to mete out punishment! In His wisdom He has decided to punish them in a concealed manner in order to leave room to doubt that perhaps the punishment does not come from Him. This leaves room for free will. Moreover, sometimes these evil men are used as Divine agents, the staff of His anger, to punish people for their evil actions. So therefore, not only does He not destroy them, but He even puts in their hands power and control to perpetrate mass destruction and mass annihilation until His plan to afflict and reprimand the nations is completed. Then the staff itself is broken and the rod of the wicked is destroyed. It is enough for us to know that the Holy One, blessed be He, is very patient, but eventually collects all that is due Him. "Anyone who says that the Holy One, blessed be He, forsakes (overlooks) punishment, forsakes his own life" (*Bava Kama* 50a; see also *Mesillas Yesharim, perek* 4).*

In the third section of Elihu's reply, he addresses the great question Iyov proposed in chapter 24: There, Elifaz had said that the wicked cannot be punished on the spot, for that would remove free will from Mankind. Every person would act as perfectly as possible, knowing that if he took one wrong step he would immediately suffer the consequences. On this, Iyov had countered, Do we not find *resha'im*, murderers and bandits, on the sea and in the wilderness, who are destroying the world? Why does He not wipe them out from under His skies to eliminate their evil and preserve the human race from destruction? Especially since they dwell like wild animals, completely separated from people, God could wipe them out in the darkness of their dwellings. Nobody would even know, so there would be no damage to the concept of free will.

Secondly, Iyov had in general questioned the concept of reward and punishment. He had proved that everything is dependent upon the Heavenly order, even Man's seemingly independent actions, for Man is compelled in everything. Therefore he deserves neither reward nor punishment, just like no reward is paid to the millstone which is turned by the flow of the river and grinds the flour; and certainly it cannot be punished if it crushes the skull of one who came too close.

Elihu now replies that both Iyov and his companions have erred in their understanding of the concepts of reward and punishment. They assumed that reward and punishment are something separate from the action. They imagined that God commands Man and cautions him to do certain actions because they benefit God, like a king who orders and warns his servants. Those who perform jobs benefit the king; those who rebel against his commands cause the king damage. Because of this he gives them a reward or a punishment, which are separate from the actual act. All this is a mistake, Elihu ex-

* He has abandoned his body and life by teaching the populace to sin — Rashi.

plains, for God is not influenced by men's actions. And He doesn't need their service. Their rebellion has absolutely no effect on Him. Rather, He is like a doctor instructing a patient. Whether one listens to the doctor or chooses to ignore his words, the reward or punishment — health and life, or illness and death — is a direct result of the action itself. So, too, the reward and punishment for Man's actions are intrinsically tied to those actions. One who subdues his lusts and desires will be as healthy as a bull, while one who chases the pleasures of the flesh will fall ill and be afflicted with pain.

Likewise, a society which makes an effort to do goodness and kindness, to do justice on behalf of the oppressed, and to eradicate evildoers from the land, will have peace and security, and not suffer evil in its midst. But the moment justice and righteousness are taken away, then you will see an increase in murderers and bandits in the country.

Divine *Hashgachah* has prepared for each living creature an ability to save itself from its predators and enemies, such as the tools with which to fight them, or strategies to guard themselves from them. For example, we see that God has given certain weak birds the instinct to raise their voices in song at night in order to arouse each other to be prepared against their enemies and those who seek their lives.

So, too, has God prepared an instinct in Man, that society, and the human race in general, help each other and arouse themselves to eradicate the thieves and murderers who would destroy civilization, as well as an instinct to do justice and charity throughout the land. This guarantees Mankind's survival. When they are united in defense of society as a whole, they are stronger than those few who act like wild animals, devouring and destroying, stealing and murdering. Because of this, the obligation to bring to justice those *resha'im* who would destroy civilization has been handed over to men who naturally seek to obliterate them and eradicate the evil from their midst. When we see evil overpowering the good, and lack of law and order in the land which leaves people as helpless as the fish in the sea, the reason is that they brought this evil upon themselves. Why should they be angry at God if their foolishness twisted their path?

[It is unclear how the Malbim has answered the questions. He seems to be saying that the question posed as to God's reluctance to eliminate the Wicked, and in general the concept of Man's free will, are questions only in relation to our understanding of reward and punishment. If reward and punishment are something separate from the action and the person, then the question has validity. However, once we understand that reward and punishment are an intrinsic part of the action itself, then all the questions disappear. The very existence of marauders and pirates is the result of the evil of society. If humanity would follow its instincts and people would unite to create a good and just society, then they would be able to band together and eradicate these marauders themselves. Or perhaps, society would be so good that no one would become marauders. Moreover, perhaps the marauders' existence is His way of giving Mankind the opportunity to act on the universal instinct to create a good society. When people create a just society, they are rewarded by the very virtues of that society. The fear of marauders who threaten to annihilate the society forces the people to unite and respond to this instinct.

On an individual basis as well, we should not be confused by the apparent lack of reward for the *tzaddik*'s good actions, and the lack of punishment for the *rasha*'s evil. The reward and punishment are not entities which are separate from the action; rather, the action itself is the reward or the punishment. Acting in a good manner benefits the person. And conversely, the punishment of the wicked is the very act they have perpetrated, and the evil which naturally derives from it.

However, the answer is still obscure. Marauders and other evil forces sometimes overpower even good societies, through no fault of the people. And the Malbim has not explained the specific benefits of good actions to the individual, other than the fact that a healthy body results from healthy habits.

As to the first question, perhaps he is hinting at a concept similar to that found in the *Derashos Ha-Ran* (chap. 11). God loves justice — it creates harmony and peace within society. Therefore, if society practices justice, then its members are rewarded with a special blessing from above. (See the Malbim's commentary at the end of chap. 38 which seems to be alluding to this concept.)

On an individual basis, the Malbim's position may perhaps be similar to the concept expressed by Rav Chayim Volozhin, *zt"l* (in *Nefesh Ha-Chayim, sha'ar* 1, *perek* 12). Reward and punishment are the creation of the person himself, but on a very deep spiritual level. Through one's actions, the person creates his own Heaven or Hell for himself here on Earth, and not only on a physical or sociological level, but also on a spiritual plane. That is, as one's spiritual level increases or decrease, so too does the spiritual light or darkness surrounding him. This spiritual aura is his Next World. Moreover, his actions have tremendous influence on this world, increasing or decreasing the flow of Divine Blessing from its Heavenly source.]

With this Elihu has hinted that all that came upon Iyov, in the loss of his possessions through bandits and robbers, was his own fault — for he had not tried to the best of his ability to work for the cause of justice and elimination of criminals. And his receiving additional blows was due to his foolishness, to not repenting from this evil. Finally, Iyov added insult to injury by complaining against God about that which he himself was to blame for; he had prepared his own death trap.

Elihu's fourth address is divided into two parts. In the first he informs Iyov of the truth about the real cause of his suffering: that it was all a test. Then he goes on to explain the concept, and how the ways of God are just. Finally Elihu reveals to Iyov the Satan's accusation (which has already been discussed at the beginning of this book).

In the second part, he reprimands Iyov for being arrogant in pursuing topics greater and deeper than his understanding: the concept of the eternity of the soul, Divine knowledge, free will, etc. Elihu shows him that Man cannot fathom God's wisdom, even in regard to nature, which is right before his own eyes. Even though Iyov did not venture behind the door of the Holy of Holies to try to gaze directly at God and to analyze the metaphysical, Elihu says, he should have covered his face and not risen up to the Mountain of God or even touched its extremities.

With this ends the Debate.

GOD ANSWERS FROM A WHIRLWIND

IYOV 38-41

Now that they have finished this whole debate of pure intellect and reason, God reveals Himself to Iyov from a whirlwind❖ and commands him to gird his loins and gather his strength, for now the torments will depart from him and then God Himself will debate with him. And with God's personal revelation, the whole debate collapses. For now, God speaks personally to Iyov, and He proves:

1) That God oversees the lives of men in all their details, to such an extent that He was listening to all that Iyov said and now has come to join the debate and teach him true wisdom. This, in and of itself, testifies to *Hashgachah Pratis*, God's personal overseeing and intervention in all of Man's steps, and with this collapses Iyov's stand that God takes no notice.

2) From this it is obvious that Man's soul is Divine and eternal, alive, and highly capable, for only thus — the fact that his soul is really connected to the Divine — can it be conceived that He would speak with Man. At the moment that Man divests himself of the "clothing" of the body, his soul gazes at the Divine image, for the soul is part and parcel of His blessed Being. With this are overturned all of Iyov's doubts about the eternity of the soul and reward in the Next World, since he has

---

❖ Why did God have to answer Iyov from a whirlwind? The *gemara* in *Bava Basra* 16a tells us: Raba said, Iyov blasphemed with a *se'arah* (a storm or whirlwind), so God answered him from a *se'arah*. He blasphemed with a "storm," as it says, "He Who would crush me with a storm and multiply my wounds for no reason" (9:17). He said in front of Him: Master of the World, perhaps a storm-wind passed in front of You and You got confused between *Iyov* (איוב) and *Oyev* (אויב, enemy). God answered him with a "storm." "Then Hashem answered Iyov from the storm-wind and said,...Now gird your loins like a man, I will ask you and [you] will answer Me."

experienced while alive how the soul can discard itself of the body at the time of a vision, and attach itself to the Divine to bathe in the spiritual pleasure of the holy vision

With this all of Iyov's questions about the suffering of *tzaddikim* have been answered. For he sees that the true essence of a person is the soul, which will eventually separate itself from the body and attach itself to God to gaze upon the pleasant Divine vision and to hear His voice from the fire. This is the main reward awaiting the *tzaddikim* after they divest themselves of materiality, at the moment that the spirit returns to God Who gave it. God continues to discuss this at length with Iyov,* and tells him how Divine Providence is involved in all of His Creation, whether over Existence in general, or whether over each creature specifically, to oversee all of its needs, to prepare food and shelter, and to watch over the preservation of each species, over birth, and over provision for offspring. So certainly this Divine *Hashgachah* spreads itself over Man, the Chosen of Creation.

THE RULE OF THE WICKED — TO PROCLAIM THE ULTIMATE REIGN OF THE ALMIGHTY

After explaining all this, God goes on to answer Iyov's next question: the success of the *resha'im*, and why God does not eradicate evil men who are like predatory animals, destroying civilization. He replies that such a question can also be asked about animals: Why were the weak created, and the strong ones who prey on the weak ones? According to you [says God], it would have been better if I had created only small, weak crawling insects completely void of power!

But that would not be a sign of the greatness of the Creator. For His grandeur is demonstrated when He creates awesome and fearsome creatures, and still He arranges through His

* See the Appendix for a full quote of the *gemara* which elaborates on this discussion.

Hashgachah that even the weak species are preserved. Through this the world sees a Guardian and Single Ruler on High Who has dominion over all.

So, too, among Mankind we find tyrants and despots and awesomely powerful men. And still, God has arranged His *Hashgachah* to enable Mankind to be preserved through the fact that He created Man a social being by nature and planted within him the capability of doing justice and equity. (This is similar to what Elihu explained previously in chapter 35.)

THE TEST IS OVER

IYOV 42

ויען איוב את ה׳ ויאמר. ידעת כי כל תוכל ולא יבצר ממך מזמה. מי זה מעלים עצה בלי דעת לכן הגדתי ולא אבין נפלאות ממני ולא אדע. שמע נא ואנכי אדבר אשאלך והודיעני. [מב:א-ד]

Then Iyov answered God and said, "I knew that You can do everything and no wisdom is restrained from You. Who is this who hides counsel without knowledge? Therefore, I spoke but I did not understand; they were hidden from me and I did not know them. Hearken now and I will speak; I will ask You and You will tell me." [42:1-4]

Finally, after the end of the entire debate, Iyov reveals what he had been thinking all along: actually, his heart had been undivided in faith in God, and he had withstood the test. Really, in his heart, he had believed in *Hashgachah* and the eternity of the soul. He had believed in all the principles of faith and had not strayed from his righteousness. The whole debate which he had staged was merely philosophical and theoretical in its nature in order to illuminate the subject matter through study and examination. Since intellectual investigation is dependent upon the limits of the human being, the philosophers ask many questions concerning *emunah,* such as the paradox between Man's free will and God's foreknowledge of everything, the *tzaddik* who suffers and the *rasha* who prospers, and all the other questions Iyov posed during the debate. He does not understand or know what to answer on these questions. It is not proper, he says, to hide wisdom and leave Man without this knowledge, forced to rely on pure faith.❖

So he felt forced to speak as the adversary denying faith, and to expound upon all of the claims and proofs. He argued and claimed that he wanted God to answer him on these questions. This was all in order that, through discussion and intellectual analysis, these issues should be illuminated and he should know how to answer the *apikorus* (heretic). Others must stand in the name of the proponents of the opinion which

---

❖ Iyov has claimed to be a *tzaddik*. He has, according to the Malbim, passed the test. The Malbim seems to have chosen the interpretation of the *gemara* in *Sotah* 31a (see the Appendix). Probably it was because Iyov is referred to as "My servant Iyov" below in *pasuk* 7. This implies that Iyov is still held in God's high esteem. *Chazal* in *Bava Basra* 15b (see the Appendix), however, imply otherwise. The Gemara there states, "There was a *chassid* (saintly man) among the nations and his name was Iyov. His sole purpose in coming into this world was in order to receive his reward (in the Next World). *Ha-Kadosh Baruch Hu* brought afflictions upon him and he started cursing and blaspheming. So *Ha-Kadosh Baruch Hu* doubled his reward in this world in order to drive him out of the next." Iyov bent under the burden. Yes, he is excused for having given in only under severe duress, but this is not the way of a true *tzaddik*. Avraham was tested with ten trials. Throughout, he never once complained or questioned. He merited becoming Avraham *Avinu*, Avraham our Father. If Iyov had not complained, if he had had pure faith, he might also have merited the title Iyov *Avinu*.

upholds faith, and each must answer according to his viewpoint. In this way the truth is clarified and illuminated. He himself had played the adversary who denies *Hashgachah*, free will, faith, the eternity of the soul, and reward in the Next World. Not that he had any inclination toward these opinions in his heart, for his heart was pure in faith in all of these. He had taken this side only as a means of clarifying and crystallizing the subject. For he had wanted faith to be clear even through reason and examination. Knowledge and comprehension are greater than Faith alone without understanding and knowledge. When he had called upon God to come and argue with him, it was only a call that He should enlighten his mind in order that he should be able to understand the subject which he believed so deeply in his heart, that these concepts should not be incomprehensible to reason. As Moshe *Rabbenu*, the Master of Prophets, said, הראני נא את כבודך, "Teach me Your Glory." He had also first delved into this problem using pure reason, and wrote *Sefer Iyov*, which includes his studies and examinations on these particulars. And when he saw that it was impossible to comprehend any answer based on pure reason alone, he then asked that God Himself show him the glory of His Justice and His Rule, the same way He showed Iyov and taught him until, as it says, ונחמתי על עפר ואפר, "And I was consoled about the dust and ashes" (42:6).

לשמע אזן שמעתיך ועתה עיני ראתך. [מב:ה]

"I have heard of You by the hearing of the ear, and now, my eye has seen You" [42:5].

However, this was all until now. Iyov says, I had merely "heard of You by the hearing of the ear," but I hadn't seen You in a prophecy. I had only known You through what I had learned in tradition. Therefore, I had merely faith and not knowledge, leaving room for all these doubts. But now, "my eye has seen You." This has explained everything for me clearly, Iyov says. By revealing Yourself to me in a vision, I have seen that You oversee all the details of Man's actions. You even heard my debate! And now I know directly from You the answers to all of these questions. Besides which, this vision has proven concretely the existence of the soul beyond the body, and the ability of the soul to attach itself to the Divine. For otherwise it would be impossible for Man to comprehend God in a vision. For this requires that the soul divest itself of the body and attach itself to its roots Above, the same way that it will return to its roots after the soul leaves the body and returns to dwell with the Master of all Spirits, and this itself is the spiritual reward in the Next World.

This has proven concretely that the soul will receive its reward and its spiritual compensation.

על כן אמאס ונחמתי על עפר ואפר. [מב:ו]

"Therefore, I despise (my life), and I was consoled about the dust and ashes" [42:6].

Therefore, I despise the physical life. And I am consoled about the body since it is but dust and ashes. The physical life and success of the body are like nothing compared to the pleasure of the life of the Divine soul. That is the true pleasure which the souls of the *tzaddikim* will merit.

Therefore, now there is no question as to the *tzaddik* who suffers. Physical good or bad affecting this body of dust is nothing compared to one single moment of the soul's enjoyment of spiritual pleasure. So now the clouds have parted and a clear light is shining through. The light of knowledge has been revealed to Iyov.

ויהי אחר דבר ה׳ את הדברים האלה אל איוב ויאמר ה׳ אל אליפז התימני חרה אפי בך ובשני רעיך כי לא דברתם אלי נכונה כעבדי איוב. [מב:ז]

And it was after God had spoken these words to Iyov, that God said to Elifaz the Temanite, "My wrath is kindled against you and your two companions because you did not speak correctly, as did My servant Iyov" [42:7].

IYOV'S THREE FRIENDS: PURE ARGUMENT WITHOUT HEART

Iyov had spoken perfidy with his mouth but in his heart he spoke properly because his heart was wholly with God. His friends, however, had done the opposite. Their mouths argued on God's side, but their hearts did not reflect their words. As Iyov told them, "Will you speak unjustly for God, and will you speak deceitfully for Him?" (13:7). There, he reprimanded them because they did not really feel in their hearts what they were saying with their lips. The main communication with God is the language of the heart, not the external speech of the mouth. With this speech [God tells them], you have not spoken to Me properly, as Iyov has.

ועתה קחו לכם שבעה פרים ושבעה אילים ולכו אל עבדי איוב והעליתם עולה בעדכם ואיוב עבדי יתפלל עליכם כי אם פניו אשא לבלתי עשות עמכם נבלה כי לא דברתם אלי נכונה כעבדי איוב. [מב:ח]

"And now, take for yourselves seven bulls and seven rams and go to My servant Iyov and offer up a burnt-offering for yourselves, and Iyov My servant will pray for you, for I will favor him not to

do anything unseemly to you, for you did not speak to Me properly, as did My servant Iyov" [42:8].

He commands them to offer up burnt-offerings which atone for the thoughts of the heart, because of their having doubted in their hearts the basic principle of faith, and for the disparity between their hearts and their mouths. Also, for having cursed Iyov unnecessarily and depicting him as a *rasha* and a blasphemer, they needed Iyov to pray for them and in this way they would find favor in God's eyes so that He should not punish them.

"For you did not speak to Me properly..." Because even their sin of superficial speech in talking against Iyov required that Iyov forgive them and pray on their behalf.

וילכו אליפז התימני ובלדד השוחי צפר הנעמתי ויעשו כאשר דבר אליהם ה׳ וישא ה׳ את פני איוב. וה׳ שב את שבות איוב בהתפללו בעד רעהו ויסף ה׳ את כל אשר לאיוב למשנה. ויבאו אליו כל אחיו וכל אחיתיו וכל ידעיו לפנים ויאכלו עמו לחם בביתו וינדו לו וינחמו אתו על כל הרעה אשר הביא ה׳ עליו ויתנו לו איש קשיטה אחת ואיש נזם זהב אחד. וה׳ ברך את אחרית איוב מראשתו ויהי לו ארבעה עשר אלף צאן וששת אלפים גמלים ואלף צמד בקר ואלף אתונות. [מב:ט-יב]

Now Elifaz the Temanite, Bildad the Shuchite, and Tzofar the Na'amatite went and did as the Lord had spoken to them, and the Lord favored Iyov. Now the Lord returned Iyov's captivity when he prayed for his friends, and the Lord gave Iyov twice as much as he had [before]. Now all his brothers and all his sisters and all his previous acquaintances came to him and ate a meal in his house, and they bemoaned him and consoled him concerning all the evil that the Lord had brought upon him, and they gave him, each one, one piece of money and each one one golden

nose ring. Now the Lord blessed Iyov's end more than his beginning, and he had fourteen thousand flocks and six thousand camels and a thousand yoke of cattle and a thousand she-donkeys [42:9-12].

In the merit of forgiving his friends and praying on their behalf, Iyov received good in return. Not only were all the captives returned to him, but also everything was returned to him twofold.

According to what we understand from *Chazal*, none of his possessions were really lost. Nor did any of his children die. The Satan hid them from him and sent him messengers to bring him the bad tidings. All his possessions and children were in reality held by the Satan for the whole time. This is the meaning of the words "twice as much as he [Iyov] has."

[The Malbim is deriving this from the fact that the past tense היה is absent from the text. Rather, it says כל אשר לאיוב, literally, "everything that Iyov has" (present tense).]

This implies that they were the original possessions, and now they increased to become double, as is obvious from the numbers of his livestock, which are double what he had originally.

ויהי לו שבענה בנים ושלוש בנות. ויקרא שם האחת ימימה ושם השנית קציעה ושם השלישית קרן הפוך. ולא נמצא נשים יפות כבנות איוב בכל הארץ ויתן להם אביהם נחלה בתוך אחיהם. [מב:יג-טו]

*And he had seven** *sons and three daughters. And he named the first Yemimah, the second Ketziah, and the third Keren-Happuch. Nowhere in the land were to be found women as beautiful as Iyov's daughters, and their father gave them an inheritance among their brothers* [42:13-15].

* According to the Malbim's commentary, that these are the same sons that Iyov originally had, it seems that he is translating the word שבענה as "seven." Rashi and the other commentators, however, translate it as "twice seven," or fourteen.

According to *Chazal*, these were the same children Iyov had originally, but the daughters had doubled in their beauty. Due to their beauty which had now gained a new splendor, he called them new names indicating their extraordinary radiance.

> ויחי איוב אחרי זאת מאה וארבעים שנה וירא את בניו ואת בני בניו ארבעה דרות. וימת איוב זקן ושבע ימים.
> [מב:טז-יז]
>
> ***And Iyov lived after this a hundred and forty years, and saw his children and grandchildren for four generations. And Iyov died an old man, satisfied in days*** [42:16-17].

With all that had happened to him — the tremendous wealth that he now enjoyed, the overwhelming beauty of his daughters, and especially God's revelation to him at the end of the debate — he recognized the value of the spiritual life of the soul in the Next World. A little bit of contentment in the Next World is better than all of this world. The primary life, besides reward and punishment, is found in the Next World. So he said, "I despise (my life), and I was consoled about dust and ashes." He is no longer concerned with the loss or torment of the body, now that he sees the moment when the soul removes its "soiled garments" and returns to the Source of all spirits, where it delights in eternal pleasure.

Therefore when R. Me'ir finished reading *Sefer Iyov*, he said, "Man is destined to die...happy is he who grew in Torah..." (*Berachos* 17a). From *Iyov* he saw that the purpose of life is death, where the real life of the spirit begins. And the end is the goal. As long as Man is alive he is constantly being drawn closer to this goal. So he must prepare provisions for the appointed day, through toiling in Torah to perfect his soul.

On this, Shlomo *Ha-Melech* said in his great wisdom, טוב שם משמן טוב — "*Tov shem mi-shemen tov* — A [good] name is better than good oil." The day of death starts from the day of birth. This is the goal toward which one travels and moves from the time one is born. From all one's toil in this world, the main thing is the good name which remains with him at the end, and this is better than the finest oil.

END OF THE MALBIM'S COMMENTARY ON IYOV

POSTSCRIPT

If we could only see the truth, we would no longer have any doubts. Questions about faith or Divine *Hashgachah* arise only when the truth is clouded over. Our job is to develop our faith by cultivating humility in our thinking. Think? Yes, we must utilize all the tools we have at our disposal to uncover the truth and understand. But ultimately there is so much more that we cannot conceive, such as the eternity of the soul and reward and punishment. Just because we have questions on Divine *Hashgachah,* still we have no right to modify the truth to fit our conceptions (or misconceptions). Humility is the key to *Chazal*'s thinking. *Chazal* mold their perceptions of the world according to the truth, instead of molding the "truth" according to their perceptions of the world. We must bend our perceptions (based upon experience) in light of the basic truths which tell us that God is perfectly just. As the Chafetz Chaim used to say, "Without faith there are no answers; with faith there are no questions" ("Reb Elchonon," p. 326).

סוף דבר הכל נשמע את האלקים ירא ואת מצותיו שמור
כי זה כל האדם. [קהלת יב:יג]

The final thing, after all has been heard, is to fear God and keep His mitzvos, for this is the whole of Man [*Koheles* 12:13].

Morenu v'Rabbenu HaGaon Rav Chaim Pinchas Scheinberg, *shlita,* has often said in the name of Rav Yisrael Salanter, *zt"l*: All of man's knowledge is like a million zeros, which add up to nothing. But add just one number — a "1" (fear of God) — in front of them and it turns the zeros into millions.

Selected Essays

Excerpts from Essays by
Ha-Gaon Ha-Tzaddik
RAV YERUCHAM LEVOVITZ, zt"l
Mashgiach of Yeshivas Mir in Pre-war Poland

I

WHY SO MANY NISYONOS?

(Adapted from **Da'as Torah**, *Bereshis*, p. 136.)

Our Sages state in *Pirkei Avos* that *Ha-Kadosh Baruch Hu* tested Avraham with ten trials. Why did he need ten? If he could stand up to one, couldn't he have stood up to ten? Would one not have been enough? Also, if the *Akedah* was the most difficult, then why did *Ha-Kadosh Baruch Hu* not give him only this last one, and that would have proved everything?

This brings out a very important principle. Sometimes we find a person who is truly great in many ways, but in one specific point he is not great at all, he is even quite lowly. When we see this contradiction — on one hand, he is so great, and on the other he is even corrupt — we are tempted to try to explain the contradiction. No! This is not the right way to look at it. There is no need to answer the contradiction at all.

Chazal in *Sanhedrin* 74a revealed the answer to us. In the *Shema* we say, "And you should love the Lord your God with all your heart and all your soul and all your money (מאדך)." If a person loves God with all his heart, that is the epitome of love. He is willing to give up his life for Him. So why does it say, "with all your money"? And if someone is willing to give up all his money for Him, then what is added by saying, "all your soul"? The answer is that sometimes you can find a person who is willing to give up all his money for religious or philanthropic purposes, but his life is too dear to him to sacrifice it. Therefore, it says, "with all your soul." And sometimes you can find a person who is willing to sacrifice his life, his health, his whole being, but when it comes to his money, that's a different story. Therefore, it says, "with all your money."

These are the facts. God has given each person different and sometimes conflicting traits. Each person has within him the potential for the lowest baseness possible, beyond all comprehension. There is a type of person whose nature is so calm, that it is impossible for him to fathom how one can become angry and lose his temper. And yet when it comes to his money, to get even a penny out of this same person is like splitting the sea. This doesn't make any sense. But it doesn't have to make sense, for that's the way it is. And in this way, each person was given his place to develop. One doesn't get rewarded for doing what comes naturally (except in the aspect that God doesn't hold back reward from any creature).

One is rewarded and gets merit only from those things which are difficult for him. It is there that each person must work his whole life to purify himself. Accomplish at least something. This is the reason that Avraham needed ten *nisyonos*. One could not be brought as proof for the second. It is possible that in one specific aspect he was good, while in another, he was not.

II

IYOV'S COMPLAINT THAT IT IS IMPOSSIBLE TO FIGHT ONE'S NATURE

(Adapted from **Da'as Chochmah u'Musar**, vol. I, *ma'amar* 2)

בקש איוב לפטור את כל העולם מן הדין. אמר לפניו, רבש"ע בראת שור פרסותיו סדוקות בראת חמור פרסותיו קלוטות, בראת גן עדן בראת גיהנם, בראת צדיקים בראת רשעים, מי מעכב על ידך. (ב"ב ט"ז)

Iyov wished to dismiss the whole world from judgment [to relieve the whole world from God's judgment by saying that they are all forced by God, for He created them with the evil inclination — Rashi.] He said in front of Him, "Master of the Universe, You created the ox with cloven hooves, You created the donkey with solid hooves [*Rashi*: You made this animal kosher, and that animal *treif*; everything came about by Your hand for You created the signs of impurity in them], You created Gan Eden (the Garden of Eden, referring to the Next World, where the *tzaddikim* receive their reward), You created Gehinnom, the place where the wicked are punished. You created *tzaddikim* [*Rashi*: through their good nature], You created the wicked [*Rashi*: through their evil nature]. Who can resist Your hand?" [*Bava Basra* 16a]

Iyov complained that just as it is impossible for the ox to change to uncloven hooves, and the donkey to change to cloven hooves, since that is a change of nature, so too is it impossible for the *rasha* under any circumstances to become a *tzaddik*.

Iyov had a very valid point. The nature of a person is so ingrained within him that it requires a miracle to change it.

What did Iyov's friends answer him?

"Surely you will do away with fear and increase speech before God" (15:4). The Holy One, blessed be He, cre-

> ated the evil nature of man. He created the Torah as an antidote. [*Rashi*: Torah is the medicine which repels the urge to sin, as it says in *Kiddushin* 30b, "If you meet that disgusting fellow (the *yetzer ha-ra*), drag him to the *beis ha-midrash*. If he is a stone, he will melt...." Therefore, people are not compelled involuntarily, for they have a means of protecting themselves] [*Bava Basra* 16a].

Yes, Iyov was right. According to the strict laws of reality, to change one's nature requires a miracle. But God has given us the Torah to be the antidote — meaning, through the Torah we can create the miracle.

Chazal said, "Beloved is Yisrael, who were given the precious instrument...with which the world was created" (*Pirkei Avos* 3:18). This is not empty poetry praising the Torah through which the world was created. *Chazal* are teaching us how beloved Yisrael is, because they have been given that precious instrument which created the world — meaning that *Ha-Kadosh Baruch Hu* used the Torah to create the universe. If the Torah can be used to create worlds, then most certainly Torah has within it the virtue of changing nature. Was not the very Creation of the world a change in nature? If so, then by using Torah, we also can change nature. This was the reply of Iyov's friends: Yes, it is true what you said. Man's nature is completely impossible to change without a miracle. But *Ha-Kadosh Baruch Hu* gave us the means through which to bring about this miracle. "*Ha-Kadosh Baruch Hu* created the *yetzer ha-ra*, and He created the Torah, the medicine against it" (*Kiddushin* 30b).

Everything within nature follows certain rules. So, too, in the realm beyond nature there are certain rules, without which the miracle cannot take place. Rav Yisrael Salanter, *zt"l*, in his famous *Musar* Letter, wrote that there are two ways in which Torah breaks the *yetzer ha-ra*: a physical aspect and a spiritual aspect.

The spiritual aspect is what *Chazal* referred to in *Sotah* 21a: תורה בעידנא דעסיק בה מצלא, "Torah saves a person (from his *yetzer ha-ra*) while he studies it." It doesn't matter what he is learning — Torah has the power to protect the person from transgression. If a person studies *Bava Kamma* and the Laws of Damages, he is protected from speaking *lashon ha-ra*.

But the spiritual aspect of Torah is not active unless the person gets involved first in the physical aspect, which Rav Yisrael Salanter spoke about at length: the study of Halachah in all of its details. When a person tries to stand up against the trait of haughtiness, he must learn all the *halachos* related to the "laws of haughtiness." In order to practice honest business dealings, he must first learn the laws between man and man. For each *averah* and each mitzvah, he must learn that mitzvah and its laws. "The main cure (for the *yetzer ha-ra*) is a deep and detailed study of the *halachos* related to that subject, with the intent of carrying them out" (Rav Yisrael Salanter in the *Iggeres Ha-Musar*).

According to what we said above, we can explain this simply. One of the rules of creating a miracle is intending and knowing that you are about to perform a miracle. A person must approach the study of Torah with the explicit intent that through this he is about to change his very nature. Without this, it is impossible to create the change. If a person involves himself in this physical aspect of Torah with all its fine details, then the spiritual aspect will come automatically, and the more he continues studying, the more he will be protected from sin.

III

IT'S GOOD ONLY WHEN THE EVIL TESTIFIES TO IT

(Adapted from **Da'as Chochmah u'Musar**, vol. II, *ma'amar* 42)

Normally, a son finds it easy to gain approval from his father. There is hardly any father who sees anything wrong with his son. Love covers over all the misdeeds (*Mishlei* 10:12), and he can find some saving factor in even the most improper actions. On the other side of the coin is one's enemy. It is almost impossible to approve of even his best behavior. Each of his deeds is dissected to find what's wrong with it, and in even the best and most excellent behavior one finds defects and doubts. It is an accepted fact that what is said by an enemy is disregarded as being totally biased.

> "Now the day came about, and the Heavenly powers came to stand before God, and the Satan, too, came among them. And God said to the Satan, 'From where are you coming?' And the Satan answered..." (*Iyov*: 1:6-7).
>
> He (the Satan) said in front of Him, "Master of the Universe, I have floated around the whole world, and I have not found one faithful like Your servant Avraham, to whom You said, 'Arise and walk through the land, its length and breadth, for I have given it to you,' and yet at the time when he was not able to find a place to bury Sarah until he bought one for 400 silver shekels, still no doubts entered his mind as to the justice of the Divine ways."
>
> "And the Lord said to the Satan, 'Have you paid attention to My servant Iyov? For there is none like him on Earth...' " (*Iyov* 1:8).
>
> R. Yochanan said, "What was said about Iyov was greater than what was said about Avraham. About Avraham it was written, 'For now I know that you fear God' (*Bereshis* 22:12), while about Iyov it is written, 'He is a sincere and upright man, God-fearing and shunning evil.' "

> "And the Satan answered God and said, 'Does Iyov fear God in vain? Haven't You protected him, his household, and all that he has all around him?... However, stretch forth Your hand and touch all that he has. Will he not blaspheme You to Your face?' And God said to the Satan, 'Behold, all that he has is in your hands; only upon him do not stretch your hand...' (*Iyov* 1:9-12)" [*Bava Basra* 15b].

Let us imagine someone slandering a person whom we considered to be a great *tzaddik*, such as the Chafetz Chaim. Even one who usually accepts *lashon ha-ra* would be embarrassed to hear such talk, especially if this came from someone who hated the slandered person heart and soul. It would be obvious that one should not listen at all to what this person is saying, for his hatred is just oozing out of his throat. *Chazal* said that Iyov was praised by God *more* than was Avraham. If that is the case, then all of the Satan's accusations are as if he had come to slander Avraham *Avinu* himself. And the speaker here is the Satan, the most notorious and hostile enemy possible. The most logical reaction would be to ignore everything he said. And yet we see here the most amazing thing. Not only did God listen very carefully to the Satan's accusations and everything that he said, but He immediately handed Iyov over to him!

Moreover, even after He took everything away from him, causing Iyov to say, "Naked did I come from my mother's womb, and naked shall I return there. God gave, and God took. Let God's Name be blessed," we read, "still Iyov did not sin, and he did not attribute a blemish to God" (*Iyov* 1:21-22). "And God said to the Satan, 'Have you paid attention to My servant Iyov? For there is none like him on Earth, a sincere and upright man, God-fearing and shunning evil, and he still maintains his sincerity. Yet you incite Me against him to swallow him in vain?' " (*Iyov* 2:3). God showed no anger against the Satan for his empty provocation. He didn't reprimand him. Instead we find in the Gemara, "R. Yochanan said, 'If it weren't explicitly written, it would be impossible to say it. It is as if a person can incite Him and succeed in His being incited' " (*Bava Basra* 16a). Even after such a claim that God Himself testified that the Satan incited Him over nothing, an empty provocation, with all this, He again listened to his accusations! "Now the Satan replied to God and said, 'Skin for skin, and whatever a person has, he will give for his life. But, stretch forth Your hand now and touch his bones and his flesh; will he not blaspheme You to Your face?' And God said to the Satan, 'Here he is in your hands, but preserve his life' " (*Iyov* 2:4-6). Is this not frightening?

This teaches us a tremendous principle: A person is required to act on such a level that even his greatest enemy gives his approval to him and admits that his actions are good. *A good act is such only* if, even upon hearing God Himself say, "Have you paid attention to My servant Iyov, for there is none like him on Earth," the Satan agrees and says, "That's right! There is no one like him on all the Earth." Even Man's greatest enemy, the Satan himself, cannot find any deficiency or doubt. But if he still doesn't consent, if he still finds something missing, some defect within the individual, *this is not yet considered a "good deed"*!

This is the fine dividing principle of good and bad. "Good" isn't good unless the absolute evil attests to it, and says that it is good. It goes so far as to say that even the most deranged lunatic must not be able to find any claim or libel against it. And if so, if this "meshuganeh" can still find something to complain about, then this isn't yet the "good" demanded from the individual. Then the Heavenly Powers of Judgment listen to the complaints and examine the Satan's claims.

This is an overwhelming revelation. Here we are, usually scrutinizing our actions under the magnifying glass of...a father! Our outlook on our personal actions is like the benevolence of a father to his son's behavior, characterized by love and endearment. And now we see that this is not the case. Our actions have to be able to stand up to the scrutiny of our worst enemy! He, the Satan himself, must consent to them. And if he doesn't give his approval, they aren't considered good. And they listen and pay close attention to everything he says.

This is a terrifying revelation! Who can stand up to this test! Is there to be found on this Earth actions of such a caliber that even one's worst enemy will confirm and consent to them?

IV

THE WORLD HAS BEEN HANDED OVER TO AN EVIL POWER

(Adapted from **Da'as Chochmah u'Musar**, part 2, *ma'amar* 44)

Imagine those who lived before World War I.* If someone had come to them, while they were still enjoying a life of peace and tranquillity, and told them of how life would be during the War, of the pain and poverty with all the terrible tragedies and bitter suffering, no one would have believed at all that it would be possible to live under such circumstances. And yet, those who were born during that period managed to get through life even in that situation.

A free man, when he tries to imagine life in a prison, believes that it would be better to die than to suffer such a fate. Yet those born in prison live their lives and wile away their days even there, as if there were some flavor and enjoyment in their lives. The explanation is quite simple: they have never experienced any other way of living. To them, this is the way it is supposed to be.

When we honestly contemplate our everyday life, we realize what a prison it really is — a life of impatience, a life of hate, jealousy, lust, etc. It's a very bewildering phenomenon that we can live like that. But we are merely like those who have been born in a prison and have never seen any other way of life. We think that this is the picture of life. That this is the way it has to be, and that it's impossible otherwise.

A person who contemplates this honestly and intelligently discerns that he has been living in a prison. With each step he takes, he comes up against the prison walls. Evil fills up every inch of this world, until there is no fresh air left to breathe. One constantly breathes in "evil," until this "reign"**

* This was written before World War II.

** See the following two footnotes.

has conquered the world.

When we think about all the mistakes and confusion so prevalent in civilization, it is staggering. Life is almost a constant stream of errors. For hundreds of years men live with one system of thought, until the "wise man" comes along and proves with clear evidence that they were completely mistaken. Then a new system is discovered. Life continues according to this for another few hundred years, when again someone else comes along and proves the mistakes of the previous one. Isn't that simply amazing!

The individual, also, is constantly living with errors. Today he sees yesterday's mistakes, and tomorrow he will consider living differently, and then again he will find out that even that was a mistake. They say of Rav Sa'adyah Gaon that every day he did *teshuvah.* And when his *talmidim* asked him why, he told them that every day he considered that yesterday wasn't the way it should have been, according to his understanding and realization of this day. Therefore, he did *teshuvah* every day. It appears that Man passes his whole life in mistakes.

Now one comes to the realization that this history of mistakes which characterizes civilization is not an accident, but an essential part of Creation. That is the situation of this world — *olam ha-zeh,* a world of error and mistake! All of our questions regarding the world, even though they are tremendous questions, and even though the intelligent person may know how to answer, still remain questions. Moshe *Rabbenu* was perplexed and asked, "Let me know Your ways" (*Shemos* 33:13), and *Chazal* explain (*Berachos* 7a) that he was asking about the *tzaddik* who suffers and the *rasha* who prospers. The intellectual who contemplates sees these problems as being an intrinsic part of the world. The world was created specifically with these problems as part of the very fabric of Creation.

How are we to understand the Satan's ability to accuse and incite? We read in the Gemara:

> "Yet you incite Me against him to swallow him in vain?" R. Yochanan said, "If it weren't explicitly written, it would be impossible to say it. It is as if a person can incite Him and succeed in His being incited" [*Bava Basra* 16a].

Here was a man "sincere and upright, God-fearing and shunning evil," and yet, as soon as the Satan accused him, he was immediately handed over to him. "Behold, all that he has is in your hands; only upon himself do not stretch your hand." "Here he is in your hands, but preserve his life." Is it possible to say anything else except that the whole world was given over to the wicked Satan! This was Iyov's complaint, that the world has been given over to this power of evil, that everything has been given over to him.❖ Iyov was right. The impetus of the world is completely in his hands. There is absolutely nothing one can do about it; there is no way out:

> "And with all this Iyov did not sin with his lips." Rava said, "With his lips he did not sin, but he sinned in his heart." What did he say (meaning, how did he express himself later on, revealing the basic trend of his thinking)? "The Earth has been given into the hands of the

---

❖ Here Rav Yerucham, *zt"l*, has begun developing his theme that the whole world has been handed over to the dominion of the Satan. He is, in a certain manner, the so-called "ruler" of the world and, within the sphere appointed to him, has control over everything. He creates darkness and influences everybody and everything. Our job in Creation is to fight his rule and break through the darkness. This is what the *tefillah* (in the *Amidah* prayer for Rosh Hashanah) refers to when we pray that everyone finally recognize that in reality God has reign over everything, when finally כי תעביר ממשלת זדון מן הארץ, "You will abolish the rule of evil from the Earth." (See also the following footnote.)

> wicked one; he covers the faces of its judges. If not, then who is he?" Rava said, "Iyov wanted to turn the pot upside down (and spill out the food)" [to uproot all respect of the Almighty by his cursing and blaspheming — Rashi]. R. Yehoshua said to him, "Iyov was only referring to the Satan" [*Bava Basra* 16a].

The principle expressed by R. Yehoshua, this secret, that "The Earth has been given into the hands of the wicked one," embraces all of this world: it is entirely under his hand. Here, things are run his way. All the questions, mistakes, and confusion which are prevalent in the world, everything is based on this one secret: "The Earth has been given into the hands of the wicked one."

> In a *baraysa* it states, "He (the Satan) goes down and causes one to err, then he goes up and angers (the Almighty), then he gets permission and takes his soul." [He goes down below and misleads the populace into sin, then he rises above and incites the anger of the King with his prosecutions. Then he gets permission to kill the transgressor. This is the meaning of the verse, "Yet you incite Me" — Rashi] [ibid.].

With this statement, *Chazal* revealed to us the great secret of "The Earth has been given into the hands of the wicked one." This is the meaning of "He (the Satan) goes down and causes one to err." The errors are his realm, his kingdom, which he is constantly demonstrating. "Then he goes up and angers (the Almighty)" — and why should they listen to him up there? The answer is that the world has been given over to him — it's his; therefore, what he says is listened to.

"Then he gets permission and takes his soul." The secret which encompasses everything is "The Earth has been given into the hands of the wicked one." This is the basic principle of all of *olam ha-zeh*. It must be this way, for the conduct of evil permeates each step of the way. This is the path that we must travel and emerge from intact. This is the explanation of the statement of *Chazal* that *olam ha-zeh* is a world of *nisayon*, of constant tests. This is the fact of the whole of this Existence.❖

This principle encompasses all of *olam ha-zeh*, from its beginning to its end. It was present immediately at the beginning of the Creation, with the first man, Adam, even before the sin, while he was still in a state in which "the serving angels (*malachei ha-shares*) wanted to say *Kedushah* before him" (*Bereshis Rabbah* 8:9). There was no evil yet at all, and there was no room for the *yetzer ha-ra* to take effect, except to create an error. And that is exactly what happened — Adam erred. This "error" had its origin in "The Earth has been given into the hands of the wicked one." This is an amazing fact, that even the first man, before the sin, was already under the hand of "the wicked one." His sole job in this world was to stand up against this test and conquer the difficulties. And when he did not succeed, it just got harder, because now he was more in the hand of this *rasha*. Now he had to overcome the additional difficulties. This has continued on until today, when we find ourselves in a situation where we are completely in the hand of the *rasha*. And still, the demand applies even to us: to pass

❖ Rav Elchonon Wasserman, *zt"l*, also discussed the concept of the power of the Satan in this world. He stated that the affairs of the world are conducted in two ways: 1) by God, and 2) by the Satan. Not, God forbid, that there are two deities, but rather that the Satan is granted permission to fight, so to speak, against God. Therefore, in every situation, the person must ascertain, under direction of the *Gedolim* of that generation, whether what is occurring to him is being conducted by God or by the Satan. If he is at war with the Satan, the course of action required is completely different than if he is being dealt with by what he calls "an act of Divine Providence" (*Kovetz Ma'amarim, "Omer Ani Ma'asai l'Melech,"* (cited in "Reb Elchonon," p. 322).

through this garbage dump of evil which reigns over us, and come out intact!

Avraham was tested so many times. "Arise and walk through the land...for I have given it to you" (*Bereshis* 13:17). And then afterwards, when he came to bury Sarah, he couldn't find even four *amos* of land to call his own. He was promised, "For in Yitzchak will be called your seed" (*Bereshis* 21:12), and afterwards he was told, "Offer him up as a sacrifice" (*Bereshis* 22:2). Where is the consistency in God's actions? It must be that all this was a result of this secret of "The Earth has been given into the hands of the wicked one." The holy *Avos*, who were "clever in mind, and yet made themselves innocent like animals" (*Chullin* 5b), withstood the test and came out whole. But Iyov said, "The Earth has been given into the hands of the wicked one," and it is impossible to stand up against him.

It goes so far that *Chazal* state (*Arachin* 17a) that if *Ha-Kadosh Baruch Hu* would have held the *Avos* accountable according to strict justice they wouldn't have been able to stand up. This is not talking about the Next World. Rather, with this statement *Chazal* have revealed to us the depth of the secret of "The Earth has been given into the hands of the wicked one," how encompassing it is, how far it goes, and how dreadfully frightening it all is. Even the *Avos* did not yet encounter all the difficulties there are, even after all their *nisyonos*. After all of the ten tests of Avraham, and those of Yitzchak and Ya'akov, still, all the evil has not yet been poured out for them. They still haven't traveled the full gamut of "The Earth has been given into the hands of the wicked one." For if so, they wouldn't have been able to withstand it. That's why Avraham said to *Ha-Kadosh Baruch Hu*, "Swear to me that You won't test me any more!" (*Bereshis Rabbah* 56:18).

From all this it is clear that *nisyonos* are not accidental. Rather, all of one's life is a constant barrage of tests. Such is the makeup of the world: "The Earth has been given into the hands of the wicked one." There isn't one hairbreadth of Creation which isn't a test. It is total *nisayon*. It is impossible to comprehend anything except with the concept of *nisayon*. Only from evil can one perceive good.

Chazal knew this secret of *olam ha-zeh*, that its purpose is purely to test. The concept of *nisayon* was at the head of their consciousness. Every event that occurred to them was immediately judged accordingly, as if all of what was happening to them was a test. And we? We say everything about whatever situation we are in. It is completely analyzed. But *nisayon*? The idea never occurs to us. It is difficult for us to conceive of all of *olam ha-zeh* being only a test. This concept is distant from Man and never enters his mind.

The makeup of this world is based upon *nisayon*. "There will come days when you will say, I have no desire for them" (*Koheles* 12:1). *Chazal* commented (*Shabbos* 151b), "These are the days of the *Mashiach*, when there will be no merit and no liability (חובה)." It is understandable why there won't be any liability — nobody will be doing anything wrong. But why no merit? The answer is that without evil, without having to travel the path of evil, there is no good. *Olam Ha-Ba* can come only out of *olam ha-zeh*.

Three Essays from

Derech Emunah u'Bitachon, *parashas Lech Lecha*

by Morenu Maran Ha-Gaon Ha-Rav
CHAIM PINCHAS SCHEINBERG, Shlita
Rosh Yeshivas Torah Ore, Jerusalem

[There is some repetition from one essay to the next; these parts were not edited out, in order to allow each essay to be self-contained and retain its continuity.]

I

A *NISAYON* AS AN INDICATION OF A PERSON'S INNER MIND

The Gemara in *Nedarim* 32a asks, "Why did Avraham *Avinu* deserve to have his children enslaved in Mitzrayim for 210 years? Shmuel answers, 'Because he overstepped his bounds by saying, "How can I know that I will inherit it (Eretz Yisrael)?" ' "

Avraham *Avinu* was the first to achieve proper belief in *Ha-Kadosh Baruch Hu*. Therefore, how are we to understand such a tremendous criticism against him, that his *emunah* was faulty? Moreover, why was it deserving of the terrible punishment of his descendants being enslaved in Mitzrayim? In order to understand the severity of the transgression, we must first understand another point.

Rabbenu Yonah (*Pirkei Avos* 5:3) considers the incident of Ur Kasdim as the first of the ten *nisyonos*. Nimrod threw Avraham *Avinu* into a fiery furnace because he dared believe in *Ha-Kadosh Baruch Hu*.

The normal course of testing an individual is to test him first on the easy things, and then, if he stands up to that, to test him with something harder. But once he has stood up to the difficult test, there is no need to subject him to an easier test; it is obvious that he will withstand it. That is the logical way of doing things. If so, how can *Rabbenu* Yonah count Ur Kasdim as the first *nisayon*? Once *Ha-Kadosh Baruch Hu* had required him to completely sacrifice his life for his faith in God, then what was the need to further test him with the episode of the wanderings and to command him to leave his home? Certainly the *nisayon* of the furnace was much greater than being forced to leave home.

Secondly, the Alter of Kelm, in his book *Chochmah u'Musar*, asks another penetrating question on *Rabbenu* Yonah's position: Being that this was one of the ten *nisyonos*, why was it not written about explicitly in the Torah, instead of just being hinted at?

Moreover, *Rabbenu* Yonah's opinion is even more perplexing in that he counts the episode of Sarah's burial as the tenth *nisayon*. This after he has already listed the *Akedah* as the ninth (unlike the Rambam, who lists the *Akedah* as the tenth). What place is there for the *nisayon* of Sarah's burial after he has already withstood the tremendous *nisayon* of Yitzchak's *Akedah*, when *Ha-Kadosh Baruch Hu* personally testified, "Now I know that you are a God-fearing man"? And *Rabbenu* Yonah himself wrote that the *nisayon* of the *Akedah* was the most difficult of all the *nisyonos*. So why wasn't it the last?

The Rambam, however, doesn't even mention this incident in his count of the *nisyonos*, but rather starts counting from the *nisayon* of the wanderings, when God told him, "Go out from your land...." Why didn't he list Ur Kasdim as one of the ten *nisyonos*? Was this not a true example of self-sacrifice? Both of these opinions, *Rabbenu* Yonah's and the Rambam's, apparently need explanation.

The Concept of *Nisayon*

Perhaps we are wrong in understanding that the argument between the Rambam and *Rabbenu* Yonah is a simple matter of what to list. Perhaps they are arguing about the basic concept of *nisayon*. The *Sefer Ha-Yashar* (*sha'ar* 2) writes that there are ten criteria which test the love of a lover for his beloved. It was by these criteria that Avraham *Avinu* was tested.

Rabbenu Yonah: A *Nisayon* is an Expression of One's Love

This is an entirely new perspective which we must understand. A *nisayon* is not simply a "test" to determine if one loves the Creator. Rather, it is an expression of the depth of that love. Each time one stands up to a test, he expresses how deeply he loves God. Even though it may be well-known that one has reached the highest pinnacle of love of God, still the *nisayon* serves to further express that love. This can help us understand *Rabbenu* Yonah. For if a *nisayon* is not a dry test, but rather an external expression of the great love lying within one, then even a light test can come after a difficult one, for each situation is independent of the other. Whether in one situation or another, a person expresses his great love to God.

The *Shav Shemattsa* notes in his introduction that before the *Akedah,* Avraham *Avinu* was commanded to take "your only son whom you love, Yitzchak." After the *Akedah,* it states, "and you did not spare your only son from Me." After having withstood this *nisayon,* the concept of love toward his son is no longer mentioned. Pure love exists when it is directed toward only one person. If one loves someone else, it detracts from his love of the first one. Before the *Akedah,* Avraham had an only son, and his love toward him was tremendous. This detracted from his love toward God. This is the reason he was commanded to slaughter his son — to lessen this love and allow room for complete devotion to God. Having withstood this *nisayon* by being willing to slaughter his son, his great love was rechanneled in one direction — toward God.

According to the way we have understood *Rabbenu* Yonah, we can take this one step further. Actually, even before the *Akedah,* Avraham had this same love, but it was just lacking the proper expression, as pure love undiluted by love for anything else. Through the *Akedah,* he was able to express this love — "Now I know that you are a God-fearing man." This is *Rabbenu* Yonah's view of a *nisayon.*

The Rambam: A *Nisayon* is an Indication of one's *Emunah*

The Rambam views a *nisayon* as a way of determining the strength of one's *emunah* in God. A *nisayon,* then, is such that one's willingness to follow that faith, even against reason, is tested.❖ If one's intellect dictates that a certain path be fol-

---

❖ In a similar vein, the Brisker Rav (cited in the Haggadah *Me-Beis Ha-Levi* and quoted in the Haggadah *Yalkut Lekach Tov*) explains the section of the Haggadah which says, "Originally our forefathers were idol-worshipers... and I took your forefather, Avraham, from across the river...." The Midrash explains: R. Yitzchak said, "This is like one who was traveling on a path, and saw a brightly glowing palace. He said, 'Is it possible that this palace exists without someone running it?' The owner of the palace peered out and said to him, 'I am the owner of this palace!' So, too, since Avraham *Avinu* said, 'Is it possible to say that this world has no one running it?,' therefore, *Ha-Kadosh Baruch Hu* peered out and said to him, 'I am the owner of the world!' " (*Bereshis Rabbah* 39:1).

This *midrash* needs explanation. Once Avraham *Avinu* had recognized that there is a Ruler to Creation, what was added by *Ha-Kadosh Baruch Hu* appearing to him and telling him, "I own the world"? Whatever was possible for a human being to understand on his own had already been achieved by Avraham. And as for concepts beyond the human intellect, we know that a person cannot fathom concepts beyond his limited grasp, as the verse tells us: "A person cannot see Me and live."

The Brisker Rav's father, Rav Chayim Brisker, *zt"l,* explained the difference between knowledge and faith. Knowledge includes only what a person is able to comprehend with his intelligence, while faith is what is lowed, then this is not a *nisayon*, but rather the result of logic. Therefore, according to the Rambam, the test of Ur Kasdim cannot be listed as one of the ten *nisyonos*. For once one's intellect recognizes a unique Creator, then it is obvious that even if you are thrown into a fire, you cannot change your mind. It is a well known fact that many great men, of many nations, sacrificed their lives for their beliefs. If one feels that

---

impossible to understand with one's intelligence. Real faith begins from the place which the mind alone cannot fathom.

With this we can understand the Midrash. Avraham *Avinu* understood on his own that there is a ruler running the world. However, being that this knowledge was an intellectual concept, it was by necessity limited and only touched what the human intellect could comprehend. In return for this personal elevation on his own, he was rewarded in that the "owner of the palace" peered out to him and said, "I am the owner of the universe!" The connotation of the word "peered" is God's personal revelation, which granted Avraham a level of faith beyond human intellect and comprehension.

It is possible, said the Brisker Rav, that this is the intent of the words of the Haggadah, "and I *took* him." Yes, Avraham *Avinu* recognized the Creator on his own, but the level of *emunah* that he finally attained was rather the result of *Ha-Kadosh Baruch Hu*'s personal "taking." He lifted up Avraham *Avinu*, His loved one, and granted him the exalted level of pure and true *emunah*.

We see thus that Avraham *Avinu* attained a level of faith beyond the human intellect. It was in this level of faith that Rav Scheinberg wishes to explain that the *nisayon* lay: to retain this pure faith in spite of the apparent contradictions.

something is the truth, how can anything cause him to change his mind? Thus it is not possible for Ur Kasdim to have been a *nisayon*.

On this point *Rabbenu* Yonah agrees that self-sacrifice dictated by reason is logical, and therefore the Torah didn't write about this test openly — to answer the Alter of Kelm's question. However, since *Rabbenu* Yonah defines a *nisayon* as an expression of one's inner self, Ur Kasdim does deserve to be listed. The Rambam, however, understands the definition of a *nisayon* as a test to determine if a person is willing to follow God's Will even against the dictates of reason, and not to take account of logical considerations. For example, the *nisayon* of the famine: here was an apparent contradiction to what God had promised him — "And I will bless you and I will make your name great" (which Rashi interprets as monetary wealth). He could have felt that the famine was a contradiction of God's promise, but in spite of everything, he did not harbor any questions about God's ways.

The Midrash also substantiates this. It states (*Bereshis Rabbah* 56:12) that Avraham had the ability to answer back, against God's command to offer up his son as a burnt-offering. He could have said, "Yesterday You told me that 'through Yitzchak you will see descendants,' and now You tell me to offer him up as a sacrifice?!" But he did not say this. Instead, he followed God's commands completely, even against all laws of reason. This was the point of the *nisayon* of the *Akedah*, and not the actual offering up of his son. On this the Torah states, "And You found his heart faithful..." (*Nechemyah* 9:8). This is faithfulness, to follow God's Will even against reason.

Now we can understand the tremendous criticism against Avraham *Avinu* which brought about the punishment that his children were enslaved for 210 years. The purpose in each of his *nisyonos* was for him to follow God with no doubts, no second thoughts, no logical considerations. And here we find him asking, "How can I know?!" This was a contradiction of his purpose. This was the terrible criticism.

> R. Chiya bar Chanina said, "Avraham was not complaining [when he said, 'How can I know...?']; rather, he was asking, 'What merit do I have...?' " [*Bereshis Rabbah* 44:14].

There seems to be a contradiction between this statement of R. Chiya and that of Shmuel (mentioned above, at the beginning of this essay). According to Shmuel, Avraham was criticized for questioning the Divine plan, while according to R. Chiya there was nothing wrong with what he said. Upon deeper examination, however, we can say that there really is no dispute between them.

In explaining the *pasuk* הנה א-ל ישועתי אבטח ולא אפחד כי עזי וזמרת יה ויהי לי לישועה, "Behold, He is the God of my salvation, I will trust and not be afraid," the *siddur Ha-Gra* asks: It says (referring to Avraham), "and he believed in God, and it was considered *tzedakah*." What was so great about what Avraham had done? It seems relatively trivial. We find that with Ya'akov, even though *Ha-Kadosh Baruch Hu* had promised him, "And I will watch you wherever you go," still he was afraid, for perhaps he had committed a transgression which nullified the promise. Avraham, however, viewed the promise to him as *tzedakah*, and not based on his own worthiness of it. Therefore, he did not fear that a transgression would negate it, for God's *chesed* is forever and always, even if one sins. This is what is meant by א-ל ישועתי, "God of my salvation": א-ל, which is the Divine attribute of *Chesed*, should be my salvation — this is what I rely on to be the reason for my salvation, and not the merit of my actions. Therefore, אבטח ולא אפחד, "I will trust and not be afraid." For there is no reason to fear that perhaps a transgression has nullified the promise.

Following this course, we can understand the criticism against Avraham *Avinu* for asking what merit he had, instead of trusting that God would help him out of pure *chesed* and not because of the merit of his actions. The point of the criticism was that he showed a lack of pure faith, and he should not have wanted to understand through reason. Faith which follows pure reason would obligate one to have *bitachon* only when he merits it. But pure faith, independent of reason, allows one to have trust even when reason doesn't permit *bitachon*, when there isn't enough to merit it. Even in such a situation one should believe and trust in God's salvation.

(Thus we can answer that R. Chiya was not arguing with Shmuel. Avraham *Avinu* was not demonstrating lack of faith; he was merely asking, "For what do I merit that God will be with me?" However, that in and of itself was, for Avraham, a small blemish in the purity of his faith.)

Each individual encounters situations which are difficult to bear, to stand up against — one person in one situation, another person in a different situation. These may appear to be a great disturbance to one's spiritual ascent, but really one should look at them from the opposite perspective. This is the time and place that one can express his love of God. This is the point of one's personal *nisayon*. Whether the difficulty consists of a physical or material hindrance such as financial problems, or whether it is a spiritual difficulty such as studying Torah and not being able to understand the subject in depth, still one must be strong. And the stronger one is, the more he expresses his willingness to sacrifice out of his love toward God.

The *Even Shelemah* (compilation of commentaries of the Vilna *Gaon*), chap. 3, section 4, writes that "there are two types of strength found in those who serve God. They are called the strong — גבורים — and the powerful — אנשי חיל. The 'strong one' is one who conquers his nature when he is inclined to sin, while the 'powerful ones' are those courageous individuals with perfect trust which enables them to pore over the Torah day and night, and not to be diverted by their household crying for bread, as *Chazal* have interpreted the verse 'as black as a raven' (*Shir Ha-Shirim* 5:11) to refer to one who makes himself 'merciless on his children like a raven' (*Eruvin* 22a). What does *Ha-Kadosh Baruch Hu* do? He prepares for such a person someone who will support him, as Yissachar supported Zevulun." We can understand the *Gaon* along the lines that we presented above. Even if one has nothing to eat, or nothing with which to support his family, and according to pure reason there is no alternative except to leave his studies, still he should gird himself in strength and have pure and simple faith in God — the very opposite of reason.

Chazal, in their use of the word "merciless," did not mean that one should actually develop within himself the trait of being merciless, for this is very perverted. After all, the Torah commands us to develop the trait of lovingkindness. *Chazal* meant that one should act *as if* he were merciless, and in people's eyes it would appear that he is merciless. But in reality there is no greater love than the love of one who conducts himself according to full *bitachon* in God. The more one overcomes the difficulties of his situation and sacrifices himself in order to sit and engage in Torah study, the more he expresses his great love for God. He will naturally receive his full reward for this and will not be considered "merciless," since *Ha-Kadosh Baruch Hu* will send him someone to support him, as Yissachar supported Zevulun.

The *Gaon*, in several places,* comments that full *bitachon* in God is a fundamental principle of Torah. Most people think that *bitachon* is a means of fulfilling Torah and mitzvos, but just the opposite is the case. *Bitachon* is the basic principle of everything. Certainly, then, it is very important to strengthen oneself in this, even against the dictates of reason. For then רוצה ה׳ את יראיו את המיחלים לחסדו, "God will be pleased with those who fear Him, those who await His *chesed*."

* See Aderes Eliyahu on the *pasuk*, "And the nation feared God and believed in God..." (*Shemos* 14:31). See also the commentary of the *Gaon* to *Mishlei* 22:19, where he writes that *bitachon* is the essence and basic principle of all the mitzvos.

II

THE PURPOSE OF A *NISAYON*: TO PERFECT ONE'S NATURE

"Avraham *Avinu* was tested with ten *nisyonos* and he withstood them all. [This is recorded] to make us aware of how dear he was [to *Ha-Kadosh Baruch Hu*]" (*Pirkei Avos* 5:3). The *Rishonim* argue as to how to count the ten *nisyonos*. Rashi and the Maharal explain them according to *Pirkei d'Rabbi Eliezer*: "(1) First Nimrod attempted to kill him, so he hid underground for thirteen years. (2) Then Nimrod threw him into the fiery furnace (Ur Kasdim). (3) Next he was sent away (banished) from his homeland [to a land where] (4) *Ha-Kadosh Baruch Hu* brought a famine during his lifetime. (5) Sarah was taken from him. (6) The kings came and captured his nephew Lot. (7) During the *bris bein ha-besarim* he was shown how the four kingdoms would subjugate his descendants. (8) He was commanded to circumcise himself and his son. (9) He was told to send away his son with his wife Hagar. (10) He was commanded to slaughter his son Yitzchak. Ten *nisyonos*, and he had no second thoughts about God's ways, due to his tremendous love."

According to Rashi, one of the *nisyonos* was that Avraham agreed to be thrown into a burning furnace in order to sanctify God's Name (*kiddush Hashem*). It stands to reason, after having withstood such a difficult *nisayon* as this — having been prepared to give his life on behalf of his faith in God — that the other *nisyonos* are in no way equal to this one. If God were to instruct him to abandon his homeland, would he not certainly go, having been prepared even to be killed for *kiddush Hashem*? Simple logic dictates that the concept of *nisayon* go from the easy to the more difficult, in order to elevate one to ever higher levels through ever more difficult *nisyonos*. After having withstood the *nisayon* of Ur Kasdim, and after having hidden underground from Nimrod for thirteen years, the *nisayon* of "Leave your land" does not compare.

In discussing the *nisayon* of Sarah being taken by Pharaoh and Avraham's accepting this out of his love for God, the Ramban makes a powerful and yet mystifying comment:

> ויהי רעב בארץ וירד אברם מצרימה לגור שם כי כבד הרעב בארץ. ויהי כאשר הקריב לבוא מצרימה ויאמר אל שרי אשתו הנה נא ידעתי כי אשה יפת מראה את [בראשית י״ב:י-י״א]

> "And there was a famine in the land, and Avram went down to Mitzrayim to dwell there, for the famine was heavy in the land. And it was when he neared coming to Mitzrayim, and he said to Sarai his wife, 'Behold, I know that you are a beautiful woman to look upon' " [*Bereshis* 12:10-11].

On this the Ramban comments:

> Know that Avraham *Avinu* inadvertently transgressed a terrible sin by bringing his righteous wife close to stumbling over an iniquity due to his fear that they would kill him. [She was a married woman and he rightfully feared that someone would kill him in order to marry her. However, by saying that she was his sister, he almost guaranteed that someone would take her as a wife and would be living with a married woman.] He should have been secure in his faith in God that He would save him and his wife and everything he had, for God has the power to help and rescue. Moreover, leaving the Land in which he had been instructed to dwell was in itself considered a sin. Even though he left due to the famine, still, God redeems one from death during famine. Therefore, due to this incident, the Exile in Mitzrayim at the hand of Pharaoh was decreed on his descendants. "The place where you find the judgment, that is the place where there was the wickedness and the sin" [*Koheles* 3:16].

On the one hand, we have the powerfully innovative explanation of the Ramban that Avraham's going down to Mitzrayim and the incident there with Sarah were the causes of the Exile in Mitzrayim. On the other hand, *Chazal* count this as one of the *nisyonos* of Avraham *Avinu* and claim that he passed all the tests and had no misgivings about the ways of *Ha-Kadosh Baruch Hu*. This is a blatant contradiction which demands clarification.

Avraham Made Peace with the *Yetzer Ha-ra*

In order to understand the fundamental principle of *nisyonos*, we must first study the following statement of the Talmud Yerushalmi, which explains that there are two levels: acting out of fear (awe) and acting out of love.

> The most beloved of all is one who abstains [from transgression] out of love, like Avraham. Avraham *Avinu* made his evil nature good, as it says, "And You found his heart faithful before You." R. Acha said, "He struck a balance with his evil inclination (made a compromise and made peace with it — *P'nei Moshe*), as it says, 'And You found his heart faithful before You.' However, David was not able to stand up to it [meaning, he was not able to make peace with his evil inclination], so he killed it from within his heart [meaning, he forced it to do his Creator's Will]. What is the source? 'And my heart is empty within me' " [*Yerushalmi, Berachos* 9:5].

The *Yerushalmi* distinguishes between Avraham *Avinu*, who made peace with his *yetzer ha-ra*, and David, who banished it from within his heart. This, I believe, can shed some light on the subject of *nisyonos*. This world (*olam ha-zeh*) is a world of *nisyonos*, a path full of hardships. We stumble and fall and fail to understand the basis and purpose of each situation. If we contemplate all the things that happened to Avraham, we most likely would not see them as *nisyonos*. Here Avraham arrives in Mitzrayim, a land full of incest, and his wife is beautiful and attractive. There is nothing more natural than that she should be taken to the king. "There was a famine in the land." In a year of drought without rain, of course there would be a famine — such is nature. However, *Chazal* define situations such as these as *nisyonos*, for Man experiences no accidents in this world.

A *Nisayon* Makes One Great

The *Midrash Rabbah* (55:1) states:

> "And it came about after these things and God tested Avraham." It is written, "You gave those who fear You a banner (נס) to raise on high (להתנוסס) in order to be adorned, *selah.*" *Nisayon* after *nisayon*, growth after growth, in order to raise them up in the world (a play on the word נס which implies either a *nisayon*, a test, or a banner raised on high), in order to make them great in the world, like the mast (נס) of a ship.

It is a complete mistake to think that there is any accident in the world. If there are difficulties, it is because God has sent them to test one and to make him great through them. This is Man's purpose in this world.

The Essence of Torah is *Bitachon*

The popular understanding is that the purpose of performing mitzvos is to be a servant of God, and *emunah* and *bitachon* (faith and trust) are merely the means for doing so, because how is it possible to serve God without having *emunah* in Him? Therefore, faith is merely a means. The Vilna *Gaon*, on *Mishlei* (22:19), states just the opposite: "The essential reason in giving the Torah to Yisrael was in order that they should put their *bitachon* in God..., because the essence of everything is complete *bitachon*, and that is the principle of all the mitzvos...."

This is what we see in the *nisyonos* of Avraham *Avinu* — they were all tests in *emunah* and not in the application of mitzvos. Avraham was a *talmid chacham* who had his own yeshiva, and *Chazal* in *Avodah Zarah* 14b state that his *Masechta* of *Avodah Zarah* contained 400 chapters. He even fulfilled the laws of *eruv tavshilin* [even though this is not a Torah law, but rather a later Rabbinic decree]. So his *nisyonos* were not about fulfilling the mitzvos; rather, they were all in the realm of *emunah* and *bitachon*. This is what the Vilna *Gaon* meant in telling us that the essential purpose of the mitzvos is to bring one to *emunah* and *bitachon* in God. And this is what *Chazal* meant (at the end of *Makkos*): "Chavakuk came and based them (mitzvos) on one (basic mitzvah): A *tzaddik* lives with his *emunah*." The principle of the whole Torah, and the aim of all the mitzvos, is to become close to *Ha-Kadosh Baruch Hu* and to have *bitachon* in Him. It is therefore clear that all of Avraham's *nisyonos* were in his *emunah* and *bitachon* in God.

A *Nisayon* — to Oppose One's Nature

We were bothered above by the fact that the *nisyonos* of Avraham *Avinu* went from the difficult to the easy. The Maharal, in his book *Derech Chayim*, (on *Avos* 5:3) says,

> According to *Chazal*, all the *Avos* were tested, as we see in *Sanhedrin, perek Chelek* (107a), even though the Torah only mentions Avraham. This is a tremendous statement, for the *Avos*, being *Avos*, weren't like other men in the natural sense of the term, but rather they were Divine men. And that's why they were tested. The term *nisayon* comes from the word נס (miracle). Just as a miracle is not natural, so too is a *nisayon* unnatural. If the one being tested doesn't act outside the boundaries of nature, he will not be able to stand up to the *nisayon*, just as nature doesn't permit one to slaughter his own son. And so too with all other *nisyonos*. Therefore it was impossible for the *Avos* not to be tested! For they are not natural men like the rest of Mankind, and if they had conducted themselves in a natural fashion, they would not have been fitting for their high level.

We see from the Maharal that the definition of *nisayon* stems from the concept of נס (miracle), which is the opposite of nature. The usual course of a person is to go along with his nature. Greatness, however, consists of acting against nature. To quote the metaphor of the recent commentaries: *Mikveh* water purifies only when it is gathered together, whereas spring water (מי מעיין) purifies even while moving. What is the sign of spring water? The water rises from the earth. Rainwater will only flow downwards, for this is the nature of freely flowing water. But if the water flows upwards, that is a sign that it has life. This is the makeup of a *nisayon* — to go against nature. Therefore it is quite well understood that *nisyonos* do not necessarily have to go specifically from the easy to the more difficult, for each *nisayon* is a situation against the person's nature: to leave the country where he lives, to slaughter his son, etc. These weren't merely logical tests; they were trials against nature. If a person believes in God and is prepared to be killed for *kiddush Hashem,* this is something that reason can understand.

The commentaries actually do explain that this is why the Torah doesn't mention the *nisayon* of Ur Kasdim, because a person's willingness to die for his faith is something that reason comprehends. As we see with the nations, there are many who are prepared to be killed for their beliefs or convictions. At the time of the Inquisition, even simple people ran into the fire and cried out *Shema Yisrael,* because reason dictated such conduct. But to break and subdue one's nature, to break one's connection with his family, or to slaughter one's own son — these are against nature and here it is not possible to compare one against the other and say which is easy and which is difficult. For example, there are individuals to whom their money is more dear than their bodies, and they are willing to die of hunger while their bank accounts are filled with money. Even though logic doesn't comprehend this, still this is their nature and it is difficult for them to break this nature. Therefore, *nisyonos* come in various forms in order to break various aspects of one's nature. That is why it is impossible to determine which is easy and which is difficult.

The *Akedah* — to Channel Avraham's Devotion

The introduction of the *Shav Shemattsa* (end of section B) explains the *nisayon* of the *Akedah*:

> The essential *nisayon* was that God saw that he [Avraham] loved his son who had been born to him at 100 years of age. This spread out his love so that it wasn't entirely with God. Therefore, He told him to slaughter his son whom he loved, in order to put an end to the love of his son and to make that love completely directed to God. Once he had withstood the test and completely devoted his love to Him, so much so that he was willing to slaughter his only son out of his love for God, this was proof that now his love for his son had departed and he had totally devoted all of it toward the Creator. This is why the Torah no longer mentions his love for Yitzchak ('your only son whom you love') but merely 'your only son.'❖

❖ When the Chafetz Chaim's son Avraham passed away, the Chafetz Chaim was in Warsaw. He received a telegram saying that he should return immediately to Radun, but when he arrived he met the people returning from the funeral. The Chafetz Chaim did not sigh or cry, but he called out in a loud voice, "God gave, and God took, let the Name of God be blessed from now unto eternity." He then added these words: "It is told that during the time of the Inquisition in Spain they took a mother and slaughtered her two sons in front of her. The mother raised her eyes toward Heaven and said, 'Master of the Universe, as long as my sons were alive my love for You was not pure, because there remained a corner in my heart for the love of my sons. Now that my sons are gone, all my love is given over to You. From now on I will be able to perfectly fulfill the commandment, "And you shall love the Lord your God with all your heart." ' " The Chafetz Chaim concluded, "Master of the Universe, the love that I felt until now for my son, I sanctify for You!" (*Ha-Meoros Ha-Gedolim*, sec. 172).

Avraham's perfection came about through his uprooting all natural attachments in the world which prevented his complete attachment to *Ha-Kadosh Baruch Hu*. How many *tefillos* and how many tears did he shed until finally, at the age of 100, he merited the son who would continue his career and spread faith in God throughout the world! That is why God tested him, to see if his love of God would be strong enough to be able to cut off this natural attachment to his son. Avraham, having withstood this test, was told by God, "And you have not withheld your only son...," and no mention was made of "the only son whom you love." Avraham had achieved perfect love of *Hashem Yisbarach* and eradicated his love for his own son.

Nisyonos Which Counter Nature Draw One Close to *Ha-Kadosh Baruch Hu*

Nisyonos which oppose nature are the ones which draw the person close to *Ha-Kadosh Baruch Hu*. The more one cuts off a part of himself, the closer he gets to *Hashem Yisbarach*. This will help us understand the apparent contradiction in the Ramban mentioned earlier. Avraham was lauded for having stood up to the test in his *nisayon* with Pharaoh. And yet it was considered that he had erred unintentionally by reckoning that he would save himself through Sarah's claiming that she was his sister. And the Ramban sensed that this was a defect in his *bitachon* in God. This is no contradiction. At first he had indeed erred. However, after he realized that he had made a mistake in his actions, he had no second thoughts about God's dealings with him and he exploited the situation to draw himself closer in his love for God.

This is the way a person grows: through breaking his nature and his personal makeup (מדותיו). This is what our Sages taught us in the *Talmud Yerushalmi* about the difference between Avraham *Avinu* and David *Ha-Melech*. Avraham *Avinu* stood up to all of the tests through his love of God. This is what was meant by saying that he made peace with his evil inclination. For example, everyone has difficulty learning Torah or getting up for prayer. However, for one who attains a sweetness in his learning, and a love of God, how easy are these things for him! He would not even consider them a *nisayon*. That was Avraham *Avinu*, whose love of God was so great, that the *nisayon* was not in the category of "hard" at all.

David *Ha-Melech*, however, had to kill his evil inclination, because he was not able either to go with his nature or to completely oppose it. As the Vilna *Gaon* explains in *Even Shelemah* (*perek* 1, sec. 7): "Even one whose nature is bad should not go completely against it because [his efforts] will not succeed completely. Rather, he should train himself to go in the straight path according to his nature. For example, one who was born under the sign of *Ma'adim* (Mars, which astrologically is the sign of war and bloodshed) is inclined to be a shedder of blood. Therefore he can train to be a *shochet* (who is on a middle level) or to be a *mohel* (who is a *tzaddik*), but not to be a robber." The note there adds, "And that is why David trained himself to constantly wage wars of mitzvah, because he was born under *Ma'adim*. (It is also possible that this is the reason that the downfall of Edom will be by the hands of the *Mashiach ben David*, because Esav was an Edomi [red, the symbol of *Ma'adim*].) Therefore David, who was also an Edomi, obligates him (meaning, he had the same difficult nature and yet he used it for good, so that creates a condemnation of Esav, who was not able to better direct his nature)." Consequently, David was not able to make peace with his nature as Avraham did.

Love — the Way to Overcome All Difficulties

From Avraham's stand in relation to *nisyonos* we see the way to overcome all difficulties. "If one would give all the riches of his house for his love, he would be scorned" (*Shir Ha-Shirim* 8:7). *Chazal* in *Midrash Rabbah* (8:7) state:

> When R. Yochanan passed away, his generation applied to him this *pasuk*: "If one would give all the riches of his house for his love," because R. Yochanan loved the Torah to the disdain of everything else.

Chazal tell of the very difficult tribulations R. Yochanan passed through. He had ten children, and all of them died. The last and youngest fell into a cauldron of boiling water and nothing remained except a small piece of bone (see *Berachos* 5b and the commentary of R. Nissim Gaon). Yet, through his love of the Torah, he stood up to all the tests. The Vilna *Gaon* in *Even Shelemah* (*perek* 2:9) states, "It is impossible to attain the sweetness of the Torah without afflictions and distancing oneself from the passions (lusts)." The person who attains the sweetness of Torah has absolutely no interest in this world, and so all *nisyonos* evaporate due to this love. Therefore, Avraham's love — meaning his love of *Ha-Kadosh Baruch Hu* — was the basis for his standing up to all the trials and all situations.

Nisyonos — Constant Growth

Each individual experiences in his lifetime trials and difficulties. The greatest pleasure is knowing that these are the foundation of life, and that spiritual greatness is dependent upon *nisyonos*. *Chazal* call this "growth upon growth," because the development of greatness in the person involves breaking his nature. If he remains with his nature, it is clear that he has no connection to spiritual life.

We pray that "He should open our hearts to His Torah and put within our hearts love and fear of Him and the ability to do His Will, and to serve Him with a whole heart, in order not to labor for vanity and not to bring forth confusion" (*Shacharis* service, in the *tefillah* "*U'va l'Tzion*"). If one performs mitzvos while his heart is closed, all of his efforts are in vain. If he doesn't sacrifice a part of himself, he has no relation to spirituality. This is a frightening thought, that one can perform mitzvos and still have absolutely no connection to Torah and mitzvos. The goal of mitzvos is to bring one closer to God, to trust and have faith in Him. If this is lacking in the person, why then were mitzvos given to him? Mitzvos are merely the means to reach love and faith in God, "and to serve Him with a whole heart." The heart must be entirely and completely devoted to God. Avraham *Avinu* gained for himself a whole heart, as it states, "And You found his heart faithful before You." The Radak comments on the *pasuk* "The seed of Avraham My beloved" (*Yeshayahu* 41:8) that "he loved Me and clung to Me." The purpose of the Torah is attachment to God, and without this a person has nothing from the mitzvos. If mitzvos are not bringing him closer to God, then, God forbid, he is "giving birth to confusion," and even the Torah he learns is in vain — with no chance of enduring.

We live in a world of *nisyonos*. When one encounters difficulties, these are his tests. If it is difficult to study, or to get up for *tefillah*, this is the nature of Man. The obligation is to "be strong like a lion" to break this nature. The sign of a *ben Torah* is that there are *nisyonos*, for when one has no *nisyonos*, this is a sign of his bankruptcy and he is far from *ruchaniyus* (spirituality). For example, *meshulachim* (fund-raisers) go out from quite a large number of yeshivos collecting money in America. If one says of a yeshiva that it has no need for *meshulachim*, I don't think that it could be called a yeshiva. "This is the way of Torah," to toil and trouble oneself, for this is the very being of *ruchaniyus*. If all goes easily, without difficulties, it isn't a yeshiva.

The *Maskilim* once complained to Rav Chayim Ozer that according to the rules of nature it is impossible to maintain Torah. Rav Chayim Ozer answered them, "Torah is never maintained according to the laws of nature." In business it is possible to keep a natural accounting, but Torah stands on miracles and the opposite of nature. Therefore, each *ben Torah* must be prepared for trials and difficulties. If not today, then tomorrow. Happy is the one who understands that this is the way it must be for the proper development of the individual. Then, when he goes out into the world and encounters difficulties, he will be prepared for them and they will not break him.

The Alter of Kelm said that the best soldier is the one who is tested on the battlefield. There we see his strength. So, too, the real *ben Torah* is tested with *nisyonos* and obstacles. The yeshiva is the place to prepare for life. "Void of all transgression and clean from all sin" (*Shemoneh Esreh, Ma'ariv* of *motza'ei Shabbos*) — this is the goal of everything. Through all the mitzvos a person can merit to cling to *yiras Hashem* (fear of God), and then He will "Grace us with [His] wisdom, understanding, and intelligence" (*Shemoneh Esreh, nusach Ashkenaz*).

III
TO DEFINE A *NISAYON*

"Avraham *Avinu* was tested with ten *nisyonos* and he withstood them all. [This is recorded] to make us aware of how dear he was [to *Ha-Kadosh Baruch Hu*]" (*Pirkei Avos* 5:3). The *Rishonim* argue as to how to count the ten *nisyonos*. Almost all of the *Rishonim* are of the opinion that Avraham's first *nisayon* was the fiery furnace in Ur Kasdim, and, according to Rashi, even the thirteen years he hid in a cave. As *Rabbenu* Yonah comments on the above *mishnah:* "The first was Ur Kasdim, when Nimrod threw him into the furnace of fire, and he was saved. This is not explicit in the Torah, but is known from Tradition. There is a hint to this in the Torah itself (when it mentions Ur Kasdim — the fire of Kasdim, *Ur* meaning fire). This was to let you know that it was because he stood up to this test that God promised him and brought him to Eretz Yisrael."

Rashi comments on the above *mishnah*: "First Nimrod tried to kill him and he hid underground for thirteen years. Then he threw him into the fire of Kasdim. Afterwards he went into exile from his homeland."

The Rambam, however, in his commentary to the above *mishnah*, explains it differently: "The ten trials with which Avraham was tested are all explicitly written in the Torah. The first was his exile when the Blessed One told him, 'Go out from your land....' " So we see that the Rambam considered that the first *nisayon* was not that of Ur Kasdim, nor the thirteen years he spent underground, but "Go out from your land...."

One of the great *Musar* teachers asked why the Rambam completely ignored the miracle of Ur Kasdim in his recounting of the ten trials. How is it possible that the great sacrifice necessary to pass through the fire of Kasdim in order not to engage in *avodah zarah* (idol-worship) was not in the category of a *nisayon*? And even if it wasn't explicitly written in the

Torah, nevertheless it is cited in the Tradition, as *Rabbenu* Yonah mentioned above, and as we see in the *Midrash Rabbah*:

> "What shall we do for our sister on the day that she will be spoken about?" (*Shir Ha-Shirim* 8:8). This was the day that Nimrod decreed to throw him into the fiery furnace [*Bereshis Rabbah* 39:3]. Also, in *Bereshis Rabbah* 38:19 the whole incident is cited in its entirety, about how Avraham came to recognize his Creator, the incident when he broke the idols, and the trial with Nimrod when he was condemned to the fire.

Even more problematic is that the Rambam himself cites the whole episode of Ur Kasdim in the first chapter of *Hilchos Avodah Zarah*:

> The world continued in this way until the Pillar of the World was born, Avraham *Avinu*. Once this giant was weaned, his mind started soaring even though he was still young. He started thinking day and night. He was astounded: How is it possible that this globe should be turning constantly without one to direct it and turn it? It is impossible that it should turn by itself. No one taught him, because no one was there to inform him. He was in Ur Kasdim, surrounded by foolish idol-worshipers...and he himself worshiped idols. But his mind was constantly working until he understood the Truth. He had a straight mind and understood that there is only one God Who directs the Earth and Who created everything. There is no other Deity in existence besides Him. He understood that the whole world was mistaken.... When he was forty years old, he came to a clear recognition of his Creator, and once he recognized Him he knew, and started to answer the people of Ur Kasdim, and to argue with them and tell them that they weren't going in the true direction. He broke the idols and started telling everyone that it is not worth worshiping anything except the God of the world. To Him it is fitting to bow down, and to offer sacrifices and libation. All this he did in order that all future Existence should recog-

> nize Him, and that it is proper to destroy and break all images in order that people shouldn't be mistaken by them....Since he overpowered them with his proofs, the king tried to kill him. A miracle occurred and he escaped to Charan.

We see that the Rambam himself refers to the miracle of the furnace and that this was a tradition that the Rambam was aware of. Therefore it is quite perplexing why he didn't include it in the list of the ten *nisyonos*.

We have to understand the greatness of Avraham *Avinu*. From the time he was a little boy, he had already begun to ask questions. He thought; he used his head; he was astounded. He looked at the sun and the moon and the stars and their constant and consistent movements. How is it possible, he asked, for them to move so systematically without someone moving them? Every day the sun rises and sets, everything so perfectly following the "laws of nature." How is it possible that there is no *Manhig*, no one causing them to move? All this with no teacher, immersed in the *avodah zarah* of Ur Kasdim. His father, his mother, everyone worshiped idols. We can imagine Avram, sitting in a temple with his family, sitting there during the service, thinking, How ridiculous! Until he came to the Truth, that there is a Prime Mover Who created everything, and there is nothing that He did not create and that He does not rule over. When he was forty years old he came to the recognition of God. Imagine, living in such a place and coming to his own recognition of God. Because of this they threw him into the fire. And yet, with all this, the Rambam did not include this in the list of the ten *nisyonos*!

Perhaps we can learn an important principle from this. *It isn't considered a nisayon if the person being tested understands what is demanded of him*. If the demand on the person is something the normal human mind can comprehend, then it is not a *nisayon*. Avraham *Avinu* understood that idols are foolish and vanity, as the Rambam wrote, "But his mind was constantly working until he understood the Truth....When he was forty years old, he came to a clear recognition of his Creator." The *Kesef Mishneh* explains that at forty he completed his recognition, meaning that he reached a complete and clear understanding, with no doubts, that idols are vanity of vanities. It is very understandable that a person would be willing to give up his life for a clear cause when others are trying to force him to believe in what is vanity of vanities. Therefore the Rambam held that the fiery furnace was not yet in the category of a *nisayon*. We even find among the nations those who give up their lives for foolishness which they understand to be the "truth."

A *nisayon* according to the Torah, holds the Rambam, specifically consists of something that the human mind cannot understand. At least for that moment, a person doesn't understand why it is being demanded of him.

The Alter of Kelm, *zt"l*, commented that it is a surprise that the *nisayon* of the *Akedah* is explicitly mentioned in the Torah, and at such length, and yet the miracle of Ur Kasdim isn't mentioned explicitly at all, only in Tradition. According to what we have just explained, it is quite understandable. Regarding the *nisayon* of the *Akedah* it says, "That he suppressed his feelings of mercy in order to fulfill Your Will with a full heart" (*Musaf* service for Rosh Hashanah). Moreover, *Chazal* explain that Avraham *Avinu* could have claimed a very strong argument: "Yesterday You told me that 'in Yitzchak you will see descendants.' And today You tell me, 'Take your only son.' " Yet he suppressed his feelings of mercy and didn't ask and didn't doubt.

The greatness of the *nisayon* of the *Akedah* was the apparent contradiction in God's commands. This was a tremendous question. And yet, with no hesitation, Avraham suppressed his natural emotions and no question could detract from his faith. Therefore, the great sacrifice of being thrown into the fire was not in the category of a *nisayon*. Thousands of people give their lives for their opinions and ideologies. The *nisayon* of the *Akedah* was that he stood up against it in spite of the tremendous questions, even in light of the open contradiction: Yesterday You told me...and today You tell me....

> "And Avram took...." Happy is the man who fears God. Why should he be happy? Because he did not fulfill the mitzvos begrudgingly, but with joy. "In Your mitzvos he had great desire...." *Ha-Kadosh Baruch Hu* told him, "Go out from your land," and he didn't do it begrudgingly, but immediately — "And Avram took his wife Sarai" [*Midrash Tehillim,* quoted in *Yalkut Yehudah* 12:5].

This explains how he was able to pass the *nisayon* of *Lech Lecha*. At the time it wasn't at all clear what exactly the *nisayon* was. He had been promised wealth, children, and prosperity. Who wouldn't go to any place in the world, even for the remote possibility of turning into a millionaire? Do we not find men willing to travel great distances even on the slightest chance that they will find gold? So where was the *nisayon* of *Lech Lecha*?

ויהי כאשר התעו אותי, "And it was when God caused me to go astray" (*Bereshis* 20:13). Ibn Ezra comments on the word התעו, "This word is *lashon kodesh*. It means that he traveled from place to place not knowing where he was going." This was the *nisayon*: that he had to travel without knowing to where, like a person wandering around. Then each step is a test, walking and not knowing the destination. And yet he didn't simply walk, but "in Your mitzvos he had great desire." This is also stated in the *Midrash Tehillim* (section 119):

> "He went in wholeness" — this was Avraham, of whom it says: "Go before Me and be whole." What did *Ha-Kadosh Baruch Hu* tell him: "Go out from your land, your birthplace," and he didn't answer back to Him, saying, "What's the difference if I sit here or go to a different city? Why? One who moves from house to house suffers. Even more so from city to city." And yet he didn't

> delay, but immediately did everything that He told him, as it says, "And Avraham went, just like God had told him."

So, too, the Rambam understood that the greatness of Avraham *Avinu* was in this point, that he stood up against a *nisayon* where human reason cannot comprehend, even though he was able to criticize and ask questions.

We find this in our everyday lives. These are the daily *nisyonos* — for example, in the development and growth of a *ben Torah*. Who wouldn't learn with burning desire if he had the ability to become a *gaon* overnight? All of us believe in the *kedushah* of the Torah. Certainly each one of us wants to elevate himself in his learning. But the reality is as the Vilna *Gaon* states (*Even Shelemah*, chap. 4, section 10): "Sometimes a person starts going in the straight path, but afterwards drops out, because it is too hard. And he complains to God that he didn't have any inspiration." The *Gaon* is referring here to one who came to learn, and studied, and sacrificed over his studies, and yet has complaints: "*Ribbono shel Olam*, where is my inspiration?" Without a doubt, he is suffering from the *nisayon* of *Lech Lecha*. No one can argue this. And he complains that he doesn't have any inspiration!

The Vilna *Gaon* concludes, "Really, he himself was the one who ruined it, by wanting to reach the highest level in one jump." This person ruined it for himself because he didn't understand how *ruchaniyus* is developed. How much sacrifice and strain are required for each laborious step of the way in the spiritual life! How many obstacles and *nisyonos* stand in the way and oppose one's rise! A person should be strong and persistent. Many powerful questions and contradictions arise to sway the individual and he begins to question, Where is my inspiration? Why aren't I succeeding? Why is this so hard for me? He does not see that this is the right path, this is how to learn, and this is how to develop.

This is not even so hard to understand. Normal reason comprehends that difficulties are encountered in all studies. However, when it pertains to the subject of Divine *Hashgachah*, then a person doesn't understand that "This is the way of Torah, eat your bread with salt, and drink a bit of measured water, and sleep on the floor..." (*Pirkei Avos* 6:4). Just look at all the difficulties in everyday life. One comes to learn and all of a sudden he gets sick, or he suffers from the cold, or from other disturbances. And he doesn't understand what happened — why all the disturbances?

If only it would be possible to attain Torah easily. If only a person understood why learning is so hard for him, when for his friend it is so easy and he succeeds in his learning more than he does. Why is he different from his friend? Because if he were not, then it wouldn't be a *nisayon*. He must understand that we cannot understand, and we don't have to understand, the *nisyonos* of life which are the success of *ruchanius*. Each one of us is born with his own destiny and a special Divine *Hashgachah* (*Iggeres Ha-Gra*).

The Vilna *Gaon*, in *Even Shelemah* (chap. 3, section 4), writes that "there are two types of strength found in those who serve God. There are the גבורים (strong) and the אנשי חיל (powerful). The strong person is one who conquers his nature when he is inclined to sin, while the powerful ones are those courageous people with perfect trust which enables them to pore over the Torah day and night, and not to pay attention to their household crying for bread, as *Chazal* have interpreted the verse 'as black as a raven' (*Shir Ha-Shirim* 5:11) to refer to one who makes himself 'merciless'* in regard to his children, like a raven (*Eruvin* 22a). What does *Ha-Kadosh Baruch Hu* do? He prepares for him someone who will support him, as Yissachar supported Zevulun." These are the most difficult of all *ni-*

* See p. 159 above for the explanation of this concept of "merciless."

syonos. But with *bitachon* and God's *Hashgachah*, this is the way to develop into a *ben Torah*. As the Vilna *Gaon* labeled them, the powerful ones have complete *bitachon* which enables them to hover over the Torah day and night.

This is the path of the Torah. The *nisyonos* of the Torah are not things which the mind can comprehend. This was the greatness of Avraham *Avinu*: even though he didn't understand the *nisyonos*, nevertheless, as it is written, "and You found his heart steadfast before You."

Rav Chayim Volozhin writes (in *Ruach Chayim* on *Pirkei Avos* 5:3):

> "Avraham *Avinu* was tested with ten *nisyonos*" (*Pirkei Avos* 5:3). Here it says, "Avraham *Avinu*" (our forefather), while above it says, "There were ten generations from Avraham until No'ach," and it doesn't call him "*Avinu*." We can explain this by applying the verse "A *tzaddik* walks in his sincerity, happy are his children after him" (*Mishlei* 20:7). How many mitzvos did a *tzaddik* work hard and toil to achieve, which to his children after him are engraved in their nature — and with just a little bit of effort they reach the same level! As we see in real experience, so many Jews show real acts of Jewishness. Even simple laymen give up their lives for *kiddush Hashem*. This is something that we inherited from our forefather Avraham, who was willing to give up his life in Ur Kasdim for the sake of his faith. All of the ten tests smoothed the path for us. Also, how many people get a sudden urge to go to the Holy Land, to Eretz Yisrael! This is from the test of *Lech Lecha* ("Go out from your land"). And as for a Jew's ability to accept everything that happens from Heaven as good, this comes from the *nisayon* of the famine, when Avraham did not question God's commands.

All of the tests which passed over Avraham made it easier for us to do mitzvos, even though we don't understand. We have inherited this from Avraham *Avinu*. Rav Chayim

Volozhin emphasizes, "With just a little bit of effort we are able to accomplish great things." This is not anything new for us. It is already part of our nature, which we inherited from Avraham *Avinu*. He paved the way and made it easier for us. Therefore this should be our job as *b'nei Torah,* to ignore all the difficulties which pass over us in our spiritual development. Just like the soldier whose courage is shown specifically on the battlefield when the bullets are flying all around him, so too the *ben Torah* should know that he has to pass through a world of tests and it is his job to excel in them, until he attains a sweetness in his learning and becomes great in Torah.

Only a fool gives up. He doesn't understand any of this. With the first test that stands in his way, he packs his bags and leaves. When he sees his friends succeeding more than he, it is very hard for him. However, as we said, it is specifically within this very test that his development is hidden and in this way will he acquire greatness. Even with Avraham *Avinu,* it was the tests which made him into Avraham *Avinu*. He didn't merely stand up to the test and overpower it; rather, with each test that he passed through, he grew and developed and thus he accomplished.

Through *nisyonos* one gains a courageous heart. Through *nisyonos* one gains strong faith, *emunah*. This builds the person. Don't ask, "Why is it so much easier for my friend?" On the contrary—perhaps because I merit more, therefore it is harder for me. "God tests the one He loves." Can we fathom the way of *Hashgachah*? It is not our job, or within the grasp of our understanding, to understand God's ways. Why is it so hard specifically for me? No, it is just the opposite! That's the proof! That shows that I have found favor in God's eyes. This is my way of growing, this is my path to greatness!

This is what *Chazal* themselves said:

> "Go out from your land...." R. Berachyah introduced this *parashah* thus: "Your ointments have a goodly fra-

> grance; your name is as ointments poured forth" (*Shir Ha-Shirim* 1:3). R. Berachyah said, "To what was Avraham *Avinu* similar? To a flask of fine oil sealed and put aside in the corner. Its fragrance was not spreading. But as soon as it was moved, it gave forth its fragrance. Thus *Ha-Kadosh Baruch Hu* said to Avraham *Avinu*, 'Move yourself from place to place and your name will become great in the world' " (*Bereshis Rabbah* 39:2).

This is Man's greatness, not to worry about difficulties. Just the contrary — if we understood, they wouldn't be tests. If Avraham *Avinu* had been shown where he was going, what *nisayon* would this have been? Certainly he would have gone in order to inherit the land of Kena'an which had all of the promise and success of the world. Instead, how much torment did he suffer? He traveled from place to place, wandering and straying in his journey, not knowing where he was going, where to direct his feet. And there was also the *nisayon* of the *Akedah*: "Yesterday You told me...and now...." *Nisyonos* are what cause us to grow, and we cannot compare one person's *nisyonos* to another's. Each person has his own talents and strengths. Each person has to reach a different greatness. It isn't something one can understand; rather, it depends purely upon Divine Providence.

This is why the Rambam headed his list of the ten *nisyonos* specifically with God's commandment: *Lech Lecha*. There it was possible to recognize Avraham's great desire to do God's mitzvos, for that test was where he was led to stray. It was an act of great sacrifice. His greatness wasn't expressed by his self-sacrifice in being thrown into a fiery furnace, for when a person understands what is happening to him, there are no difficulties preventing the person from bringing out his inner desire. After all, people constantly travel long distances for big business ventures in spite of the greatest difficulties involved.

We pray that God grant us the merit to stand up to the

tests, and to understand that through them we can attain the standing of the courageous of heart. This is our strength, in spite of all hardship. We will accept everything that we encounter with love and with a willing soul. With the help of God we will attain true greatness.

Excerpts from a Speech*
By RAV AVRAHAM PINCUS, shlita
former *Menahel*, Yeshiva Torah Vodaas, New York, and Yeshivas Kaminetz, Yerushalayim

Parashas Vayishlach, 5752

It says in *parashas Vayishlach*: ויותר יעקב לבדו, "And Ya'akov was left alone." Now, we know that there is only One Who is alone (לבדו): ונשגב ה' לבדו, "God stands alone" (*Yeshayahu* 2:11). We can infer from this that Ya'akov attained a level of לבדו. What is this level? Simply put, it means that just as *Ha-Kadosh Baruch Hu* needs no one else, so too Ya'akov needed no one else. What is this level?

In *Pirkei Avos* 4:1, we read: איזהו חכם, הלומד מכל אדם....ואיזהו גיבור, הכובש את יצרו....ואיזהו עשיר, השמח בחלקו. "Who is wise? He who learns from everyone.... Who is strong? He who conquers his *yetzer ha-ra*....And who is rich? He who is happy with his lot." We tend to think that a *talmid chacham* is one who learns from a lot of books, goes to a lot of lectures. And who do we think is strong? The one who builds up his muscles! And rich? Oh, he is the one who made a lot of money. But the *Tanna* tells us, No! For each one of those has to depend on someone else or something else to attain his goal. If you take away the books or the lectures from the *talmid chacham*, he is nothing. If you take away the muscle-building program from the strong man, or if he falls sick and loses his strength, he is nothing but a weakling. And what happens to the rich man when the stock market crashes? All gone! The *Tanna* tells us that with *Klal Yisrael*, the Jewish Nation, there is a special level they can reach, לבדו — alone. They don't need anything from the outside, for they have everything within themselves. If you are a מבקש חכמה, one who really seeks wisdom, you will receive

* Delivered to a group of yeshiva students. Rav Pincus originally heard this speech directly from the *mashgiach*, Rav Yerucham Levovitz, *zt"l*, while he was attending the Mir Yeshiva in Poland.

something from everyone. Strength is that inner strength with which the *ben Torah* has to conquer his *yetzer*. And we all can be rich if we develop the trait of being satisfied with what we have.

Many *bachurim* are dissatisfied with what they have. Their *chavrusa* isn't good, the *shiur* also.... If only I had a different Rebbe, and isn't that other yeshiva so much better? No! Everything is there, within you. On one Purim, Rav Naftali Amsterdam, *zt"l*, came over to Rav Yisrael Salanter, *zt"l*, and took advantage of the occasion to present a problem to his Rebbe: "If only I had the Sha'agas Aryeh's head, and the Yesod V'Shoresh Ha-Avodah's heart, and the Rebbe's *middos*, then I would be something!" So his Rebbe answered him, "No, Naftali. With your head, with your heart, and with your *middos*. When you get to *Shamayim*, they're not going to ask you why you didn't become the Sha'agas Aryeh, or the P'nei Yehoshua. They are going to ask you, 'Why didn't you become Naftali Amsterdam!?' "

There is a new approach in the world at large today. It permeates all of the scholastic world, all of psychology, everything and everyone. "I'm a victim of circumstance!" "It's all my parents' fault!" "I had bad friends, my school was no good, society didn't give me a break." "It's not my fault!" "You can't blame me." People look everywhere else but at themselves. And that's the place they should look. It doesn't matter who your parents were. Nor your friends, nor your school. Everything you need is within you. When you get to *Shamayim* the question will be, Did you become yourself and everything that you could become? That's all that is asked of you. Work on yourself — become yourself!

Your Rod and Your Staff, They Shall Comfort Me*
by Y. BEN DAVID

Rav Shach, *shlita*, frequently quoted the explanation offered by Rav Isser Zalman Meltzer, *zt"l*, on the words in *Tehillim*, "Even though I walk in the valley of the shadow of death, I will fear no evil, for You are with me. Your rod and Your staff, they shall comfort me," as follows:

To what can this be compared? To a father who was traveling with his son through a thick forest. Before entering, the father cautioned his son strictly not to wander off for even a moment, lest he endanger his life.

At first the child heeded his father's warning and held on tightly to his father's hand. But after a while, something caught his attention. He let go and went off to explore. Not realizing that his son was absent, the father continued on. Soon the son tired and wished to return to his father, but could not find him. The more he floundered about in the thicket, the more confused he became and the further he strayed from his father. Night fell and darkness swallowed everything up. The night creatures ventured out of their lairs: owls, wolves and bears, each emitting its peculiar and frightening sounds. The boy was terrified.

Suddenly, the boy felt a sharp pain on his cheek. It was a stinging slap. Before screaming his protest, he looked up and saw his father. "Oh, Father! Father!" he cried, forgetting his pain. "How happy I am to have found you!" Indeed, he welcomed his father's punishment, for it meant that his father had been looking for him and still cared.

Similarly, a Jew in distress is not afraid of evil, for he realizes that this is the chastising rod of Hashem, the Father Who is concerned for his welfare. The very punishing rod is his consolation, that Hashem still cares.

* Reprinted with permission from *Yated Ne'eman*, March 27, 1992.

When the *Divrei Chayim* returned from Sanz after the funeral of his beloved son, Arye Leibush'l, who passed away at the age of seven, he said:

"A man is walking innocently along when he suddenly feels a forceful blow on his back. Turning around to identify his attacker, he is surprised to see his best friend thumping him affectionately upon the back. Even if he first meant to scold the striker, he now accepts the blows with a smile and is veritably happy at his friend's exuberant show of affection. I, too, have received a stunning blow. But when I looked around to see who struck it, I said to myself: 'Why, it is none other than Hashem Himself, Whom I love so much! There is no question about my accepting it with love and joy.' "

"I Paid No Attention to Worldly Problems"

Rav Moshe Mordechai Schlesinger told the following anecdote in his eulogy on Rav Yisrael Ya'akov Kanievsky, the Steipler *Gaon, zt"l*:

"My master (the Steipler) once told a person who was in need of fortification, encouragement, and comfort not to concern himself overly with problems that have to do with worldly matters. 'I myself,' he said, 'would have undoubtedly remained an ignoramus, had I taken to heart those matters that preoccupy a person's attention. Do you know what troubles I suffered? For years, I lived in abject poverty. We had no more than black bread to eat on Shabbos, to say nothing of proper clothing to wear. In addition, I had considerable anguish in raising my children. And so, if you think you have troubles, let me tell you that my *tza'ar giddul banim* (difficulty in raising children) alone was great enough to be parceled out to a hundred people!' (He went into some details and then continued:)

" 'Hashem provided me with a son-in-law who was taken from us, leaving eight destitute orphans behind and a baggage of medical problems.... But Hashem was kind to me, perhaps because I studied *Musar*, perhaps in the merit of the Torah I learned in my youth...

" 'I regarded all my problems in the light of the Seforno's explanation on the verse "Even though I walk in the valley of the shadow of death, I will fear no evil, for You are with me. Your rod and Your staff, they shall comfort me," as follows: David *Ha-Melech* said: "I know that it is You Who smites me. Therefore, Your rod — with which You struck me in the past — and Your staff — upon which I leaned for support — strengthen me with the knowledge that no matter how debilitating the blow, it is always followed by the supporting staff. This is my comfort and reassurance in the face of each succeeding adversity. It is the source of my faith and hope that this time, too, Your staff will be waiting to console and bolster me."

" 'There is no other resort but to ignore worldly afflictions,' he concluded, comforting the person before him. The latter left him, a new man."

Everything is for the Good

Adapted from **Shomer Emunim**
by Rebbe Aharon Rotte, *zt"l*
(*Derush Ha-Bitachon*, chaps. 7-9)

INTRODUCTION

In order to understand the concepts mentioned in *Shomer Emunim*, we must first make ourselves acquainted with two *gemaros*:

BERACHOS 60b

We learned in the name of R. Akiva, "A person should always be in the habit of saying, 'Everything that the Merciful One does is for the good.' " For instance, when R. Akiva was traveling on the road, he came to a certain town and decided to spend the night there. When no one would take him in, he said to himself, "Everything that the Merciful One does is for the good." He went and slept in the forest. He had with him a rooster, a donkey, and a candle. The wind came and blew out the candle, a wildcat came and ate the rooster, and a lion came and ate the donkey. He said, "Everything that the Merciful One does is for the good." That night soldiers came and captured the whole town. He said to them (his *talmidim*), "Didn't I tell you, everything that *Ha-Kadosh Baruch Hu* does is for the good?" (If the candle had been lit, the soldiers would have seen me, and if the donkey had brayed or the rooster crowed, the soldiers would have come and captured me — Rashi.)

TA'ANIS 21a

Why was Nachum Ish Gamzu called by this name? Because on everything that happened to him, he said, "*Gam zo l'tovah*" (גם זו לטובה), "This too is for the good" (therefore he was called Nachum, the man of "This too"). Once, the Jews wanted to send a present to the Caesar. They asked themselves who should go to deliver it for them. They decided to send Nachum Ish

Gamzu, because he was used to miracles. They sent him with a chest full of precious jewels and pearls. As he was traveling, he stayed at a certain inn. That night the innkeepers got up, emptied out the chest, and filled it up with dirt. The next day, when he saw this, he said, "This too is for the good." When he arrived at the palace of the Caesar, he opened the chest. Seeing that it was filled with dirt, the Caesar wanted to kill all the Jews. He said, "The Jews are making fun of me." Nachum said, "This too is for the good." Eliyahu *Ha-Navi* came disguised as one of the courtiers. He said to the Caesar, "Perhaps this is the dirt that Avraham their father used. When he threw it, the dirt turned into swords and the straw turned into arrows." There was one country that the Caesar was unable to conquer. He went and tried out the dirt there and it enabled him to conquer them. He came back to the palace and went into his treasure-house and filled the chest with precious jewels and pearls and sent Nachum back home with great honor. On the way back he again stayed over in that inn. They asked him, "What happened to you, that they honored you so much?" He answered them, "What I took from here I brought to them." Consequently, the innkeepers tore down their whole inn and brought the dirt to the Caesar. They said, "That dirt that Nachum brought you was from us." They tried it out and it didn't work, so they executed the innkeeper.❖

❖ This *gemara* taken literally is quite extraordinary. Moreover, it is difficult to understand how Nachum was permitted to rely on a miracle and bring the dirt to the Caesar, thus putting the entire Jewish nation in jeopardy. The Maharal (*Nesivos Olam, Nesiv Ha-Bitachon, perek* 1) explains it in simpler terms. The purpose of the story was to show Nachum Ish Gamzu's towering level of *bitachon* in God. He was so steeped in *bitachon* that nothing appeared bad to him; rather, everything that happened was

You should know [writes the *Shomer Emunim*] that it is cited in the name of the Ba'al Shem Tov that *bitachon* has two levels, that of "This too is for the good," and that of "Everything that the Merciful One does is for the good." And there is a fundamental difference between them. "Everything that the Merciful One does is for the good" implies that evil cannot

---

good. When they stole the gift that had been prepared for the Caesar, he said that this too was good, and left the dirt alone, with the intention of showing the Caesar that they had stolen the Jews' gift. Therefore, when he came, he made believe that he still had the jewels. He then proceeded to open the chest as if he didn't know anything, and intended to tell them there was a robbery.

But the Caesar became furious, in total disbelief that anyone had stolen the present. That was when one of his counselors (Eliyahu in disguise) advised the Caesar that perhaps this was a good sign. The ancient nations were very well-versed in sorcery and especially regarding the art of war. He said that it wasn't likely that a nation under the rule of the Caesar would do such a thing as ridicule him by sending him a present of dirt. It was more likely that this was some sort of witchcraft which could be used as weapons.

They listened to his advice and took the dirt to melt it down to make iron for their swords and arrows, and it was very successful. From that moment on the tide of victory turned in their favor, and the Caesar was able to conquer his enemies wherever he turned. Really it was the Holy One, blessed be He, performing miracles for those who trust in Him. God made it seem as if Nachum Ish Gamzu was the source of all the miracles, for from the moment he appeared on the scene, the Caesar saw only victory. Certainly the Jews must have sent him specifically for this purpose, that he should bring his special good fortune with him into the Caesar's court. Therefore, he was sent home with great honor and esteem.

come from God, but only love and goodness. However, as the good travels down to reach our lowly world, many impure forces come with their accusations caused by our many sins, and the good is reversed. However, they are really waiting in Heaven to see the faith of this person. If he remains strong in *bitachon* and *emunah* that God would not send him anything bad, then definitely this evil will bring forth good and it eventually will turn around. It's just that the good hasn't been demonstrated yet. Through *emunah* and *bitachon,* the strict judgment is sweetened and turned to mercy, and the person merits having it turned into good. Then the good and the salvation are revealed to him. However, if he doesn't accept it....

The category of "This too is for the good" is a deeper one. It is when one believes with such great faith that all his suffering is in reality a wonderful benefit and was never bad at all.

These are very deep concepts, but perhaps we can, with God's help, explain them a bit. Let us say, for example, that suddenly a person loses money or experiences suffering. On the first level, he should believe with perfect faith that nothing bad can come from God, even though he is suffering right now. Out of this suffering will definitely come forth good for him. Sometimes a certain good is decreed upon the person, either physical or spiritual. But his actions do not merit his receiving the good yet. Then he is sent suffering. This is preparation for him to receive the good from God. This is the case only if he doesn't destroy everything with his thoughts, and if he doesn't complain like a fool. Then definitely, without a doubt, good will come out of this, with God's help.

The second level is slightly different. For this a person has to be completely engrossed in faith in *Hashgachah Pratis*. He has to know and believe that the essence of this existence is not physical, but spiritual. At each step that the person takes there is some purpose, something in Creation to rectify. Sometimes this occurs through a mitzvah, sometimes through Torah, sometimes through *tefillah*. And sometimes the precious time has come to lift up a holy spark which has sunk into spiritual desolation. Or perhaps one's personal faults have caused him to descend there, and it is impossible to lift himself up without suffering. If the person accepts all this with joy, then not only will these sufferings be a stepping stone for his good, but rather, these sufferings themselves will become a bright and magnificent light for him and perhaps the entire world.

We can illustrate this concept with a *mashal*. Imagine a person with a toothache, who goes to the dentist to relieve the pain. There are two possibilities. The dentist can work to correct a problem within the tooth itself, i.e., a cavity or an infection. Even though this causes pain, the person is willing to accept it because this is the way to heal the problem and enable him to have a strong and healthy tooth. This involves benefit to the object itself. It can also be that the infected tooth was affecting the rest of his teeth, in which case it would be necessary to remove it in order that the rest of his teeth not become ruined. Then the suffering incurred by the removal of this tooth is not for the sake of the tooth itself, but rather for the benefit of the other teeth. Here too it is difficult for him to bear the pain of the dentist's treatment, but he accepts it for the eventual good that will come from it.

So, too, if a person sins against God, then one sin leads to another and, God forbid, this eventually can lead to other terrible and greater transgressions. The punishment for this can be terrible and dreadful, God forbid. Then God, in His great mercy, sends the person some suffering to cleanse him of his impurity in order that the person realize that he has done something wrong, and return to the right path. If he returns and accepts the Divine Judgment with love, then he is forgiven and through this enters into the boundaries of holiness. Sometimes, the Creator appraises the impurity and must cause the person suffering for an extended period. He cries out but is not answered immediately. The Holy One, blessed be He, is sending him this relatively small amount of torment in order to save him from even greater and more dreadful suffering. The purpose of these torments is to save him from other, greater suffering in this world or the next. This is the level of "Everything that the Merciful One does is for the good." One should believe that through this suffering will come good.

However, sometimes the torment is for a purpose and benefit in itself. Perhaps it is to cleanse his soul from all blemish in order that it be totally pure before God and able to be imbued with the light of Torah and service to God. This level cannot be acquired without suffering to purify the person from his attachment to the physical.* In such a case, the suffering has a purpose in and of itself, and it is not coming for the benefit of something else.** This second category is the level of "This too is for the good," where the suffering is not to protect him from imminent punishment, but to purify him and illuminate his soul. Here not only will good eventually come out of his suffering, but the suffering itself is good. For example, in the incident of R. Akiva, not only was he rescued from his predicament by the seeming misfortunes that befell him, but perhaps his suffering in some way accomplished a definite function in his goal in this world. It raised him up to a level he could not have attained without it.

This is the meaning of "*This too* is for the good." Not only will good come from this, but "*this too*" is in itself good.

* See Epilogue: Three Wonderful Gifts.

** These are the "torments of love" mentioned in *Berachos* 5a, and one has the option to relieve himself of these torments if they are disturbing his service to God, as is mentioned in the Gemara.

EPILOGUE

TO APPROACH SUFFERING WITH AWE

The Greeks had a very sophisticated society. Greek culture abounded with objects of art, which were intended solely to bring pleasure into the lives of the beholders. And yet we also find the art form called the Greek tragedies. These were plays whose themes centered on suffering. It seems strange that a culture revolving around beauty and joy should find a need to express tragedy.

The answer is probably relatively simple. Everyone experiences some sort of suffering during his lifetime, and we are all searching for some means to cope with it, some insight into the question "Why me?" Love of beauty was the hallmark of Greek culture. So their means of expression, their means of "working out the problem," was to develop an art form that would in some way give them a means of coping. By "speaking out" the problem and putting it in front of them, by seeing plays whose theme was "I am not alone," they felt they were coming to grips with the overriding issue.

True, there is some validity in this. The Gemara mentions the virtue of speaking out what is on one's heart: דאגה בלב איש ישחנה, "If there is worry on one's heart, speak it out" (*Yoma* 75a). But ultimately, this is a temporary and shallow way out of the problem. It doesn't touch the basic issues and give us an answer to the nagging problem of "Why?!"

Greek culture was diametrically opposed to the Torah. This conflict took concrete form during the time commemorated by Chanukah, when the Jews fought against the Hellenistic influences which were so prevalent then. The war against the Greeks was a reflection of a much deeper conflict between the two peoples. The world-renowned *Gaon Morenu Maran Ha-Rav* Chaim Pinchas Scheinberg, *shlita,* on several occasions during his *Musar* talks, has elaborated on this difference. He asked, What was the meaning behind the battle of the Jews against the Greeks? What lesson are we to gain from the holiday of Chanukah?

If we search for the origins of Greek society, we discover that the Greeks' love for beauty was inherited from their forefather Yefes (one of the three sons of No'ach): יפת אלקים ליפת, "God will give beauty (*yaft*) to Yefes" (*Bereshis* 9:27). Here we discover that the descendants of Yefes, the Greeks, were imbued with an intrinsic love of the beautiful, which was the major impulse behind their culture. However, this *berachah* raises a difficult question. How can one say that the driving force behind Greek culture was beauty, when we find that the Greeks were exemplary in the realm of thought? Greece boasted of great learning. In world history, Greek philosophy is still reputed to be the paradigm of wisdom.

The answer is that the wisdom of the Greeks emanated from their *berachah,* from their appreciation of beauty. Thus even their knowledge was an expression of beauty — beauty of thought. However, just as beauty is a superficial quality, an external cover which can mask an empty core, so too was Greek philosophy. There was a basic lack of an intrinsic element, of a true understanding of the hidden workings of the universe: knowledge of the Divine.

Yefes' brother Shem was the ancestor of our forefathers Avraham, Yitzchak, and Ya'akov. When No'ach gave Yefes the above *berachah,* he gave a different *berachah* to Shem: וישכון באהלי שם, "And the *Shechinah* will dwell in the tents of Shem." Yefes was blessed with love of beauty; the Divine Presence rests with Shem. As the descendants of Shem, we were blessed with a unique vantage point. We were given the holy Torah, the blueprint of the world. With the Torah we have the "key" to understanding the spiritual "soul" of the material world. Our mission is to delve into the Torah, and not be satisfied with a superficial understanding of the universe. We should, we must, try to understand events in their true light and not take things at face value.

LIFE IS A MISSION

וישכון באהלי שם, "And the *Shechinah* will dwell in the tents of Shem." Where are these tents of Shem? ועשו לי מקדש ושכנתי בתוכם, "Make for Me a *Mikdash*, a Holy Place, and I will dwell within them" (*Shemos* 25:8). This, on first reading, is a very difficult verse. One would think it should have read, ושכנתי בתוכו "and I will dwell within *it*" — that God is telling us to make a Holy Place so that He can dwell there. *Chazal* say that the *pasuk* is hinting at a very deep concept: Make for Him a Holy Place, and He will dwell within *them*, within each and every one of us.* Our job on this lowly earth is to accomplish a holy mission by sanctifying ourselves to the *highest level possible* while still living our physical existence.

Our whole existence must be raised up above the mundane. Our task is to view our lives not as simple means of attaining as much pleasure as possible while avoiding pain to our utmost ("Eat, drink, and be merry for tomorrow we die"). Rather, we should see our lives as missions, a form of worship, with very high standards and very important goals. Anything which interferes with this job can only be detrimental.

Our mission is to study the Torah, and thereby raise ourselves to a level in which we attach ourselves to the Divine. Therefore, our way of "coping" cannot be the way of the rest of the world. Just to look at actors in a play suffering and say, "So I'm not alone" is not enough. Just as there is a purpose in

* Rav Chayim of Volozhin, *Nefesh Ha-Chayim, sha'ar* 1, chap. 4.

our living, so too there is a purpose in our suffering.

TO UNDERSTAND AND TO ACCEPT

The Gemara (*Berachos* 7a) relates that one of the three requests Moshe *Rabbenu* made of God was to understand the suffering of the righteous and the prosperity of the wicked. There is a debate in the Gemara over whether or not he was answered, whether he finally came to a real understanding. This hints to us that there are two ways to approach the problem: to understand it, or to accept it. Both approaches are necessary. Yes, we must try to understand it. With the tools the Torah has given us to understand the universe, our job is to try to understand as much as we can. *Iyov* was written specifically for this purpose, to address this problem. By attempting to understand somewhat how we fit into the Divine plan, we develop an acute sense of constant *Hashgachah Pratis*. Yet, it is with trepidation that we tread on this holy ground. Relying on our limited intellect may eventually lead us astray when in the final analysis our questions remain unanswered. Ultimately, deep within ourselves we must truly believe, with *emunah shelemah*, that as much as we understand, we really don't understand. Ultimately, our answer to the trials of life must be Avraham's answer to the Satan when he came to stop him from the *Akedah*: "I simply accept it."

TO UNDERSTAND

Chazal have used their great minds and spiritual awareness to delve into the concept of *nisyonos*. In the process, they have revealed to us some keen insights into the Divine plan. Understanding that everything has a definite purpose gives us the strength to use everything that happens to us as a growing experience, instead of collapsing under the burden. Our job is to develop an understanding of events that will strengthen our *emunah* and help us to see the *Hashgachah Pratis* behind the events. We can never really delve into God's vast intellect and truly understand everything. That is beyond the comprehension of one bound by the limitations of this material world. But we can, to a certain extent, peek behind the curtain and get a glimpse of some of the script. We have already seen a bit of the Torah perspective on the inner workings of the world. Here we offer a few more of *Chazal*'s observations on *nisyonos*. No one of them will answer all the problems. And we are sure that there is much more that we don't understand. What we do offer is a beginning, a direction.

MIDRASH ON *NISYONOS*

> ***"God tests a tzaddik, but His soul hates a rasha and one who loves theft" (Tehillim 11:5). R. Yonasan said, "One who makes linen out of flax, when his flax is rotten he doesn't beat it too hard because it will burst. But when his flax is fine, he beats it very hard because in that way it becomes finer and finer. So, too, Ha-Kadosh Baruch Hu does not test the wicked, because they are not able to withstand it. But He does test the tzaddikim, as it says, 'God tests a tzaddik.' "***
>
> ***R. Yochanan said, "When the potter tests his wares, he doesn't test the weak pots because even if he strikes one only once, it will break. What does he test? The strong pitchers, for even if he strikes them several times, they don't break. So, too, Ha-Kadosh Baruch Hu does not test the wicked, only the tzaddikim, as it says, 'God tests a tzaddik.' "***
>
> ***R. Elazar said, "This is like the farmer who had two cows, one strong and one weak. On which one does he put the yoke? Is it not on the one which is strong? So, too, Ha-Kadosh Baruch Hu tests only the tzaddikim, as it says, 'God tests a tzaddik' "*** [Bereshis Rabbah 32:3, 55:2].

The commentary *Etz Yosef* explains that this midrash depicts three opinions on the purpose of a *nisayon*.

TO REFINE THE PERSON. One way of looking at a *nisayon* is to compare it to flax. The linen maker's concern is purely for the sake of the linen. He wants it to come out as fine as possible. If he works it out beyond its limits, it will disintegrate, and thus he doesn't even bother to beat the poor-quality flax. Fine flax, however, is made finer specifically by being beaten. This breaks down the fibers and makes it soft and delicate. This is the analogy of a *nisayon*, the purpose of which is to refine a person who thereby atones for his sins, or to make him more aware of the spiritual. When a person experiences *nisyonos*, they purify him and train and adapt him for his special role in serving God. A *nisayon*, according to R. Yonasan, is for the benefit of the person.

TO BRING OUT HIDDEN QUALITIES. R. Yochanan takes a different approach. A *nisayon* is not for the benefit of the person himself, but is to show others the special qualities of the *tzaddik*. Therefore, he brings the analogy of the potter. When the potter wants to demonstrate the quality of his wares to potential customers, he takes a stick and strikes them. The resulting ring shows off their quality. (This is like slamming the door of a used car and listening to the thud: if it's a solid sound, this is a sign that the car is solid.) However, the owner knows the true quality of his merchandise, and if it is below standard, he won't strike it. He knows that it will not stand up to the beating and will only break, so there is no purpose in it. So, too, God tests the *tzaddikim*, to reveal to the world their hidden qualities, and to show the world why He gives them special favor (Alshich).

TO PROTECT THE WORLD. Lastly, R. Elazar's opinion is that a *nisayon* is really intended for the benefit of the world. Just as the farmer puts the yoke only on the cow who can bear the burden, so too does God put the burden of the transgressions of the world on the *tzaddik*. This serves to protect the world.

Even though we cannot truly understand how this works, the great Jewish philosopher and Kabbalist Rav Moshe Chayim Luzzatto, *zt"l*, in his work *Derech Hashem*,* has given us some insight:

"All men were originally bound to each other, as our Sages teach us, 'All Yisrael are responsible for one another.' As a result of this, each individual is bound to everyone else, and no man is counted separately....

"As a result of this principle, suffering and pain may be imposed on a *tzaddik* as an atonement for his entire generation. The *tzaddik* must then accept this suffering with love, in order to benefit his generation, just as he accepts the suffering imposed upon him for his own sake. In doing so, he benefits his generation by atoning for it, and at the same time is himself elevated to a very great degree. For a *tzaddik* such as this is made into one of the leaders in the community of the Next World (*Olam Ha-Ba*), as discussed earlier.

"All this refers to a case in which a *tzaddik* is stricken because his generation were fitting for a terrible punishment and were about to be annihilated, and would be destroyed if not for his suffering. Through his suffering he atones for them and greatly benefits them in this world and in the World to Come.

"Within this same category, however, there is a class that is even higher than this. There is the suffering that comes to a *tzaddik* who is even greater and more highly perfected than the ones discussed above. This suffering comes to provide the help necessary to bring about the chain of events leading to Mankind's ultimate perfection" (*Derech Hashem* 2:3:8). [See also *Shomer Emunim, ma'amar Hashgachah Pratis, perek* 8; *Derush Ha-Bitachon, perek* 7; and see also *Reshis Chochmah, sha'ar Ha-Teshuvah,* end of *perek* 3.

Nisyonos have a purpose. They are God's tools to accomplish some hidden goal, whether it be the betterment of the individual, or the betterment of Mankind and the world. Al-

* *The Way of God/Derech Hashem* (Jersualem and New York: Feldheim Publishers, 1977).

ways, we must believe that God's *Hashgachah* is ever present and that He is constantly looking out for our welfare.

GOD IS BUSY PREPARING HISTORY

Sometimes what appears to be the worst possible tragedy is actually just the small part of what is ultimately a most profound event. When Yosef, king of Mitzrayim, was testing his brothers, he took Shimon as a hostage until the brothers would bring Binyamin back, to prove they weren't spies. When the brothers returned to their father, Ya'akov, with the bad news, Ya'akov was struck by the severity of the blow. Yosef was gone, killed by wild animals...now Shimon was a prisoner in Mitzrayim, and his sons want to take his youngest son, Binyamin, away from him to an unknown fate. Binyamin, the only remaining son he had from his late wife Rachel! He cried out to his sons in his agony, "Why have you caused this evil to me!?" (*Bereshis* 43:6). On the surface, it seems that Ya'akov was justified in his anguish. The worst possible sequence of events was unfolding before his eyes. He had worked so hard to raise his twelve children to be the foundation of a great nation, as he had been promised by none other than the Almighty Himself. This had been his life's mission: to build *Klal Yisrael*. And now everything was collapsing around him. His sons had added to his misery by revealing to this king of Mitzrayim that there was another, younger brother living in Kena'an. This slip had unleashed the recent chain of events and brought only torment to their father. "Why have you caused this evil to me?" — that is the superficial appearance. But what was the real story, the truth behind the scenes? The Midrash comments:

> **למה הרעותם לי, *"Why have you caused this evil to me!?" R. Levi said, in the name of R. Chama bar Chanina: Ya'akov Avinu never said an idle word (except for here). Ha-Kadosh Baruch Hu answered***

> ***him, "I am busy making his son king of Mitzrayim and he asks, 'Why have you caused this evil to me?' " This is what he (Ya'akov) said: "My way has been concealed by God" (Yeshayahu 40:27). [Bereshis Rabbah 91:13]***

The *Etz Yosef* explains that Ya'akov had never attributed anything to mere accident. Here, as well, he should not have blamed the unfortunate turn of events on his sons but rather on *Hashgachah Pratis*. Ya'akov seemed to be assuming that God had removed His *Hashgachah Pratis* from him.

This is a rather harsh criticism of Ya'akov *Avinu*. Knowing the extremely high esteem in which the Torah held our fore-fathers, it is difficult for us to pass over this without trying to lessen the criticism against Ya'akov. The *Avos* were on such a high level of spiritual perfection that they were held account-able for even the slightest mistake or slip. Everything they did was held up to the microscope of Divine criticism. However, God forbid that Ya'akov forgot *Hashgachah Pratis* for even one minute! Ya'akov surely understood the concept of *Hashgachah Pratis* and *hester Panim* better than we. Most certainly he knew the basic principle expressed by *Chazal* (*Chullin* 7b) that "a person doesn't bruise his finger down in this world unless it has been decreed upon him from Above." There is a direct Divine supervision over everything that happens to us. (See also *Chovos Ha-Levovos*, *Sha'ar Ha-Bitachon*, chap. 3.)

Secondly, the term used by the Midrash, "an idle word," is very mild. If there really were a criticism regarding Ya'akov *Avinu*'s *bitachon*, why would it be referred to as his "idle words"?

There are several ways we can answer this. The *Etz Yosef*, as mentioned above, explains that since Ya'akov had never related anything to mere accident, here, too, he should not have done so. Thus we can explain that Ya'akov's criticism of his sons wrongly implied that he thought God had removed His *Hashgachah Pratis* from him. But a person of such caliber should not say the slightest thing which could be misconstrued as overlooking *Hashgachah Pratis* (heard from *Maran Ha-Mashgiach Ha-Gaon Ha-Rav*, Rav Zeidel Epstein, *shlita*).

Or perhaps, in the heat of the torment of all the tragedies unfolding before him, he may actually have lost himself and out of grief blamed the unfortunate turn of events on his sons. Many times the stress of a situation causes a person to say things he really doesn't mean. "A person cannot be held responsible for what he says when under duress" (*Bava Basra* 16b). Ya'akov, however, was on such a high spiritual level that he should have had the awareness of God's goodness before him at all times, even during such an ordeal. On his level, he should not have lost his sight and interpreted what was happening to him as *"hester Panim."* For this God rebuked him — for not having peered through the curtain and seen the light within the darkness (*Morenu Ha-Gaon Ha-Rav* Chaim Dov Altusky, *shlita*).

Morenu Maran Ha-Rav Ha-Gaon Chaim Pinchas Scheinberg, *shlita* (in his book *Derech Emunah u'Bitachon*), explained it like this: We know that there are two levels of God's supervision of this world. There is הארת פנים, *he'aras Panim*, when God, so to speak, "shines His face" upon us and deals with us in a very direct manner, openly causing everything that happens to us. But there is another way, called הסתר פנים, *hester Panim*, when God "hides His face" from us, so to speak, and it seems as if He is not looking. Everything then seems to run according to "blind nature."

In *Chovos Ha-Levavos* we find a very profound principle, which is the key to our understanding of *bitachon*: When a person trusts in anything outside of God, then God removes His direct supervision from him and leaves him in the hands of whatever it was that he was trusting.

Mori v'Rabi Rav Scheinberg, *shlita*, wrote that according to this, it is possible that a person can be worthy of having such direct, enlightened supervision from Heaven that he should have received miraculous, supernatural intervention, and yet he is treated from within the realm of nature, from a stand of *hester Panim*. And even when finally he is granted the good that he merits, it is not brought to him directly and clearly, but rather obliquely, in a roundabout manner.

The reason for all this is that the person was trying to act and work things out himself in a purely "natural" way, without the *bitachon* that he is really worthy of. Therefore, *Ha-Kadosh Baruch Hu* acts in kind toward him, also within the framework of nature, and not within a higher, supernatural plane, even though he may have been deserving of such.

This will help us explain the above *midrash*. Ya'akov *Avinu* said, "My way has been concealed by God." Heaven forbid that there was any blemish in his *bitachon* or his belief in God's direct intervention in the world. Certainly he knew all this, and trusted fully that everything comes about through Divine decree. However, he thought that God was acting toward him in a hidden manner, with *hester Panim*. Everything seemed unclear to him. He couldn't see clearly how God was bringing about the redemption.❖

This view was labeled by the Midrash as "idle words." "I am busy making his son king of Mitzrayim and he asks, 'Why have you caused this evil to me?' " Ya'akov meant to say that Heaven was dealing with him in a way which, to our eyes, seems bad. *Ha-Kadosh Baruch Hu* answered him that, No! It's not like you think. Really, it is all *he'aras Panim*. I'm busy

---

❖ [*Mori v'Rabi* Rav Scheinberg, *shlita,* learns from this that it is possible that a person can be worthy of a very direct connection to God's *he'aras Panim,* that he can be on a very high spiritual level and should have *bitachon*. And yet, he can get discouraged and have the mistaken idea that everything is dark, that everything is *hester Panim*.]

making your son into a king! (*Derech Emunah U'Bitachon, Parashas Vayeshev*).

All the troubles that occurred to Ya'akov *Avinu* regarding his son Yosef were really causing Yosef to become king. From these troubles blossomed the salvation. How could he ask, "Why have you caused this evil to me?" One shouldn't label difficulties as "troubles" since they are the salvation itself (Rav Yerucham Levovitz, *zt"l, Da'as Chochmah u'Musar*, vol. 1, *ma'amar* 4).

The truth is that everything that was happening was pure miracle. God used the very sale of Yosef, which was supposed to prevent him from gaining power, to make him king and fulfill his dreams. God was personally directing history in order to bring the *Ge'ulah*. Yosef was not dead, but was very much alive. He was becoming a king!

Perhaps we can understand this in another way as well. God had told Avraham that his descendants would have to suffer bondage in Mitzrayim. But this was to be a temporary ordeal. *Klal Yisrael* would need ideal circumstances in Mitzrayim to keep them together so that they would be ready when the time came to take them out. Therefore, Yosef was taken from Ya'akov, made a slave to one of the highest-ranking officers in Pharaoh's government, and afterwards made chief jailer over the political prisoners. He rubbed shoulders with aristocracy and learned the ins and outs of the whole gamut of Egyptian politics. When it came time for his family to move down to Mitzrayim, he had already been set up as second only to the king himself and he maneuvered the whole country in order to settle his family comfortably in an isolated area, Goshen, so that they would remain untouched by the corrupt Egyptian society. This maneuver was the basis for *Klal Yisrael*'s redemption. They retained their purity for 210 years and finally left Mitzrayim to receive the Torah. Here God is personally creating history, making preparations for the greatest redemption of *Klal Yisrael*, and Ya'akov says, Why did my sons say the wrong thing and cause me this anguish?!

[Our *emunah* is often strengthened when we can "understand" all the details and retrospectively see how they fit in. Therefore this explanation relates the incident in very human terms. However, this gives it elements of simplicity and superficiality. God didn't need all this to teach Yosef how to be a king. He could have given him royal abilities in one second. (See Gemara *Sotah* 36b — the angel Gavriel taught Yosef seventy languages the night before he was taken before Pharaoh.)

Moreover, we haven't fully taken care of the problem. Granted, God wanted to make Yosef king. But why did He do it in such a way as to cause Yosef the anguish of being enslaved and imprisoned? He could have brought him to Egypt and shown Pharaoh Yosef's great capabilities in a more dignified manner. Ya'akov had, seemingly, room for asking, Why has God dealt with me and Yosef in such a concealed manner?

The answer is, like all *Hashgachah Pratis*, that each incident is extremely complicated, with many accounts being dealt with all at the same time. On the one hand, God wanted to make Yosef king. On the other hand, Yosef had to be a slave in order that — instead of Yosef going to visit Ya'akov in Kena'an — Ya'akov would come down to see Yosef and dwell in Egypt (because a slave was forbidden to leave Egypt, as we see by Yosef's entreaties to Pharaoh to be granted permission to leave to bury his father). Moreover, there were certain accounts to be taken care of with Yosef regarding certain things he had done which, for a person of his high spiritual caliber, were considered transgressions. הצור תמים פעלו, "He is a rock Whose actions are pure." Everything God does is weighed out carefully: so much mercy, so much Divine Justice. In every incident, as much as we understand, ultimately we come to the point where we must rely on pure faith and say that there definitely are deeper reasons for everything that happened. The *tzaddik* who has trained himself to look for God's hand in everything, will see through the darkness and understand that "Everything the Merciful One does is good."]

WHAT LOOKS GOOD AND WHAT LOOKS BAD

The following story is cited in the *Yalkut Sippurim,* quoting from the *Sefer Ha-Ma'asiyos* of *Rabbenu* Nissim Gaon.

R. Yehoshua ben Levi asked *Ha-Kadosh Baruch Hu* to teach him His ways and explain to him why a *tzaddik* suffers and a *rasha* prospers. One day Eliyahu *Ha-Navi* appeared to him. R. Yehoshua ben Levi asked his permission to go with him and watch how he carries out God's errands; perhaps in this way he would be able to understand God's ways and His *Hashgachah* in the world. Eliyahu agreed, but on one condition: "While you travel with me, you will see many things which will upset you and you won't be able to withstand it. You have to promise right now not to bother me with questions. The moment you ask me for an explanation of why I'm doing all this, we will have to part company." R. Yehoshua ben Levi agreed to the condition and the two of them set out on their journey.

Toward evening they arrived at an old wooden shack. There was a lone cow grazing nearby. As they approached the shack, the owner, an old man, and his wife came out and begged them to spend the night with them. They agreed, and the old couple tried to do their utmost to make them comfortable, but the poverty that prevailed in their house was considerable. The next day, before they left the house, Eliyahu got up to say his prayers. To R. Yehoshua ben Levi's tremendous surprise, he overheard Eliyahu pray that God should kill the couple's lone cow! They had not gone far on their journey that morning when they heard the old lady wail, "Oy! Our only cow! Oy! What's going to be with us?"

Toward evening they arrived at a beautiful mansion. They knocked on the door but nobody opened it for them. Eliyahu said, "Perhaps they didn't hear us. Let's go in." They entered and saw the *ashir* (wealthy man) and his wife sitting at a table set with expensive dishes and all sorts of delicious foods served in front of them. All around them stood servants and maids to wait on them. When the *ashir* saw them, he did not greet them, nor did he ask them to join him in his meal. In anger he turned away from them and snapped at his wife, "Who let these nuisances in? We have to make sure that the front door is locked so that creatures like these aren't able to bother us."

The *ashir*, not usually known for his generosity, was especially angry that day, since one of the walls of his house was damaged and about to collapse. He had called in some builders to fix it but they had never come. When the guests asked his permission to spend the night in his house, he agreed very reluctantly, and gave them permission to sleep only on the stone bench in the back yard. He did not give them anything to eat or drink. The next morning R. Yehoshua pressed Eliyahu to leave the house. Eliyahu agreed, but suggested that they pray first. Again, R. Yehoshua overheard a strange *tefillah* coming from Eliyahu's lips: that God should perform a miracle and the broken wall in the *ashir*'s house be fixed immediately. And within a minute, the leaning wall stood up and returned to its original condition. Once again R. Yehoshua restrained himself and didn't ask anything.

They once more walked the whole day. That evening as dusk came, they arrived in a big city. "Let's go to the shul," said Eliyahu. "Perhaps one of the people there will invite us to stay with him." The two travelers found the shul, a beautiful edifice, and entered. It was obvious from the luxury that the people of this city were exceedingly wealthy. Each one sat in his own chair, according to his position, and was quite strict that no stranger should have the *chutzpah* to sit in his place. The two guests were pushed into a corner of the shul, and there they waited until after *Ma'ariv*. Finally one of the members of the shul noticed them and said to his friend, "Look. There are paupers here again. Who's going to take care of them this time?" His friend replied, "There's no need to invite them home. It's enough to bring a little bread, salt, and water to shul." The other people praying there paid no attention to the poor guests. No one invited them home; no one bothered to notice them. They contented themselves with giving the *shamash* a few pennies to buy them some bread.

Morning came. After sleeping in shul and davening *Shacharis*, the two travelers departed from the city. As they were leaving, Eliyahu gave the people a *berachah*: "May it be His Will that you should all be leaders and important people." This incensed R. Yehoshua and he was about to ask Eliyahu for an explanation, but when he remembered the agreement which prohibited him from asking such questions, he held himself back. At the end of the day, as the sun was setting, they arrived at a different city. The people of this city spotted them and with great *simchah* and honor brought them into a large and comfortable home. They brought out the best food and drink and sat with them to enjoy the guests that had chanced to pass their way. In the morning, as they were departing, Eliyahu prayed and gave them the following *berachah*: "May it be His Will that the Holy One grant you only one leader."

R. Yehoshua ben Levi could no longer restrain himself at Eliyahu's seemingly outrageous behavior. When they had left the city, he stopped and turned to Eliyahu. "I cannot watch these strange actions of yours any longer," he said. "For the good people you pray that it should be bad for them, and for the bad you pray for the opposite, that it should be good. What is going on?"

Eliyahu *Ha-Navi* answered, "Since you have broken our agreement, I will have to leave you. But before I leave, I will explain what I did. I knew that there was a decree on the wife of the poor old man who had invited us in, and that she was to die the next day. Therefore I prayed to God that she remain alive and that their cow die in her place. True, they will suffer terribly when their only cow dies, but think for a minute: would not the old man gladly give everything he owned in order to save his wife? Not only that, but his wonderful and diligent wife will bring him much wealth and soon they will be blessed to live comfortably and affluently and then they won't even miss the cow.

"The *ashir* didn't know that underneath his broken wall was hidden a treasure of gold. If he had rebuilt the wall himself, then he would have found the treasure. But now that the wall miraculously rebuilt itself, he will never find it. But soon the wall will fall down again, never to be rebuilt, because the *ashir* will be busy with so many worries that he won't be able to even think about fixing his house.

"And as to the arrogant people for whom I prayed that they all become leaders — this will guarantee that they will constantly quarrel, because no one will want to give in to his friend and each one will want to be the head of the city. Therefore, there will never be any peace among them and they will never be blessed in anything they do. As for the people of the city who received us so wonderfully, to them I gave a *berachah* that they should have only one head: they will all agree to choose the best man among them for that job and thus they will live peacefully under him.

"And now remember this well. The ways of God are hidden. Not everything that looks like good is really good, and not everything that looks bad is really bad."

THREE WONDERFUL GIFTS

Ha-Kadosh Baruch Hu gave three wonderful gifts to Yisrael, but each of them is acquired only through suffering: Torah, Eretz Yisrael, and Olam Ha-Ba [*Berachos* 5a].

Morenu Ha-Gaon Ha-Rav Avraham Ya'akov (Zeidel) Epstein, *shlita* (*Mashgiach ruchani* of Yeshiva Torah Ore), in his book *Me-Imrei Shlomo*, vol. 1, says that this statement of *Chazal* is very perplexing. For we know that when one gives a gift, he gives benevolently, with a deep desire to benefit the recipient.

How is it possible then that God, the source of goodness, should give three wonderful gifts and yet force the receiver to suffer?!

The Maharal (in the Introduction to *Derush al Ha-Torah v'Ha-Mitzvos*) treats the topic thoroughly: Chazal have taught us here the deep meaning of Eretz Yisrael for the people of Israel. Eretz Yisrael is not simply the ideal that is commonly pictured, of everyone sitting under his grapevine or fig tree, in a land flowing with milk and honey, where one can enjoy all the possible pleasures of the world; a land where there is no toil or burden of making a living; a land where there is no subservience to any other government or foreign nation. This is not the real essence of Eretz Yisrael for *Klal Yisrael*.

Everybody understands that *Olam Ha-Ba* is a spiritual situation completely divorced and separate from all physical pleasures and notions. The Gemara in *Berachos* 17a states: "In *Olam Ha-Ba* there is no eating or drinking, but the *tzaddikim* sit with their crowns on their heads enjoying the radiance of the *Shechinah*." The Torah, also, is something holy and pure, the opposite of physical desires and lusts. The deep desire of the Jew, especially a *ben Torah*, is to cling to the "Giver of the Torah," to make every effort to enter into the realm of the *Shechinah* and enjoy the great radiance. As the *Zohar* says (*Vayikra*, p. 3), "There are three levels which unite one with the other: *Ha-Kadosh Baruch Hu*, Torah, and Yisrael."

So, too, the very essence of Eretz Yisrael is a special spiritual one, specifically for *Klal Yisrael*. It is a place of gaining attachment to the *Shechinah*.

Therefore, these three wonderful gifts are impossible to attain without first purifying oneself and completely abandoning the physical as much as is possible. If there remains some residue of attachment to the material, some sort of connection to this world, this is a contradiction to acquiring *Olam Ha-Ba*. The way to attain *Olam Ha-Ba* is only through suffering. This is what breaks and annuls the pleasures of this world. Suffering is something in opposition to the pleasures of the world, which cleanses one from the material. So, too, Torah perceptions are acquired specifically through suffering, which brings about separation from this world and annulment of one's attachment to desires and lusts.*

Chazal revealed to us that it is very possible to make a mistake and think that Eretz Yisrael is only a physical attainment: our figs and grapes, our fruit, our Land. Do not make this mistake — Eretz Yisrael provides one of the greatest connections to *Hashem Yisbarach*. It requires a complete separation from the material. Lack of cleansing oneself from the material interferes with attainment of the advantages of the Land. Therefore, it was given, and can be acquired only through suffering, and the abandonment and cleansing of the material.

Therefore, *Chazal* said (*Pesachim* 113a) that among those who inherit *Olam Ha-Ba* is one who lives in Eretz Yisrael. One who lives in the Holy Land with no interference or disturbance, meriting to connect himself to the significance and very essence of Eretz Yisrael, becomes automatically united and attached to *Ha-Kadosh Baruch Hu* and *Olam Ha-Ba*. Therefore, our forefathers, whose purity from the material was the epitome of perfection, so desired Eretz Yisrael, the same way that one who is pure and free of the material desires Torah and *Olam Ha-Ba*.

How mistaken are the individuals who desire Eretz Yisrael merely for the material benefits of the Land. This is a total contradiction to the very essence of Eretz Yisrael.

PRECIOUS SUFFERING

When R. Eliezer fell sick (with his last illness), his talmidim came to visit him. R. Eliezer said to them,

* See Gemara, *Berachos* 5-6 and Rashi.

> *"There is a fierce sun burning in the world." The* talmidim *started to cry, and R. Akiva laughed. They said to him, "Why are you laughing?" And he answered them, "And why are you crying?" They said, "Is it possible that a* sefer Torah *should be enveloped in suffering and we shouldn't cry?" So he answered them, "That's why I'm laughing. As long as I saw that my Rebbe's wine didn't become sour, and his flax didn't get ruined, and his oil didn't spoil, and his honey didn't become watery, I said to myself, Perhaps the Rebbe has already received his [reward in this] world. But now that I see the Rebbe suffering, I'm happy." R. Eliezer said to him, "Was I lacking anything from all of the Torah?" R. Akiva answered him, "Rabbenu, you taught us (Koheles 7:20), 'For there is no man on Earth who is a tzaddik and does good and does not sin' "* [Sanhedrin 101a].

R. Eliezer, one of the greatest men of his generation, also suffered. The question is, What was the cause? The great *tzaddik* searched himself through and through. With the same piercing analysis he used in learning, he searched himself for some hint of a blemish, but all he could conclude was, "Was I lacking anything from all of the Torah?" Finding himself completely pure, he came to the conclusion that "There is a fierce sun burning in the world." His pain was an atonement for the generation. This was a tragic scene, a *tzaddik* suffering not for his own sins, but for the deficiency of his era. So his *talmidim* began to cry.

But R. Akiva had a different outlook: We don't have to blame the generation. The pain is a good sign. Such a great man must have a tremendous reward waiting for him, and the best place to receive it is in *Olam Ha-Ba,* the world created specifically for that purpose (*Mesillas Yesharim,* chap. 1). But we live in a world of imperfection and there is no such thing as a perfect man. Everyone must suffer somewhat in order to prepare and purify himself for the Next World. So where was R. Eliezer's suffering? He had enjoyed life and seemingly nothing had gone wrong. That was a terrible sign. Perhaps he had forfeited his Next World, and received his reward here in this imperfect world! Therefore R. Akiva saw his teacher's suffering from a different vantage point: Suffering is good. It is a good sign. It means that one's Next World is remaining intact, and he isn't forfeiting it for a lowly substitute (*Iyun Ya'akov* and the Rif in *Ein Ya'akov*).

The Gemara (*Kiddushin* 39b) says that there is no reward in this world. How could that be? Are there not many instances in the Gemara and the Midrash in which individuals actually did receive their reward, here in this world?

The truth is that the reward in the Next World is so great that it is beyond our comprehension. "One moment of pleasure in the Next World is greater than all of the lifetimes of this world" (*Pirkei Avos* 4:22). However, if the reward is paid in this world, it is paid according to the concepts of this world, and is in relation to our short lifespan, as opposed to the eternity of the Next World. This is like a child exchanging all the gold in Fort Knox for a million marbles. In his world, the marbles are hard currency. He doesn't understand the value of gold, and he wouldn't know what to do with it. But when he grows up and gains the proper perspective, he will kick himself for having given up the real "hard currency" for children's toys.

This was R. Akiva's understanding of what was happening to his teacher. Even a *tzaddik* of the stature and holiness of R. Eliezer could be paid in the currency of this world, and that might mean simply a successful business (in the form of flax and wine). This might very well be all of his *Olam Ha-Ba*! To receive the reward of a whole lifetime of Torah and mitzvos in this world would mean forfeiting the eternal hidden treasures awaiting the *tzaddikim* in *Olam Ha-Ba* for lowly temporal pleasure (the Steipler *Gaon* in *Birkas Peretz, parashas Va-Escha-*

nan). R. Akiva saw in his teacher's suffering a sign that his future was still intact, and this was cause for joy.

"GIVE ME MORE SUFFERING!"

The famous Yerushalmi Maggid, Rav Shabsai Yudelevitz, *shlita*, tells this story (cited in *Yalkut Lekach Tov*, vol. 1, p. 142):

There was once a man who constantly suffered from various pains and agonies. He and his household were always sick; he had a difficult time making a living; and other general problems accompanied him throughout his life. One day he told his wife that he was going to the *tzaddik*, the kabbalist Rav Shalom Sharabi, *zt"l*, to ask him if he could explain why God was treating him like this, and what he had to do in order to lighten the burden.

When he arrived at the Rav's house, the Rebbetzin asked him to wait until the Rav was ready. He sat down on the couch in the waiting room and, tired from the long journey, he fell into a deep sleep and dreamed.

In his dream he saw himself in Heaven, and before him stretched a desolate road. No one was in sight all around. Complete quiet reigned in the area. Slowly he began to make his way down the road. Suddenly, from behind him, he heard a tremendous commotion. The sound grew closer and louder, until an enormous carriage passed him, filled with *malachim*, angels as pure as the snow. The carriage quickly sped ahead and disappeared beyond the horizon. Again silence fell and the man continued on his way. Soon he saw another carriage coming toward him, and behind it other carriages — each one full of white *malachim*, some of them very large and others small and thin. When the caravan of white *malachim* passed, there appeared another immense caravan of carriages, but this time they carried fierce black *malachim*. The whole scene aroused his curiosity, and he quickened his pace until he arrived at a large square, where he found all the carriages parked. The *malachim* got off the carriages and gathered in the center of the square where there stood a tremendous scale, and they proceeded to climb up onto it.

The man didn't understand what was going on until one of the *malachim* came over and explained to him: "This is where the Heavenly *Beis Din* (Court) meets, and they are presently deliberating someone's case. The *malachim* who are climbing onto the scale were created from the mitzvos and transgressions the person did during his lifetime. You see, when one does a mitzvah perfectly, a large and heavy white *malach* is created. But if the mitzvah isn't performed properly, the *malach* is defective, lacking limbs, or thin and scrawny. The same is true regarding the black *malachim*, created from one's transgressions. Those created from the *averos* done with premeditation and enjoyment appear here large and weighty, while the *malachim* created out of accidental or unintentional sins are small and thin."

Upon hearing the explanation, the man approached the carriages and saw on each one signs with the names of the mitzvos or the *averos*. On the carriage which had held the white *malachim* was written: *talmud Torah, tefillah,* honoring one's parents, *gemilas chesed, shemiras Shabbos,* etc. On the carriage which had held the black angels were signs stating the names of various sins: *bittul* (laxity in the learning of) *Torah, lashon ha-ra,* desecration of Shabbos, theft, jealousy, etc.

In the meantime the scales filled with white *malachim* on one side, and black ones on the other. As they continued to climb onto the scales, the man became curious and asked who exactly was being judged at this trial. "You!" they answered him. He turned pale, and as he watched, he saw that just about all the *malachim* had climbed on, and the scales were leaning toward the side of the black *malachim*. He realized that if this was to be the final decision, he would be judged as a *rasha*. He began to tremble.

An announcement was made, asking if there were any

more *malachim* who had not yet climbed onto the scale, and the answer was no. Again an announcement was made: perhaps this Jew had suffered during his lifetime, and if so, then his sufferings could be added to the side of merit.

Immediately a huge carriage full of *malachim* created from his sufferings arrived and they climbed onto the white side. At the same time a few black *malachim* got off the scales, because suffering cleanses one from his *averos*.

He began to feel a bit better as he saw the scales start leaning toward the white side. Now they were almost even, but as the last of the *malachim* from his suffering climbed on, the scales still leaned a bit toward the side of the *averos*. He knew that his situation was desperate. Any minute they would announce the verdict, and the scale was still leaning toward the bad! Out of desperation, he cried out, "Please, give me more suffering!"

His cry woke him up. The Rav's family, who had been frightened by the scream, rushed in and asked what had happened. The man realized that everything had been a dream, rose from the couch, and hurried to the door. The Rebbetzin called after him, "Wait! Didn't you want to speak to the Rav?"

"There's no need for that," he replied. "He has already sent me the answer."

"IF ONLY HE HAD BEAT ME MORE!"

Rav Yisroel Lubachinsky, the son-in-law of the Alter of Navardok, related a remarkable *mashal*. There was once a *poritz* (a wealthy landowner) who hired a Jew to work some of his land. He treated the Jew like a slave, and one day beat him mercilessly. A few days later the Jew met a friend of his who saw how distressed he was and asked, "What's wrong?" The Jew told his friend about the terrible beating he had suffered at the hand of the *poritz*. "Why don't you take him to court — maybe they will do something about it," his friend suggested. The Jew took his friend's advice. The judge ruled in his favor and handed down the verdict: for every blow the Jew had received, the *poritz* was to pay him a generous amount of rubles.

A few days later, the Jew again met his friend, and again he looked upset. "What's wrong now?" his friend asked him. "I thought you won the case and got a pretty reward from the *poritz*!"

"I did," the Jew answered, "and that's exactly what's bothering me. Before, I was upset about the beating he gave me. But now that I've been compensated for each blow, I'm very upset. If only he had beat me more!"

If only we knew what really awaits us in return for all the pain and suffering we endure in this world, then we wouldn't complain so much. (Quoted by Rav Chaim Pinchas Scheinberg, *shlita,* in his book *Derech Emunah u'Bitachon, parashas Vayeshev.*)

LIFE IS A BRIDGE

One of the basic things necessary for an understanding of the total picture is putting "this world" into its proper context. Rav Yechiel Michel Tucazinsky, *zt"l,* explained this quite vividly. Life on this Earth, he writes, begins with man being transported from a human womb, the womb of his mother, and ends with his restoration to the womb of the earth, the mother of all life, from which he was formed and to which he must return. This life on Earth constitutes no more than a bridge connecting two basic forms of life at either end of our life — the past and the future. Although both are the essential forms of life, they are completely separate and distinct. The past is a completely passive life, while the future depends upon the individual, and is determined by the nature of what he has gained by his own choice during his life on Earth.

This bridge through which we pass is called "Life"; the emergence from the womb, "Birth"; and the return to earth, "Death." The reason for this nomenclature is that during this transition stage, man is only aware of the substance of his present life. He is incapable of forming any conception of a spiritual life, one unassociated with breathing or any physical functions. He knows nothing of his past and, having no idea of the long future ahead, man imagines his short transition period as his entire world, with nothing behind or beyond.

During those early months when man is hunched over with his head between his legs within his mother's womb, his mouth closed and his food all prepared and ingested through his navel, were he to be mentally developed to the same degree as human beings outside the womb are, there is no doubt that he would regard his mother's womb as the only world. He would think of the period of gestation as one of long duration (as in the case of a child, for whom, with a life unburdened by cares, time passes very slowly). For him this short transition period would seem to be a "lifetime." He could not imagine a world extending beyond the expanse of the womb.

Now suppose that there were twin brothers lying together in the womb, asking each other what would happen to them once they left their mother's womb. They would not be able to form any conception whatsoever of what awaited them — of all their eyes would see and their ears hear here on Earth. Let us imagine that one of them believed in the tradition which he had received, that there was a future life beyond the womb, while the other, a "rational" being, would only accept what his own intelligence could grasp and he, accordingly, would only acknowledge the existence of what he experienced, of "this world" alone. The two would disagree and argue, very much as men do on Earth — some believing that man continues to live, others denying that man has any life other than in this world of the present. Suppose that the "believing" brother were to repeat what had been transmitted to him, that with their emergence from the womb they would enter a new and more spacious realm. He tells him of his tradition that they would eat through their mouths, see distant objects with their eyes, and hear with their ears, that their legs would straighten, that they would stand erect and traverse vast distances on a gigantic nurturing Earth, replete with oceans, rivers, etc., with all sorts of vegetative growth and mountains, while above them would stretch a sky with its starry hosts. The other, who only believed in what he could sense, would jeer at his brother's naivete in indulging in such fantasies. He would retort that only a fool would believe all of this ridiculous nonsense which makes no sense to the rational mind. The more the "believer" would elaborate on the variegated features they would encounter in this world, the more would the "rational" brother mock and ridicule him.

"What then, my enlightened brother," asks the "believer," "do you believe is in store for us when we leave the womb?"

"Simple and obvious. Once this enclosure opens and you are torn away from this world where your food and drink are provided, you will fall into an abyss from which there is no return. You are as if you had never existed at all," the "rational" brother would reply.

As they continue their argument, the womb suddenly opens. The "naive believing" brother starts slipping and falls outside. Remaining within, the other brother is shaken by the "tragedy" that has overtaken his brother, and bewails him bitterly. "Brother, where are you? How did you manage to fall to your destruction? Your folly that these contractions were birth-pangs caused your downfall. That is why you did not clutch at anything to stop yourself." As he bemoans the misfortune, his ears catch the cry of his brother, and he trembles. "Oy, this must be his last gasp as he dies...." At that very moment when inside the womb there is wailing and grief on the death of the brother, outside, at that very moment, joy and celebration fill the home of the newborn baby. The new parents are joyous and shout with joy, *"Mazel Tov, Mazel Tov,* a baby...we have a son!" (*Gesher Ha-Chayim,* beginning of vol. 3).

THE SPIRITUAL REALITY

Once we master the idea that the essential reality of the person is his spiritual dimension — his soul — and that even after he rids himself of his physical body, still his soul lives on, then we can go on to another concept: that of the possibility of another lifetime after death. Many people are really visiting this world for the second (or third) time.* With this we can come to grips with many seeming tragedies. The great kabbalist Rav Moshe Cordevero, *zt"l* (in *Shiur Komah,* sec. 54: 5, 6, cited in *Shomer Emunim, ma'amar Hashgachah Pratis, perek* 15), presented the example of a woman who miscarried. Perhaps this baby which had been formed within her had been a soul who had been judged in Heaven and had to come back again to atone for something he had done in his previous lifetime. Through his suffering in this world, he purifies himself and is able to rise up to his true place in *Olam Ha-Ba*. His parents also, for some reason, have to endure some suffering. So God puts them together to execute the Divine Justice. This is the meaning of the verse משפטי ה׳ אמת צדקו יחדיו, "The judgment of God is true, it is righteous together" (*Tehillim 19:10*).

THE DEPTH OF GOD'S WAYS

This is quite a difficult concept for us to absorb. But such is the purpose of the people of the Torah, to become aware of the spiritual realm and how it affects everything that goes on here in this world. In this world we see only the surface. We must look to our Sages for guidance in understanding the depth underneath.

* See the Vilna *Gaon's* commentary on *Mishlei* 14:1, and *Even Shelemah,* chap. 10:31. See also *Shomer Emunim, Kuntres Ha-Gilgulim*.

The Holocaust was a tremendously difficult ordeal for everybody who went through it. But besides the physical torment, it unsettled the faith of many Jews. The closest *talmid* of the Chafetz Chaim, Rav Elchonon Wasserman, *zt"l*, (who himself was later murdered by the Nazis), once discussed this. The government in Czarist Russia for many years had carried out a policy of abducting Jewish children to be raised by gentile farmers and then to serve in the Russian army for twenty-five years. It was a horrendous decree. The great Jewish leaders were confounded, and could not grasp the meaning of such an unprecedented decree. But the Chafetz Chaim understood what was hidden from others, and clearly enunciated the meaning of this infamous decree. During the period of the Judges, many Jews strayed toward the powerful enticement of idol-worship. Even in the days of the First Temple many Jews flocked to Ba'al and Ashtores. The Chafetz Chaim explained that these pitiful and errant souls had been returned to Earth once again in the form of the kidnapped children — called Cantonists — in order to be tested again. Would they remain faithful to God and His Torah even under such difficult conditions? Indeed, many withstood the test. Despite all the suffering and torture they endured for over twenty-five years, they guarded their Judaism firmly and remained loyal Jews.

"We see from this," Reb Elchonon concluded, "that someone who failed in his first lifetime is sent into this world a second time, and even a third! He is forced to endure harsh tests so that he should maintain his Judaism. It is even possible for a soul to be returned after an interval of 1,000 years. The Cantonists may have lived in the time of the First Temple. This is a very long accounting, and is impossible to comprehend. Accordingly, it is possible that the Jews of this era [during the Holocaust], who are being forced to gird themselves with heroism and undergo harsh tests of loyalty to Torah, may be reincarnated souls from many centuries ago, whose purpose in this lifetime is to endure these trials and demonstrate that they are steadfast Jews."

Rav Elchonon continued, in the name of Rav Chaim Ozer, *zt"l*: " 'The wicked grow like grass...' (*Tehillim* 92:8). With the wicked, everything grows and flourishes like grass, which grows by itself. If one wonders why this phenomenon did not occur in earlier generations, the verse then continues: 'And all the iniquitous blossom — to destroy them till eternity.' If you see the wicked flourishing, it is only because we now stand on the threshold of the final purification, just before the end, at the time of *ikvesa d'Meshicha* (the footsteps of the *Mashiach*). Souls from all previous generations have accumulated by the millions, to be put into the furnace for purification. Hence those souls have descended into a generation of a frightful, spiritual whirlpool and horrifying suffering. It is now becoming clear who is capable of withstanding this trial and remaining firmly attached to his holy roots, and who is unable to stand up to the test and mend his ways, and allows himself to be completely severed from his roots. His fate is excision, as is written, 'to destroy them till eternity' (ibid.). This is the meaning of all the strange phenomena we see in our days. We are standing at the edge of the age of purification" (Aharon Sorasky, in his book *Or Elchonon*, vol. 2, pp. 263-67, and "Reb Elchonon," pp. 396-97; see also *Kovetz Ma'amarim, ma'amar Omer Ani Ma'asai La-Melech*, sec. 3, quoted in "Reb Elchonon," p. 321).

IF ONLY WE COULD SEE

The following story, created by Rav Yom Tov Ehrlich, is based on the writings of Rav Chayim Vital, *zt"l*, who learned it from his Rabbi, the Arizal. It is taken from *Yalkut Lekach Tov*, vol. 1, p. 284.

Yosef, a young man who was married only a few years, left the shul after Shabbos services one Friday night and made his way to his mother's house to wish her a *"Gutten Shabbos."*

The house glowed with a pleasant warmth, and the candles burned brightly, as if they were proclaiming that the holy Shabbos had descended upon the world. The younger children were seated around the table, but the chair at the head of the table, where their father used to sit, was empty. He had passed away two years before, and his empty chair still disturbed the tranquillity of the house. Wistfulness mixed with pain filled everyone's heart. Their mother, Rachel, sat in her place as usual, reading a *sefer*.

"*Gut Shabbos*," Yosef greeted them.

"*Gut Shabbos*," the children replied.

"*Gut Shabbos*," said Rachel, as she attempted with all her strength to hide the tears welling up in her eyes.

"You're crying again," Yosef said. "There has to be a limit to this, Mother. Today is Shabbos and you're not allowed to make yourself suffer."

"But Yosef," his mother replied, "exactly two years ago your father left this world. How can I not cry today?"

Yosef sighed. "Today you have a good reason, Mother. But what about yesterday, and the day before? Yes, it's been two years already, and you are still constantly grieving. Think about Abba in Gan Eden — certainly he wouldn't be happy with all this! And what about the *Borei Olam*? God surely isn't pleased with this either. The *Shulchan Aruch* tells us when we should mourn deeply, when our grief should lessen, and when to stop. Acting like this is like showing that you don't agree to what Hashem wants." Yosef finished his speech. "Please forgive me, Mother, for talking to you like this."

Rachel rose, wiped the tears from her cheeks, and said, "I know you're right, Yosef. I *do* try, with all my strength, to forget — but I just can't." And again she wiped the tears away.

"Imma!" little Shoshana piped up. "We want you to always be happy!"

"So do I," answered her mother, "and I promise you that I'll really try."

Yosef wished his mother a *Gut Shabbos* again and set out for his own home. David, his younger brother, made *Kiddush* over the wine, and throughout the meal everyone felt a real Shabbos peace. Rachel even laughed a bit. The children talked about the weekly Torah reading, and Rachel smiled proudly.

Everyone went to sleep late, and Rachel felt an inner peace that she had not felt since her husband had left her. She began to think that, after all, she wasn't alone in her plight; she knew other young widows, and they were happy. She would try to make peace with her lot. Her thoughts turned to the *shidduch* that had been proposed to her recently. In the past whenever she had thought about it she had cringed. But now she dozed off into a peaceful sleep, and she dreamed.

In her dream, people all around her were running. She ran with them and they all entered a dense forest. They ran through the forest, disappearing into the darkness. She continued to run and as the forest ended,a burst of light suddenly surrounded her. The sun shone more brightly than usual, and she saw that she was standing at the entrance to a beautiful garden filled with exquisite flowers of marvelous fragrance. All around were gleaming ponds. The whole garden was bathed in the glow of intense sunlight.

Suddenly she noticed a man with a long silvery beard, wearing a white robe. He approached her and asked if she wanted to see her husband, and she followed him with her heart pounding. The old man stopped beside a large fruit tree, and in the distance she saw a wide field, enclosed with a golden fence. Inside were a group of people wearing brightly colored clothes, sitting in rows and studying Torah. In the midst of them stood a young man who was giving the *shiur*.

The old man turned to Rachel. "Wait here a few moments," he said. "Soon the lesson will be over and then you'll be able to see him." The *shiur* ended, and the teacher began walking toward her. Suddenly Rachel recognized her husband's suit. Her head spun as she realized that this was actually her husband standing in front of her.

"Avraham!" she cried faintly, and leaned against the tree for support.

"Yes, here I am," her husband answered gently. "Please calm down."

Slowly she regained her composure. "Why did you leave me so young, Avraham?"

"You must understand," he began softly, "that in the world you live in, souls are sent to complete certain missions and to endure hardships because of sins they committed previously. I was already in the world once before, you see, in another lifetime. I was a *talmid chacham* and a *tzaddik*, but I didn't want to marry and have children, so that my learning would not be disturbed. When I left the world and came here, at first they made me the head of one of the yeshivos in Gan Eden, and I started rising from level to level. But when they found out that I had never married or had children, they sent me back to the world. There I married you, and when we had our seventh child they called me back to Gan Eden to return to my yeshiva, where everybody was waiting for me. Your merit is great and when the time comes, we will be together again in this world, the real world."

"But," asked Rachel, "how can it be that you were such a *talmid chacham*, for you never had much time to learn?"

"I myself didn't know it," her husband replied. "I had been sent into the world only to correct what I had been lacking — to marry and have a family."

His wife continued to ask questions. "And can you tell me, then, why our Yosef is so unsuccessful in business?"

"Certainly you remember the *din Torah* he had? Yosef won the case, but in doing so he caused great pain to his fellow Jew. He would have been punished more harshly if I hadn't interceded on his behalf and asked them to give him only four years of difficulty in business. In another year the term of punishment will be up and he'll start to succeed."

"And what of our David, who is already twenty-four and still can't find a *shidduch*?"

Her husband smiled and said, "The reason for that is that his intended bride took her time coming into the world. Now she is only thirteen and she lives in another city. In five years she'll come to your city, she'll marry David, and she'll even pay for the whole wedding!"

Rachel began to tremble as a painful memory came to her. It took all of her might to ask her husband, "And why did that tragedy happen to us, when that drunken goy killed our precious three-year-old son?"

"Come with me," her husband replied gently. They walked together quietly, until they came to a sunny grove of little trees. From the sky emanated beams of light in different colors. Beautiful birds flew from tree to tree and she heard them singing, אור זרוע לצדיק ולישרי לב שמחה "Light is sown for the righteous, and joy for the upright in heart" (*Tehillim* 97:11), while others sang, למען יזמרך כבוד ולא ידם "May my soul praise You, and not be silent" (*Tehillim* 30:13). Multicolored insects flew around and also sang into their ears, as did swarms of little creatures running in the grass. Even the grass itself, and the trees, sang.

Suddenly she saw balls of fire swinging on chains of colors. They stopped near her and above them were little angels with wings, flying right above her head. All around she heard wonderful music coming from all sorts of instruments and she felt as if her soul would fly out, as she was about to faint. Her husband immediately took some grass from the garden and held it to her nose. She came back to herself and looked around and saw a canopy made of precious stones shining with all the colors of the rainbow. Underneath the canopy was the form of an angel, who came and stood before her. She recognized her dead son and cried in joy. She fainted, and her husband again revived her with the fragrance of the grass. She opened her eyes and saw that it was no mistake. This was her son and none other.

"Oh, why did you leave me when you were so young?" she asked him.

The child answered, "Everything has been calculated by the *Borei Olam*. I had been in the world once before, before I was born to you, Imma. I had been born to a very special family. In our city there was a pogrom and the goyim murdered all the Jews. I was six months old and the only one left alive. A gentile family took me in and raised me until the Jews from a neighboring town ransomed me and brought me back to live among them. I became a great *talmid chacham* and lived the rest of my life peacefully. When I left the world, they received me here in the real world with great joy and I rose from level to level until I reached a place where I couldn't go any higher, because I had been nursed for one year by a gentile woman. The verdict was that I should be born again and nurse for three years from a Jew and then I would be able to attain my proper high place. That's when I was born to you, Imma, and that is a great merit for you. When I finished my three years, I was taken again to my real place, because there was nothing left for me to do in that lowly world."

"But why did you have to go in such a terrible way?" his mother asked.

"When I was about to pass from the world, a terrible decree went out on the Jews of our city, and all of them were about to be killed, including you and Abba. That's when I was honored by being able to atone for the whole city, and I was killed in their place. In that way I saved the whole city, and that's why I was able to merit all the honor you see here. No one in all of Gan Eden is allowed to see me, only Abba, whenever he wants." The child laughed gleefully, flew up and was gone.

Then her husband said to her, "You have seen that all of your questions have answers. There is a Creator, and He creates no evil. Now I have to go back to my *shiur*." He accompanied her back to the place where she had first been, by the tree, and said to her, "It is wonderful here, but I cannot bear your constant grieving, Rachel. Please, for my sake, start to enjoy life again. You have been offered a good *shidduch;* don't oppose it." Her husband disappeared and the old man again appeared. He led her through the forest until they reached the city.

She woke up from her sleep as if she had been born anew. For a long time her face bore its smile, as she continued to see her fortunate husband and her smiling son. A heavy rock had been lifted from her heart and she finally was consoled.

She is now happily married and living a wonderful and pleasant life.

[Note by Rav Yom Tov Ehrlich, the creator of this story: "This story was developed from the writings of Rav Chayim Vital, *zt"l,* who learned it from his great teacher, the Arizal. It reveals to us deep concepts in the Torah, especially the concept of *gilgulim* (reincarnation). It teaches that all the creatures in the universe are like screws in the great machine called Creation. *Ha-Kadosh Baruch Hu* tightens the screws or loosens them, and adjusts their actions according to the workings of the machine. He brings *neshamos* (souls) into the world to fulfill certain tasks, and He takes away those *neshamos* which need to be above in the Next World. For this world and the Next World are really one unified concept. The *neshamos* work together with the body in the lower world, while above the *neshamos* act alone. If we could only know how everything acts together, we would never feel any suffering."]

TO ACCEPT

The following *midrash* relates the battle that was going on within Avraham *Avinu*'s mind while he was going to the *Akedah.* For three days he traveled and the whole time the Satan was working hard to stop him. Based upon the *midrash,* we can study some of their conversation.

The Satan came to Avraham Avinu and said to

him, "Old man, have you lost your mind? This son was given to you when you were at the age of one hundred, and now you're going to slaughter him?!" He answered, "I accept that." [על מנת כן, literally, "On such a condition." Perhaps we can infer that it implies, "It was on this condition that I came into the world, to accept this."*] ***"And if He tests you even more than this*** [to take your own life — Etz Yosef], ***will you be able to withstand it?" He answered, "Even more than this."*** [Even if He commands me to slaughter myself, I will do it without any second thoughts or excuses — *Etz Yosef.*] ***So the Satan tried one more argument. "You know, tomorrow, when you come back without Yitzchak, they're going to find out and call you a murderer. They will convict you of murdering your son."*** [This was a very powerful argument. The very mitzvah that he was about to perform might turn around the next day and cause him to be accused of murder, a terrible *chillul Hashem* (desecration of God's Name). In addition, perhaps we can understand it one step further. Avraham had spent his entire life dedicated to fighting the idol-worship that was prevalent then. One of the main forms of idol-worship in Kena'an was child sacrifice (see Vayikra 18:21 and the commentaries of Ibn Ezra and the Ramban). Avraham fought to teach the concept of the one merciful Father in Heaven Who abhors such actions. Now all his work was to be demolished. His whole life's mission was to be completely destroyed, as the preacher of the God of Mercy would be exposed as having committed

* See *Sefer Ha-Yashar* by *Rabbenu* Tam, chap. 6: "A person has to know and be very careful at these times (of trial), for it was on this condition that he entered a Covenant with his God."

the very thing he had fought against — human sacrifice!*] ***He again answered the same as he had before, "I accept that" [Bereshis Rabbah 56:5].***

Avraham understood that as great as the power to reason is, as much as he had become who he was because of his great mind, still, ultimately reason is limited. We cannot understand everything, and we must not try to out-think God. There comes a time when we reach the limit of our power to reason. Then the answer must simply be, "I accept that." The ultimate answer to everything is simply faith: God is right. I accept it. That was the difference between Iyov and Avraham.

Avraham was the deepest thinker that ever lived. With the power of his vast intellect, he broke through the iron facade of the false philosophy of an entire generation.** Even he knew that the ultimate answer is simply to accept. ok zpn lr — It was on this condition that I came into the world, to accept. It was for this purpose that he merited the mitzvah of *bris milah*, התהלך לפני והיה תמים, "Go before Me and be *tamim* "— pure, innocent, complete. Purity and perfection require being simple and whole. תמימות — learning to accept perfectly, with humility, is the ultimate achievement of the human race.

WHEN WILL I HAVE THE OPPORTUNITY?

When they led R. Akiva out to be executed, it was time to say Kerias Shema. As they ripped his flesh with iron combs, he accepted upon himself the Yoke of the Kingdom of Heaven (עול מלכות שמים). His talmidim asked him, "Rabbenu, even here!?" He said to them, "My whole life I was bothered by this pasuk: 'And you shall love the Lord your God with all your soul.' I said to myself, When will I

* See *Mishnas R. Aharon*, vol. 1, p. 104, and also *Lev Eliyahu* on *parashas Vayera*.

** see Rambam, *Hilchos Avodah Zarah*, chap. 1.

> ***have the opportunity to fulfill this? And now that it has come into my hand, should I not fulfill it?" He concentrated on the word "(The Lord is) One" until his soul left him, while he was still saying, "One...." Happy are you, R. Akiva, that you have gained entry into the Next World*** [*Berachos* 61b].

R. Akiva understood that there is something much deeper, much more important, than living this mundane life. He had a purpose, and every experience was an opportunity to express that purpose. He saw in the command, "And you shall love the Lord your God with all your soul," a chance to fulfill his life's calling. The ultimate goal for R. Akiva was to love God more than himself. Not only did he understand this, but he waited for it: "When will it finally come into my hand and I will be given the opportunity to achieve my goal?"

That, wrote Rav Yerucham, *zt"l* (in *Da'as Chochmah u'Musar*, vol. 1, *ma'amar* 101), is how we should view all hardships in this world. Hardships not only have a purpose, but are a necessary creation in this world. They are our way of actually living out our ideals, and not just believing them. *Rabbenu* Tam, in *Sefer Ha-Yashar*, chap. 6, explains that *olam ha-zeh*, this lowly world, is merely a path of hardships. The one who prepares himself and expects them, will succeed in his purpose. Rav Yerucham explains that not only should a person prepare himself for troubles, but he should look forward to them. He should view them as a new opportunity to test himself,❖ to see how much he can pull himself up out of the "mud" of this world. The deeper the "mud," the greater the

---

❖ "Every single object in the world and every single event in the world, have the purpose of testing men's free will. That is the reason for their existence" (Rav Avigdor Miller, *shlita*, in *Rejoice O Youth!*, section 611; see also *Mesillas Yesharim*, chap. 1).

opportunity. "The *Avos* ran before You like horses running through the shallow water" (*Sanhedrin* 96a). Even though the water is all mud, and there is no solid ground to stand on, still our forefathers ran over it, barely touching the mud. The whole measure of a person's success is only through the *nisyonos* that are all around him, while he runs through them all, barely touching the "mud."

Or, as my *Rosh Yeshiva*, Rav Chaim Pinchas Scheinberg, *shlita*, often quotes from the Chafetz Chaim, *zt"l*, "The fool turns gold into mud, while the wise man turns mud into gold."

WE WILL ALL BE LIKE DREAMERS

The Gemara (*Berachos* 7a) relates that Moshe *Rabbenu* asked to understand God's ways (*Shemos* 33:13), the suffering of the righteous and the prosperity of the wicked. *Ha-Kadosh Baruch Hu* answered, וראית את אחורי ופני לא יראו, "You will see My back, but My face you shall not see" (*Shemos 33:23). Rav Eliyahu Dessler, zt"l, in his profound work Michtav Me-Eliyahu*, explains, according to the Targum Unkelos, ותחזי ית דבתרי ודקדמי לא יתחזון, "You will see that which is behind Me, and that which is before Me you shall not see." Understanding the ways of God is possible only after the fact. Only then, retrospectively, is it possible to comprehend how everything was for the good. But for us to understand before the fact is impossible. We cannot delve into the depths of the mind of the Holy One, blessed be He, and understand the substance of His ways. It is beyond one's ability in this world to fathom the depths of God's thoughts before they have actually come into being. In this realm things are mostly concealed and hidden.

בשוב ה׳ את שיבת ציון היינו כחולמים, "When God brings us back to Tzion, we will be like dreamers." The Alter of Kelm, Rav Simchah Zissel Ziv, *zt"l*, explained that this refers to the final Redemption. When the Mashiach will finally reveal himself, everything will be clear and understood retrospectively. We will look back upon all the hardships and suffering of the *Galus* as if they had never occurred, and as if they were merely a dream and a fantasy. Our external view of the world causes us to err and imagine that there are evils and troubles. But a deeper insight shows that everything is only for the good and is truly a blessing.

When Yosef's brothers went down to Egypt, they were flooded with questions: Yosef's dreams, their decision to sell him, the famine, the strange accusations of the king, etc. When Yosef finally revealed himself to his brothers and said, "I am Yosef," all the questions instantly dissolved. All the more so, said the Alter of Kelm, will we, at that future time when the final salvation will unfold before our eyes, suddenly recognize the "I am God" that was hidden within the whole history of Mankind. Finally all of our questions of this *Galus* will disappear. But before that time we will be able to understand only that "Everything that the Merciful One does is for the good" — without any real understanding of how it is good. The light of the Redemption is hidden, and only with the coming of the *Mashiach* will it be taken from its hiding place and be revealed to all.

A true *tzaddik*, however, through his deep recognition that "Everything that the Merciful One does is for the good," reaches the ability to endure sacrifice with joy. He accepts upon himself with love the torments of *Galus*. Through this he merits having the inner light of the *Ge'ulah* revealed to him, and he clings to it. This is what raises him above the burden of suffering. This is the deep concept expressed by the Ramchal: that it is possible that the light of the *Mashiach* will be revealed to the pure *tzaddik* even before it is revealed to the rest of the world.

This is the profound secret of suffering, concludes Rav Dessler, *zt"l* — that the burden of suffering is only in the world of the imaginary, for a person who lives a life of the imaginary. But as much as a person has raised himself above the illusions of this world, in that measure will he be able to see through the suffering and banish it from his consciousness (*Michtav Me-Eliyahu*, vol. III, pp. 244-45).

TO BLESS THE GOOD, AND TO BLESS THE BAD

"A person is obligated to make a *berachah* on the bad the same way he makes a *berachah* on the good" (*Berachos* 60b). The Gemara asks, on this statement, Surely it cannot mean the exact same *berachah*? We know that on good tidings we say *Shehechiyanu*, ברוך שהחיינו וקיימנו והגיענו לזמן הזה, "Blessed are You...Who has kept us alive to arrive at this time," or the *berachah* הטוב והמטיב, "Blessed are You...Who is good and bestows good," while on bad news we say, ברוך דיין האמת, "Blessed is the Judge of Truth."❖ Rava answered, "No, this statement means that we must accept everything with joy...." חסד ומשפט אשירה לך ה׳ אזמרה, — 'On Divine Mercy and Judgment I will sing unto You O Lord' (*Tehillim* 101:1). If it is Mercy, I will sing, and if it is Judgment, I will sing." Immediately after this, the Gemara quotes R. Akiva, that "One should always say, 'Whatever the Merciful One does is for the good.' " This arouses the commentaries to ask, If that is the case, that everything is for the good, then the Gemara's original question doesn't make sense. If one should make exactly the same *berachah* on the bad as he does on the good, why are there two

---

❖ From the different *berachos*, we come to the recognition that the dimension of good is greater than the dimension of bad. On the good, we say the *berachah* "Who is good and bestows good," implying that even after we receive the good that we are deserving of, He increases the measure and sends us more. Likewise, on the bad we say, "the Judge of Truth," that is, that He punishes only what is deserving according to Divine judgment, and no more (*Sifsei Chachamim*, *Berachos* 54a).

separate *berachos*? Isn't everything really good?

Yes, everything is really good. But as long as we are clothed with this physical body and are unaware of the spiritual reality, we cannot really see the good. To us things sometimes seem to be a bitter pill. The *berachah* we make is to understand the reality behind the illusion. The job of the people of the Torah is to use our gift of intellect to see through the haze. When we suffer bitterly, we make a *berachah* (*Berachos* 54a, and *Shulchan Aruch, Orach Chayim* 230:1), and we see the *Hashgachah Pratis*, that everything is through His hand. And therefore, as we make the *berachah* on bad tidings, "Blessed is the Judge of Truth," still we are bound to raise ourselves above the superficiality of this world and to sing!

In *Pesachim* 50a it says that in this world (*olam ha-zeh*) we make two different *berachos*: on good tidings we say, הטוב והמטיב, "[Blessed are You]...Who is good and does good." And on bad tidings one says, דיין האמת, "...Who is the Judge of Truth." But in the Next World (*Olam Ha-Ba*), *we will make one berachah on everything: "Who is good and does good." Rav Eliyahu Dessler, zt"l,* explains that in this world it is impossible to see clearly that "Everything that the Merciful One does is truly for our good." Even one on the level of Moshe *Rabbenu* is obligated to make the *berachah* "the Judge of Truth" on something that he feels is bad, from the standpoint of this world. But in the Next World we will see clearly that all of God's actions are really intrinsically good. Therefore, there we will say on everything, "Who is good and does good." On this the Gemara cites the *pasuk*: "On that day God will be One...." We will recognize that everything flows only from God Who runs everything with mercy. We see that the main understanding of God's glory is in the Upper Realms (*Michtav Me-Eliyahu*, vol. III, p. 279).

There is a very interesting story about the famous chassidic Rebbe, Rebbe Zusha, and his brother, Rebbe Elimelech, *zt"l*. Once a man came to Rebbe Elimelech and asked him the meaning of the Gemara's statement, "A person is obligated to make a *berachah* on the bad the same way he makes a *berachah* on the good."

"How can a person make a *berachah* on the bad?" he asked. "How can I thank God for the terrible things He has done to me?"

Rebbe Elimelech answered, "Yes, I too was bothered by that. But if you go to my brother, Rebbe Zusha, he'll know the *peshat* (the simple meaning of that statement)." The man proceeded to hunt for Rebbe Zusha and finally found him, clothed in rags and sitting and learning in a squalid little hut, living in the worst poverty imaginable. The man approached him, and told him that his brother had said he would be able to explain the Gemara's statement, "A person is obligated to make a *berachah* on the bad the same way he makes a *berachah* on the good."

Rebbe Zusha looked at him, quite perplexed. "I don't know why my brother sent you to *me*, for I also don't understand that *gemara*. How can I tell you how to make a *berachah* on the bad? Nothing bad has ever happened to Zusha!"

TO BLESS THE BAD LIKE THE GOOD

The renowned *posek* (halachic authority) Rav Shlomo Zalman Auerbach, *shlita*, relates the following story* about Rav Eliyahu David Rabinowitz Teumim, the *Aderes, zt"l*, the Chief Rabbi of Yerushalayim. He had a son who passed away quite young. The funeral had been set for a specific time, and the members of the *Chevrah Kaddisha* knew that the Rabbi of the city was always punctual. They all were ready and waiting to proceed with the funeral.

But the Rabbi didn't appear. He remained in the room of the deceased, staring silently there, delaying the procession. This was very surprising to all. Twenty minutes later the

* Heard from Rav Auerbach, *shlita*, by someone who was present when he related it while he was paying a *shiva* call. It is also cited in *Yalkut Lekach Tov*, vol. 3, p. 82.

Aderes came out of the room and signaled them to proceed.

During the *shivah*, he explained, "I remained in the room until I succeeded in bringing myself to the same *simchah* I had felt the day that my son came into this world." The explanation could be that we are commanded to make a *berachah* on the bad with *simchah*, just as we make a *berachah* on the good. The Rabbi saw that he was still lacking the "just as." Only after meditating on the joy he had felt at the birth of his son was he able to make a *berachah* with those same feelings of *simchah* — that He is the True Judge (*Dayan Ha-Emes*).

The Chafetz Chaim used to say that a medicine can be bitter, but it shouldn't be called "bad." For really, it is good. So, too, we shouldn't call a situation bad — merely bitter.

TO SING ON THE GOOD, AND TO SING ON THE BAD

In the future, Ha-Kadosh Baruch Hu will make a feast for the tzaddikim on the day when He rewards the seed of Yitzchak with chesed. After they eat and drink, they will give Avraham the cup of berachah to bentch upon. Avraham will reply, "I cannot make a berachah, for Yishmael came from me." They will say to Yitzchak, "Take the cup and bentch." He answers, "I cannot bentch, for Esav came from me." They tell Ya'akov to bentch and he answers, "I cannot bentch, for I married two sisters, something the Torah was going to forbid." They say to Moshe, "Take the cup and bentch," and he answers, "I cannot bentch, for I did not merit to enter Eretz Yisrael." They say to David, "Take the cup and bentch." He answers them, "Yes, I will bentch. And it is befitting for me to bentch, as it says, "כוס ישועות אשא ובשם ה׳ אקרא, 'I will raise up the cup* of salvation and call upon the Name of God' " (Tehillim 116:13) [*Pesachim* 119].

* The Gemara (*Yoma* 76a) states that David Ha-Melech's cup will hold 221 *lug* (more than 20 gallons)!

At first glance this is very perplexing. Avraham *Avinu* was blessed with tremendous honor and wealth. The B'nei Ches referred to him as "a Prince of God in our midst" (*Bereshis* 23:6; see also Rashi, 23:10). The Torah relates several times the great honor Avraham received. And yet he felt himself unworthy of singing God's praises because he had Yishmael as his descendant.

David, on the other hand, felt himself lowly and broken his whole life, as we see from much of *Tehillim*. David had a life full of misfortune. First he was considered an outcast by his family, who thought that he was a *mamzer*. Then, he was hunted mercilessly by his father-in-law, Sha'ul *Ha-Melech*. Later he was dethroned and run out of the city in a rebellion led by his own son. He never even had a good dream (*Berachos* 55b). He had suffered tremendously in his lifetime. And yet he is the one who is worthy to say, "Yes, I will sing God's praise. And it is befitting for me to sing"?!

Morenu Maran Ha-Gaon Ha-Rav Chaim Pinchas Scheinberg, *shlita* (in his work *Derech Emunah u'Bitachon, parashas Vayeshev*), gives a very moving explanation which, perhaps, can serve as our model in developing our reaction to suffering. He writes that the explanation can be found upon studying the Gemara, in *Berachos* 60b. It says there that in the same way that one makes a *berachah* on the good, so too should one make a *berachah* on the bad. The source? R. Tanchum said, from here: כוס ישועות אשא ובשם ה׳ אקרא...צרה ויגון אמצא ובשם ה׳ אקרא.... "I will raise up the cup of salvation and call upon the Name of God.... I found distress and sorrow, and I called upon the Name of the Lord."

This is an amazing juxtaposition. David *Ha-Melech* didn't feel any difference between being dealt with through *he'aras Panim*, seeing the hand of God clearly maneuvering everything for our benefit, or through *hester Panim*, when God seems to hide His face. Whatever happened to him, he sang. חסד ומשפט אשירה לך ה׳ אזמרה, "On Divine Mercy and Judgment I will sing unto You, O Lord" (*Tehillim* 101:1). Whether in a situation where I see Divine Mercy, or when I see God dealing with me in Divine Judgment, I will sing! (*Berachos* 60b). This level of song is not the same as the level of one who sings upon seeing only Divine Mercy. When the song comes even when everything seems dark and God is treating us through Divine Retribution, this is the highest level of song. His hand is hidden, we see only *hester Panim*. And still one sings! This is the highest level of song.

David *Ha-Melech*, who had experienced so much trouble in his lifetime, is the one who will see himself as worthy of singing God's praises. He had fully recognized that even though it appears that God is hiding, still he must sing. Even though everything looked bleak, he understood that "Everything the Merciful One does is for the good." In all the most difficult situations, he found a way to sing. His life full of suffering created the most Divine collection of song ever composed by Man. Throughout the ages, people have covered their *sefer Tehillim* with tears, moved by the expression of hope they found there. David *Ha-Melech*, at that future feast of the *tzaddikim*, will be the most worthy of all to bless the Name of God. Through a life full of tragedy and torment, his one comment was, צרה ויגון אמצא, ובשם ה׳ אקרא, "I found distress and sorrow, and I called upon the Name of the Lord." From this deep and profound recognition, he will be able to say, "I will *bentch and sing God's praise, and it is befitting that I should sing.*" כוס ישועות אשא ובשם ה׳ אקרא, *"I will raise up the cup of salvation and call upon the Name of God."*

Appendix

Gemara Bava Basra 15b-16b

There was a *chassid* (a saintly man) among the nations and his name was Iyov. His sole purpose in coming into this world was in order to receive his reward (in the Next World). *Ha-Kadosh Baruch Hu* brought afflictions upon him and he started cursing and blaspheming. So *Ha-Kadosh Baruch Hu* doubled his reward in this world in order to drive him out of the next.

> *Now the day came about, and the Heavenly powers came to stand before God, and the Satan, too, came among them. And God said to the Satan, "From where are you coming?" And the Satan answered...* [1:6-7]

He (the Satan) said before Him, "Master of the World, I have floated around the whole world, and I have not found one faithful like Your servant Avraham, to whom You said, 'Arise and walk through the land, its length and breadth, for I have given it to you,' and yet at the time when he was not able to find a place to bury Sarah until he bought one for 400 silver shekels [an enormous amount in those days], still no doubts entered his mind as to the justice of the Divine ways."*

Iyov's Righteousness

> *And God said to the Satan, "Have you paid attention to My servant Iyov? For there is none like him on Earth..."* [1:18]

* Even though Avraham *Avinu* could have complained that God had given him the land, and therefore it wasn't right that he had to buy the property there, and for such an exorbitant price.

R. Yochanan said, "What was said about Iyov was greater than what was said about Avraham. About Avraham it is written, 'For now I know that you fear God' (*Bereshis* 22:12), while about Iyov it is written, 'a sincere and upright man, God-fearing and shunning evil.' " What does "shunning evil" mean? Rav Abba bar Shmuel said, "Iyov was lenient regarding his money. The local custom was to give half a prutah to the storekeeper. Iyov was lenient with his (half)." [When one had a small amount of work to do, he would say to the worker, I want to give you half a prutah (the smallest coin in those days was a prutah), so let's go to the store and buy a loaf of bread or some eggs for a prutah, and we'll split it up. Iyov was lenient and gave over the second half-prutah, which was rightfully his, and gave him the whole prutah, for it was improper in his eyes to be so strict with an amount so small that it wasn't even worth money — Rashi.]

Rava expounded, "What does it mean when it states: 'The blessing of the lost one would come upon me, and I would make the widow's heart sing for joy' (*Iyov* 29:13)? 'The blessing of the lost one would come upon me....' [אובד, lost one, implies that he ascertained that the orphan was ruining the field (because he didn't know how to care for it) — Rashi.] This teaches that he used to take a field away from orphans, improve it, and then return it to them. '...And I would make the widow's heart sing for joy.' Wherever there was a widow whom nobody wished to marry, he would go and put his name on her [start a rumor that she was his relative or that he himself was interested in marrying her — Rashi], and then someone would marry her."

Iyov's Prosperity

> *And the Satan answered God and said, "Does Iyov fear God in vain? Haven't You protected him, his household, and all that he has around him? You have blessed the work of his hands..."* [1:9-10]

What is the meaning of "You have blessed the work of his hands"? Rav Shmuel bar Rav Yitzchak said, "Anyone who took money from Iyov was blessed." What is the meaning of, "and his livestock has spread out (literally, 'broken through') in the land"? Rav Yosei bar Chanina said, "The livestock of Iyov broke through the fence (normal bounds) of the world. The normal way of the world is that wolves kill the goats. With the livestock of Iyov, the goats killed the wolves."

> *"However, stretch forth Your hand and touch all that he has. Will he not blaspheme You to Your face?" And God said to the Satan, "Behold, all that he has is in your hands; only upon him do not stretch forth your hand." And the Satan left from before the Presence of God. Now the day came about that his sons and daughters were dining and drinking wine at the home of their firstborn brother. And a messenger came to Iyov and said, "The cattle were plowing and the she-donkeys were grazing beside them...."* [1:11-14]

What is the meaning of "The cattle were plowing and the she-donkeys were grazing beside them"? [The term "beside them" implies that they were right next to the cattle. This teaches us that they ate the stalks from the furrow just plowed, for the seeds grew immediately at the time of planting — Rashi.] This teaches that the Holy One, blessed be He, gave Iyov a taste of the Next World. [As it says in *Yirmeyahu* 31:7 women will conceive and give birth on the same day. See *Shabbos* 30b — Rashi] (So too here — the crops grew the instant they were planted.)

> *And Iyov stood up and rent his garment, tore the hair from his head, and fell to the ground and prostrated himself. And he said, "Naked did I come from my mother's womb, and naked shall I return there. God gave and God took away. Let God's Name be blessed." Despite this, Iyov did not sin, and did not attribute a blemish to God. And the day came when the Heavenly powers came to stand before God, and the Satan, too, came among them to stand before God. And God said to*

the Satan, "From where are you coming?" And the Satan replied to God and said, "From floating around on the Earth and from walking on it." [1:20-2:2]

He [the Satan] said in front of Him, "Master of the World, I have flown around the whole world, and I have not found one faithful like Your servant Avraham, to whom You said, 'Arise and walk through the land, its length and breadth, for I have given it to you,' and yet at the time when he was not able to find a place to bury Sarah until he bought one for 400 silver shekels, still no doubts entered his mind as to the justice of the Divine ways."

And God said to the Satan, "Have you paid attention to My servant Iyov? For there is none like him on Earth, a sincere and upright man, God-fearing and shunning evil, and he still maintains his sincerity. Yet you incite Me against him."

The Satan — The Great Adversary

R. Yochanan said, "If it weren't explicitly written, it would be impossible to say it. It is as if a person can incite Him and succeed in His being incited." In a *baraysa* it states, "He (the Satan) goes down and causes one to err, then he goes up and angers (the Almighty), then he gets permission and takes his soul." [He goes down below and misleads the populace into sin, then he rises above and incites the anger of the King with his prosecutions. Then he gets permission to kill the transgressor. This is the meaning of the verse, "Yet you incite Me" — Rashi.]

Now the Satan replied to God, "Skin for skin, and whatever a person has, he will give for his life. However, stretch forth Your hand now and touch his bones and his flesh; will he not blaspheme You to Your face?" And God said to the Satan, "He is in your hand. Just [be sure to] preserve his life." And the Satan left from the Presence of God, and he smote Iyov with terrible boils from the sole of his foot to the top of his head. [2:4-7]

R. Yitzchak said, "The Satan's suffering was greater than Iyov's. This is like the servant whose master told him, 'Break the barrel but watch the wine (be careful not to spill a drop).' " [The suffering of the Satan was that he was commanded to watch Iyov's life that he not die — Rashi.] (One of the Satan's main purposes in Creation is to take lives. So telling him to act against his very nature was a terrible ordeal for him.) This tells us that he is the Satan (inciter), he is the *yetzer ha-ra* (each person's evil inclination), he is the angel of death. He is the Satan, as it is written, "And the Satan left from the Presence of God." He is the *yetzer ha-ra*, as it is written there (in *Bereshis*), "For the nature of a person is only evil the whole day...." And here it is written, "Only upon him do not stretch forth your hand" (comparing the word "only"). He is the angel of death, as it is written, "Just preserve his life." So we see that this is his domain [to take his soul, and therefore he was warned not to take it — Rashi].

R. Levi said, "The Satan and Peninah (Elkanah's second wife [his first wife was Channah, mother of the Prophet Shmuel] both had pure intentions. The Satan saw that the Holy One, blessed be He, was directing his attention toward Iyov. So he said (to himself), Heaven forbid that He should forget Avraham's love of Him. Also with Peninah, it is written (*Shmuel* I, 1), 'And her rival wife angered her greatly in order that she lift her voice up' " [that she should cry because she was barren, and pray — Rashi]. R. Acha bar Ya'akov quoted this statement in a lecture in Papunia; the Satan came and kissed his feet.

Iyov's Sin

And with all this Iyov did not sin with his lips [2:10].

Rava said, "With his lips he did not sin, but he sinned in his heart." What did he say (later on, which revealed what he had originally been thinking)? "The Earth has been given into the hands of the wicked one; he covers the faces of its judges. If not, then who is he?" Rava said, "Iyov wanted to turn the pot upside down (and spill out the food)" [to uproot all respect for the Almighty, by his cursing and blaspheming — Rashi]. R. Yehoshua said to him, "Iyov was only referring to the Satan."❖

> *It is with Your knowledge that I will not be wicked, and no one can be saved from Your hand* [10:7].

Rava said, "Iyov wished to dismiss the whole world from judgment" [to relieve the whole world from God's judgment by saying that they are all forced by God, for He created them with an evil nature (yetzer ha-ra). This is what he meant when he said, "It is with Your knowledge that I will not be wicked":

❖ According to R. Yehoshua, Iyov remained a *tzaddik*. Rava, however, seems to be of the opinion that Iyov lost his *righteousness*. This appears to be a basic dispute as to Iyov's intentions. Later on, when Iyov got back all he had lost, *Chazal* argue about whether he received the reward as a *tzaddik* (see the Malbim on chapter 42), or whether perhaps he was considered a *rasha* and received all his reward of the Next World here in this world. (As the *gemara* quoted above says, "There was a *chassid* [saintly man] among the nations and his name was Iyov. His sole purpose in coming into this world was in order to receive his reward [in the Next World]. *Ha-Kadosh Baruch Hu* brought afflictions upon him and he started cursing and blaspheming. So *Ha-Kadosh Baruch Hu* doubled his reward in this world in order to drive him out of the next.") The Gemara in *Sotah* (see below), however, states that Iyov served God out of love, and doesn't make any reference to shortcomings. The Malbim (at the very end of his commentary) presented the opinion that Iyov did not sin in his heart; he was only arguing that there appears to be no Divine Justice.

If You had wanted, I would not have been wicked — Rashi.] He said in front of Him, "Master of the Universe, You created the ox with cloven hooves, You created the donkey with solid hooves. [You made this animal kosher, and that animal *treif.* Everything came about by Your hand for You created the signs of impurity in them — Rashi.] You created Gan Eden (the Garden of Eden, referring to the Next World, where the *tzaddikim* receive their reward), You created Gehinnom (hell, the place where the wicked are punished). You created *tzaddikim* [through their good nature — Rashi], You created the wicked [through their evil nature — Rashi]. Who can resist Your hand?" [Therefore, no one can save himself from Your hand. Who can resist Your Will? All sinners are coerced into their sin — Rashi.]

What did Iyov's friends answer him? "Surely you will do away with fear and increase speech before God" (15:4). The Holy One, blessed be He, created the evil nature of man (*yetzer ha-ra*). He created the Torah as an antidote. [Torah is the medicine which repels the urge to sin, as it says in *Kiddushin* 30b, "If you meet that disgusting fellow (the *yetzer ha-ra*), drag him to the *beis ha-midrash.* If he is a stone, he will melt...." Therefore, they are not compelled involuntarily, for they have a means of protecting themselves — Rashi.]

> *If only He would weigh my anger and my broken spirit on a scale and place them together...* [6:2].

Rav said, "Throw dirt into Iyov's mouth! He thinks he can get chummy with Heaven?" [He spoke before the Divine Presence like a person who argues with a friend — "Come and let's weigh the facts and decide who really owes whom" — Rashi.]

> *There is no arbiter between us who will place his hand on both of us* [9:33].

Rav said, "Throw dirt into Iyov's mouth! Since when does

a servant reprimand his master?"

> *I made a covenant with my eyes, so why should I gaze upon a young girl* [31:1].

Rava said, "Iyov didn't look at other women, but Avraham didn't even look at his own wife. As it says, 'Now I know that you are a woman of beautiful appearance.' 'Now' implies that beforehand he didn't know."

> *Just as a cloud is consumed and goes away, so will one who descends to the grave not ascend* [7:9].

Rava said, "From here we know that Iyov denied belief in the resurrection of the dead."

> *He Who would crush me with a storm and multiply my wounds for no reason* [9:17].

Raba said, "Iyov blasphemed with a *se'arah* (סערה, storm), so God answered him from a storm. He blasphemed with a storm, as it says, 'He Who would crush me with a storm.' He said in front of Him, 'Master of the World, perhaps a storm-wind passed in front of You and You got confused between *Iyov* (איוב) and *Oyev* (אויב, enemy).' God answered him with a storm. "Then God answered Iyov from the storm-wind and said, '...Now gird your loins like a man, and I will ask you and [you] will answer Me'" (38:1,3). [The Gemara plays on the word סערה. The ס and ש are both pronounced "s," so the Gemara reinterprets the word סערה (storm-wind) as שערה (hair).] God said to him, "I have created so many hairs on a person. To each hair I created its own separate pore, in order that two hairs not suck nourishment from one pore. For if two hairs should suck nourishment from one pore, it would darken the person's eyesight. I did not get confused between one pore and the next; would I get confused between *Iyov* and *Oyev*?!"

> *Who has separated a place for the streaming raindrop...* [38:25].

[God said,] "So many drops of water did I create in the clouds. And each drop was created in its own path in order that two drops should not come through one path. For if two drops were to come down together in one path, they would soften the earth and turn it into mud, and it wouldn't give forth fruit. I did not get confused between two drops; would I get confused between *Iyov* and *Oyev*?!"

...And a path for the cloud of the thunderclaps [38:25].

"I created much thunder in the clouds. Every thunderclap was created with its own path, in order that two thunderclaps should not travel on one path. For if two thunderclaps were to travel along one path, they would destroy the entire world [because the creatures would not be able to bear the sound — Rashi on the *pasuk*.] I did not get confused between two thunderclaps; would I get confused between *Iyov* and *Oyev*?!"

Do you know the time for the mountain goats to go and give birth? [39:1].

The mountain goat is very cruel to its offspring. When the time comes for her to give birth, she goes up to the top of a mountain so that her young should fall to the earth and die. [The mountain goat's womb is narrow, and delivery is much more painful to it than to other animals. It hates the young for causing it this pain — Rashi, on the *pasuk*; see also *Metzudas David*.] "I prepare an eagle to catch the newborn in its wings and put it down safely in front of her. If the eagle were to be early by one second or late by one second, the calf would immediately die. I did not get confused between two seconds; would I get confused between *Iyov* and *Oyev*?!"

Do you watch over the labor pains of the hind? [39:1].

The hind's womb is narrow. "At the moment she crouches to give birth, I prepare a snake to bite her on her womb, which loosens it and allows her to give birth. If it were to be a second early or a second late, she would die immediately. I did not get confused between two seconds; would I get confused between *Iyov* and *Oyev*?!"

> *Iyov does not speak with knowledge, and his words are without sense* [34:35].

Rava said, "We learn here that a person cannot be held accountable for what he says in a time of distress."

> *And the three friends of Iyov heard of all this evil which had come upon him, and each one came from his place, Elifaz the Temanite, Bildad the Shuchite, and Tzofar the Na'amatite. And they met together to come and bemoan him and console him* [2:11].

What is the meaning of "And they met together"? R. Yehudah said in the name of Rav, "This teaches us that they all walked in at exactly the same time." We learn in a *baraysa*, "Three hundred *parsos* (around 1,200 miles) separated them from each other. So how did they know? Some say each one had a crown [and on each crown were three faces with the name of that person engraved on the face. When distress came upon one of them, his face would change. (The same explanation applies in regard to the following trees.) — Rashi] Some say they each had three trees, and when one tree dried up, they would know." Rava said, "This is what people [mean when they] say, 'Give me a friend like Iyov's, or give me death!' "

Iyov Served Out of Love

Mishnah Sotah 27b:

On that day (when they appointed R. Elazar ben Azaryah head of the Yeshiva), R. Yehoshua ben Hurkanos expounded, "Iyov served *Ha-Kadosh Baruch Hu* out of love, as it says, 'Even if He kills me I will look toward Him' (*Iyov* 13:15). Still the matter is in doubt. [Because the word לא is used in the verse; the Gemara explains that this word can be translated as לא, 'no,' or as לו, 'to him.'] Does it mean 'I am looking toward Him,' or 'I am not looking'? It says in the verse, 'Until I expire I will not remove my whole sincerity from Him' (27:5). This teaches that he did everything out of love."

R. Yehoshua said, "Who will come and remove the dust from your eyes, R. Yochanan ben Zakkai, because for your whole life you have said that Iyov served the Omnipresent only out of fear, as it says, 'A sincere and upright man, God-fearing and shunning evil'! And here is Yehoshua, the *talmid* of your *talmid*, teaching that he did everything out of love."

Gemara Sotah 31a:

We learned in a *baraysa*: R. Me'ir said, "The Torah called Iyov God-fearing, and the Torah called Avraham God-fearing. Just as the fear of God by Avraham was out of love, so too the fear of God by Iyov was out of love. How do we know this in Avraham's case? Because it is written, 'The seed of Avraham who loves Me' (*Yeshayahu* 41:8). What is the difference between one who acts out of love and one who acts out of fear? There is this difference, as we learned in the *baraysa*: R. Shimon ben Elazar says, 'One who acts out of love is greater than one who acts out of fear. For with the second, his merit protects him for 1,000 generations, while for the first, his merit protects him for 2,000 generations."

Glossary

The following glossary provides a partial explanation of some of the Hebrew, Yiddish, and Aramaic words and phrases used in this book. The spellings and explanations reflect the way the specific word is used herein. Often, there are alternate spellings and meanings for the words.

AKEDAH: Avraham's binding of Yitzchak on the altar.

ALIYAH (-YOS): ascent.

AMIDAH: the daily silent prayer, recited standing, which comprises the SHEMONEH ESREH.

AMORA'IM: (A.) the sages whose teachings comprise the Gemara.

APIKORSUS: heresy.

ASHIR: wealthy; a wealthy man.

AVERAH: a transgression.

AVINU: "our father."

AVODAH ZARAH: idol worship.

BACHUR (-IM): young man (men); yeshiva student(s).

BARAYSA: (A.) a Tannaic compilation, normally expanding on subjects dealt within the MISHNAH, to which it is secondary.

BEIS DIN: a Jewish court of law.

BEIS MIDRASH: a house of study.

BEN TORAH: a learned, observant Jew.

BERACHAH: a blessing.

BERESHIS: the Book of Genesis.

BITACHON: faith and trust in God.

BITTUL TORAH: the misuse of one's time in non-Torah pursuits.

BOREI OLAM: the "Creator of the world," God.

BRIS MILAH: the ritual of circumcision.

DIN TORAH: lit., Torah law; a dispute judged by a Rabbinical court in accordance with the HALACHAH.

EMUNAH: belief in God.

ERETZ YISRAEL: the Land of Israel.

GABBAI: a synagogue official.

GADOL (GEDOLIM): a person (persons) of great stature; great Torah scholar(s).

GALUS: the Exile from *Eretz Yisrael*.

GAON (GE'ONIM): (A.) a genius in Torah learning; Sage(s) of the Babylonian yeshivos.

GEMILAS CHESED: performing acts of kindness.

GE'ULAH: the redemption.

HA-KADOSH BARUCH HU: the Holy One, blessed be He.

HALACHAH: Jewish law.

HASHGACHAH PRATIS: Divine Providence.

HE'ARAS PANIM: revealed Divine benevolence and Presence.

HEFSED: a loss.

HESTER PANIM: a situation in which God's Presence is hidden or obscured.

KEDUSHAH: holiness, sanctity.

KIDDUSH: the sanctification of the Sabbath and Festivals, usually recited over a cup of wine.

KIDDUSH HASHEM: the sanctification of God's Name.

KERIAS SHEMA: the recitation of the *shema* prayer.

KLAL YISRAEL: the Jewish Nation.

LASHON HA-RA: gossip; slander.

MA'AMAR: an essay.

MALACH (-IM): angel(s).

MA'ARIV: the evening prayer service.

MANHIG: a leader.

MASECHTA: (A.) a tractate of the Mishnah or the Talmud.

MASHAL: a parable.

MASHGIACH (RUCHANI): the spiritual dean of a yeshiva.

MASHIACH: the Messiah.

MATTAN TORAH: the giving of the Torah (on Mount Sinai).

MAZAL: fortune.

MIDDAH (MIDDOS): character trait(s).

MIDDAS HA-DIN: the attribute of Divine Judgment.

MIDDAS HA-RACHAMIM: the attribute of Divine Mercy.

MIKVEH: a ritual bath.

MISHNAH: an orderly redaction and summary by R. Yehudah Ha-Nasi of the accumulated Oral Law, which forms the basis of the Talmud.

MITZRAYIM: Egypt.

MOTZA'EI SHABBOS: "the departure of the Sabbath," Saturday night.

MUSAF: additional offerings in the Temple on Holy Days; the additional prayers recited on those days.

MUSAR: Jewish ethics.

NAVI (NEVI'IM): prophet(s).

NES: a miracle.

NISAYON: a trial; a test.

OLAM HA-BA: the World to Come.

OLAM HA-ZEH: this world.

PARASHAS HA-SHAVUA: the weekly Torah portion read in the synagogue.

PARNASSAH: livelihood.

PASUK: a Scriptural verse.

PEREK: a section.

PERUSH: an interpretation.

POSEK: a halachic authority.

RABBANIM: Rabbis.

RABBENU: "our teacher."

RASHA (RESHA'IM): a wicked, evil person (persons).

REBBE: a Torah teacher.

RIBBONO SHEL OLAM: Master of the Universe (God).

RISHONIM: the Early Authorities, those scholars who flourished between the eleventh and sixteenth centuries.

RUCHANIYUS: spirituality.

SEFER TEHILLIM: the Book of Psalms.

SEFER IYOV: the Book of Job.

SEFER TORAH: a Torah scroll.

SHACHARIS: the morning prayer service.

SHAMASH: the caretaker of a synagogue.

SHAMAYIM: Heaven.

SHECHINAH: the Divine Presence.

SHEHECHEYANU: the blessing recited over new fruit, new clothing, or the performance of a mitzvah for the first time that season.

SHEMA YISRAEL: "Hear O Israel," the opening words of the fundamental prayer affirming the unity of God.

SHEMIRAS SHABBOS: observance of the Sabbath.

SHEMONEH ESREH: the Eighteen Benedictions, or *Amidah* prayer.

SHIDDUCH: a marital match.

SHIVAH: lit., seven; the seven-day period of mourning.

SHLITA: the Hebrew acronym for "May he live long and happily, Amen."

SHOCHET: a ritual slaughterer.

SHUL: (Y.) a synagogue.

SHULCHAN ARUCH: lit., "a prepared table"; the Jewish Code of Law compiled by R. Yosef Karo.

SIDDUR: a prayer book.

SIMCHAH: joy; a joyous occasion.

TALMID: a student; a Torah student.

TALMID CHACHAM: a Torah scholar.

TANNA'IM: (A.) the Sages whose teachings comprise the Mishnah.

TEFILLAH: prayer.

TESHUVAH: repentance.

TREIF: (Y.) not kosher.

TZADDIK (-IM): a righteous, pious man (men); a holy man (men).

TZEDAKAH: charity; righteousness.

YAHRTZEIT: (Y.) the anniversary of a death.

YETZER HA-RA: the evil inclination.

YIRAS HASHEM: fear of God.

YISSURIM: suffering; afflictions.

ZT"L: the Hebrew acronym for "May the memory of this pious man be for a blessing."